THE RTL & RTW CLASSES
AFTER
LONDON TRANSPORT

AN ILLUSTRATED HISTORY OF THE
POST-LONDON TRANSPORT
EXISTENCE OF THE RTL AND RTW CLASSES

THE RTL & RTW CLASSES
AFTER
LONDON TRANSPORT

AN ILLUSTRATED HISTORY OF THE
POST-LONDON TRANSPORT
EXISTENCE OF THE RTL AND RTW CLASSES

John A.S. Hambley

Published in 1998 by
JOHN A.S. HAMBLEY
7 Linden Road,
Dunstable,
Beds. LU5 4NZ

British Library Cataloguing in Publication Data
A catalogue record for this book is available from the British Library

ISBN 0 9533146 1 8

Designed and produced by Hedgehog.
Printed and bound in Great Britain.

CONTENTS

Double Deck Tours Ltd., Niagara Falls, Canada now adorns the panels of RTW148. The fleet number and British registration plate are still carried, to which has been added a Canadian equivalent, Y21-847. Other cosmetic changes include an array of marker lights along the roof line and local advertising. The bus appears to have a set of Willesden garage blinds, although the Canadians obviously have no idea of which relates to which.

ACKNOWLEDGEMENTS

The book contains all known details up to May 1998 and has been gathered from many sources. I must single out the PSV Circle, The London Omnibus Traction Society and the RT/RF Register for the bulk of the details contained herein. Individual enthusiasts and historians have also allowed the use of their personal records on certain vehicles and a big thank you is extended to everyone involved especially Maurice Bateman, Harold Bloomfield, Roy Hillyard, David Munton and Brian Wright who very generously allowed me to cross check the details of every vehicle covered allowing as accurate a history as is possible to be documented throughout the pages. David Ruddom as usual has given me much help especially with the final text and this is much appreciated.

Photographs, individually acknowledged, have been made available by:- A. B. Cross, Michael Dryhurst, John Fozard, John Gascoine, Henry Heyworth, F. W. Ivey, Kevin Lane, Ian Macdonald, Roy Marshall, Alan Mortimer, David Munton, Tony R Packer, Photobus, Lyndon W. Rowe, John G. S. Smith, Wijewardene Memorial Media Library and Documentation Centre without whose support the book would never have materialized. I hope the reader will acknowledge that there are a few dates and probably additional disposal details which are still to be uncovered and it is hoped to issue an addendum with the next book in the series if this proves to be practicable. Therefore anyone with additional information is asked to get in touch with the author at the address shown earlier.

FOREWORD

This book deals with the disposal and subsequent history of the London Transport RTL and RTW classes. It is the first in a new series which will cover other classes in a similar format in the future. It is set out in columns with fleet number, chassis number, body number which was carried at the time of disposal together with registration number followed by the known history and relevant dates to any changes in ownership, re-registrations and other useful history.

RTL

DIRECTORY

RTL1238 was one of eleven purchased in 1967 and added to earlier batches which had been acquired in 1965 and 1966 by Barton Transport Limited. In its new livery it looks very presentable although it still requires the Barton name to be added to the top of the radiator shell. (John Gascoine)

RTL1	485113	6531	JXN313		
				Bird's Commercial Motors (Dealer), Stratford-upon-Avon, Warwickshire	02/58
				A1 Service, (A.Hunter, Dreghorn), Ardrossan, Ayrshire 16	by 04/58
				Bird's Commercial Motors (Dealer), Stratford-upon-Avon, Warwickshire	02/64
				Partially scrapped at Bird's	04/65
RTL2	484906	2235	JXN314		
				Bird's Commercial Motors (Dealer), Stratford-upon-Avon, Warwickshire	03/58
				OK Motor Services (W.Emmerson), Bishop Auckland, Co. Durham	03/58
				Withdrawn	04/70
				Morley (Dealer), Shildon, Co. Durham for scrap	04/70
RTL3	484841	2077	JXN315		
				Body rebuilt to right hand side platform and left hand side staircase by London Transport – 10/58	
				Mount Blanc Auto-Rental, Geneva, Switzerland	05/64
				Noted parked at Rue-Le-Royer, Geneva, with temporary wood roof	03/69
RTL4	484842	2216	JXN316		
				Bird's Commercial Motors (Dealer), Stratford-upon-Avon, Warwickshire	02/58
				OK Motor Services (W.Emmerson), Bishop Auckland, Co. Durham	03/58
				Withdrawn and used for spares	01/69
RTL5	484839	2144	JXN317		
				Bird's Commercial Motors (Dealer), Stratford-upon-Avon, Warwickshire	02/58
				OK Motor Services (W.Emmerson), Bishop Auckland, Co. Durham	03/58
				Withdrawn	—/69
				Morley (Dealer), Shildon, Co. Durham for scrap	—/69
RTL6	484838	6594	JXN318		
				Bird's Commercial Motors (Dealer), Stratford-upon-Avon, Warwickshire	03/58
				R.C.Doughty & Sons, Kings Lynn, Norfolk	03/58
				Disused with Doughty	04/68
				J. Clarke (Dealer), Walpole St. Andrew, Kings Lynn, Norfolk	09/69
				Now derelict on site	01/70
RTL7	484986	6619	JXN319		
				Bird's Commercial Motors (Dealer), Stratford-upon-Avon, Warwickshire	03/58
				R.C.Doughty & Sons, Kings Lynn, Norfolk	03/58
				Disused	09/69
				J.Clarke (Dealer), Walpole St Andrew, Kings Lynn, Norfolk	09/69
				Still there	03/70

J.Laurie trading as Chieftain were taken over by Central SMT on the 1st October 1961 and RTL11 shows off its previous owner's identify with the fleet number of its newer owner. The radiator mounted name plate now reads Leyland, the chassis manufacturer, rather than in London Transport ownership, its operator's name. (Alan Mortimer)

RTL8	485114	6612	JXN320		
				Bird's Commercial Motors (Dealer), Stratford-upon-Avon, Warwickshire	08/58
				S.Eynon & Sons, Trimsaran, Carmarthenshire	09/58
				Arlington Motors (Dealer), Cardiff	—/63
				Jones (Scrap Dealers), Cardiff Docks	05/63
RTL9	484840	2065	JXN321		
				Bird's Commercial Motors (Dealer), Stratford-upon-Avon, Warwickshire	03/58
				R.C.Doughty & Sons, Kings Lynn, Norfolk	03/58
				Disused	09/69
				J.Clarke (Dealer), Walpole St Andrew, Kings Lynn, Norfolk	09/69
				Now derelict on site	03/70
RTL10	484984	6562	JXN322		
				Bird's Commercial Motors (Dealer), Stratford-upon-Avon, Warwickshire	03/58
				OK Motor Services (W.Emmerson), Bishop Auckland, Co. Durham	03/58
				Withdrawn	—/69
				Morley (Dealer), Shildon, Co. Durham for scrap	—/69
RTL11	484905	6621	JXN323		
				Bird's Commercial Motors (Dealer), Stratford-upon-Avon, Warwickshire	09/58
				J.Laurie t/a Chieftain, Burnbank, Hamilton, Lanarkshire 51	09/58
				Central SMT Motherwell, Lanarkshire HL189 upon take over of Laurie's business	10/61
				E.Corcoran (Dealer), Motherwell, Lanarkshire and broken up	09/64
RTL12	485162	2225	JXN324		
				Bird's Commercial Motors (Dealer), Stratford-upon-Avon, Warwickshire	09/58
				J.Laurie t/a Chieftain, Burnbank, Hamilton, Lanarkshire 52	09/58
	529296		YVA776	Reregistered and new chassis number given together with fleet number 73	06/61
				Central SMT Motherwell, Lanarkshire HL190 upon take over of Laurie's business	10/61
				Withdrawn	—/65
				E.Corcoran (Dealer), Motherwell, Lanarkshire	—/65
RTL13	485219	4460	JXN333		
				Bird's Commercial Motors (Dealer), Stratford-upon-Avon, Warwickshire	10/58
				J.Laurie t/a Chieftain, Burnbank, Hamilton, Lanarkshire 53	10/58
				Central SMT Motherwell, Lanarkshire HL191 upon take over of Laurie's business	10/61
				E.Corcoran (Dealer), Motherwell, Lanarkshire and scrapped	—/66
RTL14	485218	6530	JXN334		
				Bird's Commercial Motors (Dealer), Stratford-upon-Avon, Warwickshire	01/58
				J. Laurie t/a Chieftain, Burnbank, Hamilton, Lanarkshire 63	by 02/58
				Central SMT Motherwell, Lanarkshire HL193 upon take over of Laurie's business	10/61
				Withdrawn	—/65
				E. Corcoran (Dealer), Motherwell, Lanarkshire	—/65
RTL15	485161	2236	JXN335		
				Bird's Commercial Motors (Dealer), Stratford-upon-Avon, Warwickshire	10/58
				J.Laurie t/a/ Chieftain, Burnbank, Hamilton, Lanarkshire 54	10/58
				Central SMT Motherwell, Lanarkshire HL192 upon take over of Laurie's business	10/61
				Rebuilt with non opening top deck windows, new cab and standard CSMT indicators after accident	09/62
				Withdrawn	—/65
				E.Corcoran (Dealer), Motherwell, Lanarkshire	—/65
RTL16	484985	2214	JXN336		
				Bird's Commercial Motors (Dealer), Stratford-upon-Avon, Warwickshire	08/58
				Stephenson Bros., High Etherley, Bishop Auckland, Co. Durham	08/58
				Withdrawn, cannibalised and scrapped	12/66
RTL17	485160	2240	JXN337		
				Bird's Commercial Motors (Dealer), Stratford-upon-Avon, Warwickshire	02/58
				OK Motor Services (W.Emmerson), Bishop Auckland, Co. Durham	03/58
				Withdrawn and used for spares	03/69
				Remains to Morley (Dealer), Shildon, Co. Durham	—/69
RTL18	485220	2217	JXN338		
				Bird's Commercial Motors (Dealer), Stratford-upon-Avon, Warwickshire	02/58
				Anderson Bros. t/a Blue Belle Services, Evenwood, Co. Durham	03/58
				OK Motor Services (W.Emmerson), Bishop Auckland, Co. Durham, upon take over of Anderson's business	10/59
				Withdrawn	05/70
				G.Lister (Dealer), Bolton, Lancashire	05/70
				Martin (Dealer), Weaverham, Cheshire	05/70
				G.Lister (Dealer), Bolton, Lancashire	08/70
				Pickersgill & Laverick (Dealer), Cudworth, South Yorkshire	08/70
RTL19	485221	6287	JXN339		
				Bird's Commercial Motors (Dealer), Stratford-upon-Avon, Warwickshire	08/67
RTL20	485222	6605	JXN340		
				Bird's Commercial Motors (Dealer), Stratford-upon-Avon, Warwickshire	09/58
				T.Wright Coaches, Southend-on-Sea, Essex & used for Bata Shoe contract	09/58
				Jones t/a Audawn Coaches, Corringham, Essex	07/59
				Passenger Vehicle Sales (London) Ltd., (Dealer), Upminster, Essex	05/64
				R.Locke (Breakers), Milton Street, London E14	05/64

RTL21	485223	6593	JXN341		
				Bird's Commercial Motors (Dealer), Stratford-upon-Avon, Warwickshire	02/58
				A1 Service, (Duff, Ardrossan), Ardrossan, Ayrshire	by 04/58
				Clyde Coast Services (Shields, Saltcoats), Saltcoats, Ayrshire	05/58
				Withdrawn	05/69
				W.North (Dealer), Sherburn-in-Elmet, Yorkshire	05/69
RTL22	485225	6289	JXN342		
			23 sri 3078	Ceylon Transport Board, Colombo, Ceylon	10/67
RTL23	485227	4432	JXN344		
				Bird's Commercial Motors (Dealer), Strafford-upon-Avon, Warwickshire	03/58
				A. Hormsby t/a Primrose Coaches, Scunthorpe, Lincolnshire	03/58
				Bird's Commercial Motors (Dealer), Stratford-upon-Avon, Warwickshire	01/66
RTL24	485246	4415	JXN347		
				Bird's Commercial Motors (Dealer), Stratford-upon-Avon, Warwickshire	07/58
				A1 Service, (T.Hunter, Kilmarnock), Ardrossan, Ayrshire	08/58
				Withdrawn from service but still owned	—/66
				Returned to service	—/68
				Withdrawn	03/70
				Tiger Coaches (Dealer), Salsburgh, Lanarkshire	by 04/70
RTL25	485228	4423	JXN348		
				Bird's Commercial Motors (Dealer), Stratford-upon-Avon, Warwickshire	03/58
				OK Motor Services (W.Emmerson), Bishop Auckland, Co. Durham	03/58
				Withdrawn and cannibalised	06/69
				Remains to Morley (Dealer), Shildon, Co. Durham for scrap	07/69
RTL26	485250	4425	JXN349		
				Bird's Commercial Motors (Dealer), Stratford-upon-Avon, Warwickshire	07/58
				Harper Bros., Heath Hayes, Staffordshire 1	08/58
				Harper Bros., taken over by Midland Red and bus now operating on hire to Midland Red as crew ferry bus	09/74
				Midland Red 2201	09/74
				Never operated and withdrawn	09/74
				Longbridge Engineering (Dealer), Longbridge	—/75
RTL27	485248	4727	JXN350		
				Bird's Commercial Motors (Dealer), Stratford-upon-Avon, Warwickshire	06/58
				A & C McLennan, Spittalfield, Perthshire 94	06/58
				Tiger Coaches (Dealer), Salsburgh, Lanarkshire	03/70

RTL1 looks splendid in the livery of A1 Service in which owning member A. Hunter of Dreghorn has had it repainted. Good use has been made of the London Transport fitted slip board brackets along the lower edge of the front saloon bulkhead window beneath the canopy to which a via point is now shown. The A1 insignia is carried on the panelled over via point and route number apertures and beneath the canopy where earlier the route number would have been shown. Traversing the roads of Ardrossan on an un-numbered service to Kilmarnock the bus looks modern when compared to the background. (F. W. Ivey)

RTL28	485226	4420	JXN351		
				Bird's Commercial Motors (Dealer), Stratford-upon-Avon, Warwickshire	03/58
				OK Motor Service (W.Emmerson), Bishop Auckland, Co. Durham	03/58
				Withdrawn (last RTL with OK)	11/70
				North Eastern C.W.S. Birtley, Co. Durham as Newcastle-upon-Tyne staff bus	11/70
				Co-operative Wholesale Society, Manchester and used as a staff bus between Northampton and Newport Pagnell	05/72
				Still in use	06/74
				Believed scrapped by gypsies at Poddington, Bedfordshire	by —/78
RTL29	485247	4675	JXN352		
				Bird's Commercial Motors (Dealer), Stratford-upon-Avon, Warwickshire	01/58
				A1 Service, (McKinnon, Kilmarnock), Ardrossan, Ayrshire	by 04/58
				Caldwell (Dealer), Irvine	11/67
RTL30	485245	6642	JXN353		
				Bird's Commercial Motors (Dealer), Stratford-upon-Avon, Warwickshire	01/58
				J.Laurie t/a Chieftain, Burnbank, Hamilton, Lanarkshire 64	by 02/58
				Central SMT Motherwell, Lanarkshire HL194 upon take over of Laurie's business	10/61
				E.Corcoran (Dealer), Motherwell, Lanarkshire and scrapped	—/66
RTL31	485229	4514	JXN354		
				Bird's Commercial Motors (Dealer), Stratford-upon-Avon, Warwickshire	02/58
				A1 Service, (McKinnon, Kilmarnock), Ardrossan, Ayrshire	by 04/58
				Withdrawn	01/68
				Scrapped	by 04/68
RTL32	485251	6339	JXN355 CA 5738		
				Golden Arrow Bus Service, Cape Town, South Africa 201	08/64
				Withdrawn and used for spares	04/70
				Remains to S.A. Metal & Machinery Company (Breaker), Cape Town, South Africa	05/70
RTL33	485284	2222	JXN356		
				Bird's Commercial Motors (Dealer), Stratford-upon-Avon, Warwickshire	03/58
				OK Motor Service (W.Emmerson), Bishop Auckland, Co. Durham	03/58
				Withdrawn	01/70
				Morley (Dealer), Shildon, Co. Durham for scrap	—/70
RTL34	485249	2223	JXN357		
				Bird's Commercial Motors (Dealer), Stratford-upon-Avon, Warwickshire	07/58
				Stonier & Sons, Goldenhill, Stoke-on-Trent, Staffordshire	07/58
				Withdrawn	09/67
				Tiger Coaches, Salsburgh, Lanarkshire 2	11/67
				Tiger Coaches (Dealer), Salsburgh, Lanarkshire	—/68
				J.B.G. Irvine, Salsburgh, Lanarkshire for spares	08/68
RTL35	485224	6651	JXN358		
				Bird's Commercial Motors (Dealer), Stratford-upon-Avon, Warwickshire	02/58
				S.Eynon & Sons, Trimsaran, Carmarthenshire	02/58
				Bird's Commercial Motors (Dealer), Stratford-upon-Avon, Warwickshire	by 07/62
				Refreshment stall in field at A47/A452 junction near Castle Bromwich, in dark green livery and engineless	05/64
RTL36	485288	2101	JXN359		
				Bird's Commercial Motors (Dealer), Stratford-upon-Avon, Warwickshire	06/58
				Pulham & Sons, Bourton-on-the-Water, Gloucestershire	06/58
				Withdrawn	06/68
				Hartwood Finance (Dealer), Barnsley, Yorkshire	08/68
RTL37	485289	2234	JXN360		
				Bird's Commercial Motors (Dealer), Stratford-upon-Avon, Warwickshire	01/58
				J.Laurie t/a Chieftain, Burnbank, Hamilton, Lanarkshire 65	by 02/58
				Burnt out	—/—
				Noted at Bird's Commercial Motors (Dealer), Stratford-upon-Avon, Warwickshire	08/61
				Derelict on Bird's premises	06/63
RTL38	485286	6644	JXN361		
				Bird's Commercial Motors (Dealer), Stratford-upon-Avon, Warwickshire	03/58
				J.Laurie t/a Chieftain, Burnbank, Hamilton, Lanarkshire 60	03/58
				Central SMT Motherwell, Lanarkshire HL195 upon take over of Laurie's business	10/61
				Involved in accident and stored in Motherwell garage	—/62
				E.Corcoran (Dealer), Motherwell for scrap	—/65
RTL39	485285	4414	JXN362		
				Bird's Commercial Motors (Dealer), Stratford-upon-Avon, Warwickshire	03/58
				J.Laurie t/a Chieftain, Burnbank, Hamilton, Lanarkshire 61	03/58
				Central SMT Motherwell, Lanarkshire HL196 upon take over of Laurie's business	10/61
				W.Alexander & Sons (Fife) Ltd, Kirkcaldy, Fife	—/66
				Allocated fleet number FRB162 but withdrawn without ever being used	—/66
				E.Corcoran (Dealer), Motherwell, Lanarkshire	09/66

RTL40	485287	6683	JXN363		
				Bird's Commercial Motors (Dealer), Stratford-upon-Avon, Warwickshire	06/58
				A & C McLennan, Spittalfield, Perthshire 95	06/58
				Withdrawn	—/72
				Being cannibalised	04/73
				Remains still on site	11/74
RTL41	485254	6678	JXN364		
				Bird's Commercial Motors (Dealer), Stratford-upon-Avon, Warwickshire	01/58
				J.Laurie t/a Chieftain, Burnbank, Hamilton, Lanarkshire 66	by 02/58
				Central SMT Motherwell, Lanarkshire HL197 upon take over of Laurie's business	10/61
				E.Corcoran (Dealer), Motherwell, Lanarkshire	—/66
RTL42	485280	4412	JXN365		
				Bird's Commercial Motors (Dealer), Stratford-upon-Avon, Warwickshire	06/58
				Stonier & Sons, Goldenhill, Stoke-on-Trent, Staffordshire	06/58
				Withdrawn	06/66
				W. North (Dealer), Sherburn-in-Elmet, Yorkshire	08/66
RTL43	485283	4513	JXN366		
				Bird's Commercial Motors (Dealer), Stratford-upon-Avon, Warwickshire	02/58
				A1 Service, (T & E Docherty, Irvine), Ardrossan, Ayrshire 20a	03/58
				Rebuilt to front entrance with air operated doors, by a local bodybuilder	09/63
				Sold within group to Duff, Ardrossan, Ayrshire	06/71
				Tiger Coaches (Dealer), Salsburgh, Lanarkshire	11/73
				D.Parsons (A1 Coachways), London N22 to eventually be preserved	11/73
				E.Brakell (Dealer), Cheam, Surrey	04/75
				Phillipson, London N1 for preservation	08/75
				M.Hebard (Dealer), Morden, Surrey	05/76
				London Bus Preservation Group (Dealer), Cobham,. Surrey	—/—
				Fractional H.P. Motors, St. Leonards-on-Sea, Sussex as staff bus	05/78
				Out of service	05/80
				E.Brakell (Dealer), Cheam, Surrey	08/80
				A.Potter, Edgware, Middlesex for preservation	02/81
				A.Potter moved to Luton	03/88
				Still owned	03/98
RTL44	485282	2165	JXN367		
				Bird's Commercial Motors (Dealer), Stratford-upon-Avon, Warwickshire	02/58
				A1 Service, (A.Hunter, Dreghorn), Ardrossan, Ayrshire 17	03/58
				Withdrawn and partly cannibalised	04/68
				Keenan, Coalhall, Ayrshire for spares	07/68
RTL45	485253	6707	JXN368		
				Bird's Commercial Motors (Dealer), Stratford-upon-Avon, Warwickshire	03/58
				Stephenson Bros., High Etherley, Bishop Auckland, Co. Durham	03/58
				Into service	10/58
				Withdrawn after an accident	03/67
				Randolph Coachworks (Dealer), Evenwood Co. Durham and scrapped	04/67
RTL46	485252	6687	JXN369		
				Bird's Commercial Motors (Dealer), Stratford-upon-Avon, Warwickshire	06/58
				A1 Service, (J.Brown, Dreghorn), Ardrossan, Ayrshire 5	06/58
				Withdrawn	by 05/70
RTL47	485325	6692	JXN370		
				Bird's Commercial Motors (Dealer), Stratford-upon-Avon, Warwickshire	02/58
				A & C McLennan, Spittalfield, Perthshire 85	02/58
				Delicenced	04/73
				William Inverarity & Company (Fruit Growers), Blairgowie used by berry pickers	07/73
				William Inverarity & Company, Cransley Farm, Liff near Dundee	by 08/81
				K. Jenkinson, Queensbury, Yorkshire for preservation	by 12/82
				Still owned	07/94
RTL48	485332	6697	JXN371		
				Bird's Commercial Motors (Dealer), Stratford-upon-Avon, Warwickshire	03/58
				F.Lockey & Sons. Limited, West Auckland, Co. Durham	03/58
				A.Crammom, Evenwood, Co. Durham for preservation	08/73
				RTL48 Group (A.Crammom, S.Skuce, F.Hannock) for continued preservation	by 07/78
				R.Wright and R.Humphreys, Dagenham, Essex for continued preservation	10/80
				R.Wright, Rainham, Essex for continued preservation	by 01/87
				Still owned	05/98
RTL49	485330	8315	JXN372		
				Bird's Commercial Motors (Dealer), Stratford-upon-Avon, Warwickshire	02/58
				A & C McLennan, Spittalfield, Perthshire 86	02/58
				Withdrawn	—/72
				Being Cannibalised	04/73
				Remains burnt on ground behind McLennan depot	11/74
RTL50	485331	4806	JXN373		
				Wombwell Diesel Company (Dealer), Wombwell, Yorkshire	10/69

J. Laurie, trading as Chieftain, fleet number 63 was RTL14 and it is seen here in 1961 with a clearly readable destination blind. Note the direction indicators that have been added as this bus had been disposed of well before the introduction of the direction indicator ears fitted to the London fleet in later years. The overall size of the Golden Shred advertisement appears to suit the available space very admirably. (Alan Mortimer)

RTL51	485326	4430	JXN374		
				Bird's Commercial Motors (Dealer), Stratford-upon-Avon, Warwickshire	02/58
				J.Laurie t/a Chieftain, Burnbank, Hamilton, Lanarkshire 67	by 03/58
				Central SMT Motherwell, Lanarkshire HL198 upon take over of Laurie's business	10/61
				E.Corcoran (Dealer), Motherwell, Lanarkshire and scrapped	09/66
RTL52	485328	4464	JXN375		
				Bird's Commercial Motors (Dealer), Stratford-upon-Avon, Warwickshire	02/58
				J.Laurie t/a Chieftain, Burnbank, Hamilton, Lanarkshire 68	by 03/58
				Central SMT Motherwell, Lanarkshire HL199 upon take over of Laurie's business	10/61
				E.Corcoran (Dealer), Motherwell, Lanarkshire	—/65
RTL53	485351	5090	JXN376		
			23 sri 3276	Ceylon Transport Board, Colombo, Ceylon	08/68
RTL54	485333	4448	JXN377		
				Bird's Commercial Motors (Dealer), Stratford-upon-Avon, Warwickshire	01/58
				A & C McLennan, Spittalfield, Perthshire 87	02/58
				Withdrawn	08/72
				S & N Motors (Dealer), Glasgow	08/72
RTL55	485329	6701	JXN378		
				Bird's Commercial Motors (Dealer), Stratford-upon-Avon, Warwickshire	02/58
				F.Lockey & Sons Limited, West Auckland, Co. Durham	02/58
				Withdrawn	12/74
				Lanarkshire Travel Limited, Hamilton, Lanarkshire	by 05/75
				Noted in yard of James Hepburn Limited, Motherwell, Lanarkshire	by 05/75
				E.Beckett (Breakers), Carlton, Yorkshire	04/77
RTL56	485681	4541	JXN379		
				Pickersgill & Laverick (Dealer), Cudworth, Yorkshire	05/69
RTL57	485682	4428	JXN380		
			22 sri 3290	Ceylon Transport Board, Colombo, Ceylon	03/59
RTL58	485683	4435	JXN381		
			22 sri 2936	Ceylon Transport Board, Colombo, Ceylon	01/59
RTL59	485324	4664	JXN382		
			22 sri 2675	Ceylon Transport Board, Colombo, Ceylon	12/58
RTL60	485354	4684	JXN383		
			23 sri 1127	Ceylon Transport Board, Colombo, Ceylon	05/64
				Still in existence, but withdrawn	02/77
RTL61	485327	4441	JXN384		
			22 sri 2882	Ceylon Transport Board, Colombo, Ceylon	01/59

RTL62	485281	4434	JXN385		
			22 sri 2876	Ceylon Transport Board, Colombo, Ceylon	01/59
RTL63	485339	5076	JXN386		
			22 sri 2692	Ceylon Transport Board, Colombo, Ceylon	12/58
RTL64	485352	4555	JXN387		
			CA 125 281	City Tramways Co., Cape Town, South Africa 477	02/64
				Still in service	04/74
RTL65	485353	5051	JXN388		
			23 sri 3223	Ceylon Transport Board, Colombo, Ceylon	07/68
				Still in existence, but withdrawn	02/77
RTL66	485357	6234	JXN389		
			23 sri 3205	Ceylon Transport Board, Colombo, Ceylon	04/68
			23 sri 3205	Still in existence, but withdrawn	02/77
RTL67	485684	6383	JXN390		
			CA 80821	City Tramways Co., Cape Town, South Africa 704	08/64
				Still in service	04/74
RTL68	485356	2038	JXN391		
				Chambers t/a White City Coaches, London W12	07/68
				E.Brakell, T.Robertson, T.Hornby, Cheam, Surrey for preservation	by 03/74
				G. Wallis, Wanaka, New Zealand for continued preservation	09/93
				Still owned	02/98
RTL69	485360	6361	JXN392		
			23 sri 1315	Ceylon Transport Board, Colombo, Ceylon	11/64
RTL70	485680	2397	JXN393		
				Bird's Commercial Motors (Dealer), Stratford-upon-Avon, Warwickshire	12/67
				Partially scrapped	01/68
RTL71	485361	2224	JXN394		
			22 sri 2600	Ceylon Transport Board, Colombo, Ceylon	12/58
RTL72	485358	4562	JXN395		
				Passenger Vehicle Sales (London) Ltd (Dealer), Upminster, Essex	07/65
				G.W.Osborne & Sons, Tollesbury, Essex	07/65
				Used as a source of spares, the roof being mounted onto RT317 after the latter was damaged by a low bridge. Work carried out by Thurgoods of Ware	08/65
RTL73	485362	2117	JXN396		
				Wombwell Diesel Company (Dealer), Wombwell, Yorkshire	11/69
RTL74	485685	3524	JXN397		
			23 sri 2055	Ceylon Transport Board, Colombo, Ceylon	12/65
			27 sri 7041	Sold and rebuilt as a private lorry	06/78
RTL75	485689	4658	JXN398		
				Wombwell Diesel Company (Dealer), Wombwell, Yorkshire	11/69
RTL76	485355	4560	JXN399		
			22 sri 2942	Ceylon Transport Board, Colombo, Ceylon	01/59
RTL77	485764	4661	JXN400		
			23 sri 3206	Ceylon Transport Board, Colombo, Ceylon	04/68
RTL78	485687	4479	JXN401		
			22 sri 2665	Ceylon Transport Board, Colombo, Ceylon	12/58
RTL79	485690	4618	JXN402		
			22 sri 2872	Ceylon Transport Board, Colombo, Ceylon	01/59
RTL80	485757	4493	JXN403		
			22 sri 3248	Ceylon Transport Board, Colombo, Ceylon	03/59
RTL81	485756	4558	JXN404		
			22 sri 2599	Ceylon Transport Board, Colombo, Ceylon	12/58
RTL82	485825	4667	JXN405		
			22 sri 3260	Ceylon Transport Board, Colombo, Ceylon	03/59
RTL83	485688	4503	JXN406		
			22 sri 2933	Ceylon Transport Board, Colombo, Ceylon	01/59
RTL84	485686	4581	JXN407		
			22 sri 2616	Ceylon Transport Board, Colombo, Ceylon	12/58
RTL85	485767	5093	JXN408		
				Pickersgill & Laverick (Dealer), Cudworth, Yorkshire after mechanical units had been removed at Stonebridge garage for Ceylon Transport Board	06/69
RTL86	485822	4539	JXN409		
			23 sri 3299	Ceylon Transport Board, Colombo, Ceylon	08/68
			27 sri 4253	Sold and rebuilt as a private lorry	06/80
RTL87	485770	4492	JXN410		
			22 sri 3252	Ceylon Transport Board, Colombo, Ceylon	03/59
RTL88	485768	2409	JXN411		
				Passenger Vehicle Sales (London) Ltd (Dealer), Canvey Island, Essex	02/68
				Hall t/a Broadway Coaches, Wickford, Essex	03/68
				Passenger Vehicle Sales (London) Ltd (Dealer), Silver End, Essex	04/72
				P.Blatchley t/a Contractus, Stevenage, Hertfordshire	05/72
				Still in use	01/74
				Unknown dealer, Carlton, Yorkshire	06/74

RTL89	485823	2220	JXN412		
			CA 103 333	Golden Arrow Bus Service, Cape Town, South Africa 207	10/64
RTL90	485765	4803	JXN413		
			23 sri 1954	Ceylon Transport Board, Colombo, Ceylon	10/65
RTL91	485761	4695	JXN414		
			22 sri 2870	Ceylon Transport Board, Colombo, Ceylon	01/59
RTL92	485763	4740	JXN415		
			23 sri 1055	Ceylon Transport Board, Colombo, Ceylon	04/64
RTL93	485759	4589	JXN416		
			22 sri 3291	Ceylon Transport Board, Colombo, Ceylon	03/59
RTL94	485760	4614	JXN417		
			22 sri 2663	Ceylon Transport Board, Colombo, Ceylon	12/58
RTL95	485758	4683	JXN418		
			22 sri 2874	Ceylon Transport Board, Colombo, Ceylon	01/59
RTL96	485762	5209	JXN419		
				Wombwell Diesel Company (Dealer), Wombwell, Yorkshire	05/69
RTL97	485691	4480	JXN420		
			22 sri 3249	Ceylon Transport Board, Colombo, Ceylon	03/59
RTL98	485769	2121	JXN421		
				Pickersgill & Laverick (Dealer), Cudworth, Yorkshire	05/69
RTL99	485824	4477	JXN422		
			22 sri 2879	Ceylon Transport Board, Colombo, Ceylon	01/59
RTL100	485821	4629	JXN423		
			22 sri 2596	Ceylon Transport Board, Colombo, Ceylon	12/58
RTL101	485766	2394	JXN424		
			23 sri 3216	Ceylon Transport Board, Colombo, Ceylon	05/68
RTL102	485827	4505	JXN425		
			22 sri 2930	Ceylon Transport Board, Colombo, Ceylon	01/59
RTL103	485829	4599	JXN426		
			22 sri 2929	Ceylon Transport Board, Colombo, Ceylon	01/59
RTL104	485830	4489	JXN427		
			22 sri 3259	Ceylon Transport Board, Colombo, Ceylon	03/59
RTL105	490644	4738	JXN428		
			22 sri 2694	Ceylon Transport Board, Colombo, Ceylon	12/58
				Still in existence, but withdrawn	02/77

Walsall Corporation fleet number 201 was once RTL550 and looking very untidy and a little neglected it stands waiting further use on route 17. It was to last long enough with the Corporation to be incorporated within the Northern Division of the newly established West Midlands Passenger Transport Executive in October 1969.

RTL106	490646	4672	JXN429		
			22 sri 2934	Ceylon Transport Board, Colombo, Ceylon	01/59
RTL107	490648	4590	JXN430		
			CA 134 461	Golden Arrow Bus Service, Cape Town, South Africa 221	01/65
				Burnt out at Nyanga and withdrawn	06/65
RTL108	490649	2221	JXN431		
			22 sri 2943	Ceylon Transport Board, Colombo, Ceylon	01/59
RTL109	485833	4679	JXN432		
			22 sri 2871	Ceylon Transport Board, Colombo, Ceylon	01/59
RTL110	490647	5085	JXN433		
			22 sri 3362	Ceylon Transport Board, Colombo, Ceylon	12/68
				Still in existence but withdrawn	02/77
RTL111	485831	4593	JXN434		
			22 sri 3289	Ceylon Transport Board, Colombo, Ceylon	03/59
RTL112	485834	2427	JXN435		
			23 sri 3361	Ceylon Transport Board, Colombo, Ceylon	12/68
				Still in existence but withdrawn	02/77
RTL113	485826	4591	JXN436		
			22 sri 3288	Ceylon Transport Board, Colombo, Ceylon	03/59
RTL114	485832	5053	JXN437		
				Gradeka Saobracaine Preduzece, Sarajevo, Yugoslavia	07/64
RTL115	490656	4570	JXN438		
			22 sri 3292	Ceylon Transport Board, Colombo, Ceylon	03/59
RTL116	490653	4673	JXN439		
			22 sri 2693	Ceylon Transport Board, Colombo, Ceylon	12/58
RTL117	490654	4694	KGK781		
			22 sri 2658	Ceylon Transport Board, Colombo, Ceylon	12/58
RTL118	490655	4613	KGK782		
			22 sri 2691	Ceylon Transport Board, Colombo, Ceylon	12/58
RTL119	490652	4501	KGK783		
			22 sri 1504	Ceylon Transport Board, Colombo, Ceylon	02/65
RTL120	490790	4801	KGK784		
				Pickersgill & Laverick (Dealer), Cudworth, Yorkshire	05/69
RTL121	490788	5069	KGK785		
				Pickersgill & Laverick (Dealer), Cudworth, Yorkshire	05/69
RTL122	490786	2401	KGK786		
				Passenger Vehicle Sales (London) Ltd (Dealer), Canvey Island, Essex who fitted platform doors	02/68
				Colin S. Pegg Limited, Caston, Norfolk	03/68
				Withdrawn	11/73
				Chassis to Omnibus Promotions Limited, London EC1 who removed engine for spares	09/74
				Body remains with Pegg as a store shed	
RTL123	490785	4858	KGK787		
			23 sri 2751	Ceylon Transport Board, Colombo, Ceylon	01/67
RTL124	490789	4894	KGK788		
			23 sri 3398	Ceylon Transport Board, Colombo, Ceylon	12/68
RTL125	490787	4510	KGK789		
			22 sri 2687	Ceylon Transport Board, Colombo, Ceylon	12/58
RTL126	485835	4511	KGK790		
			22 sri 2662	Ceylon Transport Board, Colombo, Ceylon	12/58
RTL127	485828	4615	KGK791		
			23 sri 1056	Ceylon Transport Board, Colombo, Ceylon	04/64
RTL128	490642	2107	KGK792		
				St Michael's School, Ingoldisthorpe, Kings Lynn, Norfolk	09/68
				Believed scrapped by local breakers	—/70
RTL129	490645	4534	KGK793		
				Leyland Motors (Dealer), London W1	04/62
				Exported to USA on SS Arabia	04/62
				Vincent Sardi (Restaurateur), Sardi's Restaurant, New York City, USA and used for transport of clients	
				to and from West Side theatres as bus number 2	04/62
				Still owned	04/68
				Inn of the Clock Restaurant, New York City	c—/71
				Seen on 5th Avenue advertising "Municipal Bus Tours"	05/72
				Horn & Hardart Restaurant, New York City in poor condition	—/74
				Believed to be the RTL with McGiures Irish, Pub, Pensacola, Florida	03/98
RTL130	490659	4982	KGK794		
				Wombwell Diesel Company (Dealer), Wombwell, Yorkshire after mechanical units had	
				been removed at Stonebridge garage for Ceylon Transport Board	04/69
RTL131	490660	4421	KGK795		
			22 sri 2672	Ceylon Transport Board, Colombo, Ceylon	12/58
				Still in existence but withdrawn	02/77
RTL132	490657	5315	KGK796		
				Pickersgill & Laverick (Dealer), Cudworth, Yorkshire	05/69

RTL1217 was initially purchased by Edward Bowman & Son in May 1963 and its Park Royal body was immediately converted into a mobile showroom with all glazed area being panelled over. A generator for producing its own electrical power was affixed to the rear which gave it a DIY bustle effect in line with certain wartime gas producer vehicles. On the 22nd March 1964 it stands within a temporary car park which has since disappeared under the Leeds Inner Road system. (Henry Heyworth)

RTL567 is seen at the "Prince of Wales", Harrow Road, London on the 15th July 1973. Now painted in a livery for Western Waterbeds International Limited it had previously carried a paint scheme for an organisation involved with sack sewing machines. After its current use it was noted in a further livery, this time for the Children of God, a very chequered non-passenger carrying career by any standards. (John G.S. Smith)

RTL133	490658	4442	KGK797		
				Bird's Commercial Motors (Dealer), Stratford-upon-Avon, Warwickshire	01/59
				A.H.Kearsey Limited, Cheltenham, Gloucestershire 62a	01/59
				Marchant's Coaches, Cheltenham, Gloucestershire upon takeover of Kearsey's business	01/68
RTL134	490782	4588	KGK798		
			23 sri 3229	Ceylon Transport Board, Colombo, Ceylon	07/68
RTL135	490784	4408	KGK799		
				Bird's Commercial Motors (Dealer), Stratford-upon-Avon, Warwickshire	01/59
				A1 Service, (McKinnon, Kilmarnock), Ardrossan, Ayrshire	01/59
				Still there	10/64
RTL136	490651	4443	KGK800		
			22 sri 2869	Ceylon Transport Board, Colombo, Ceylon	01/59
RTL137	490783	4918	KGK801		
			23 sri 3256	Ceylon Transport Board, Colombo, Ceylon	07/68
				Still in existence but withdrawn	02/77
			27 sri 569	Sold and rebuilt as a private lorry	12/79
RTL138	490661	4437	KGK802		
				A.H.Kearsey Limited, Cheltenham, Gloucestershire 63a	03/59
				Withdrawn	07/66
RTL139	490868	4850	KGK803		
				Louwman & Porqui (Motor Vehicle Importers), Leidschendam, Holland	12/67
				Netherlands National Automobile Museum, Leidschendam, Holland (which closed c. 1980)	12/67
				Het National Automobile Museum, Raamsdonksver (which opened 1982)	12/80
				Still owned	03/97
				H. Sjoerds t/a Steamline, Hulversum	by 10/97
RTL140	490871	5199	KGK804		
				Pickersgill & Laverick (Dealer), Cudworth, Yorkshire	05/69
RTL141	490650	2116	KGK805		
			23 sri 3278	Ceylon Transport Board, Colombo, Ceylon	08/68
RTL142	490643	2428	KGK806		
			23 sri 3230	Ceylon Transport Board, Colombo, Ceylon	07/68
				Still in existence but withdrawn	02/77
RTL143	490791	2059	KGK807		
				Pickersgill & Laverick (Dealer), Cudworth, Yorkshire	05/69
RTL144	490874	2104	KGK808		
				Wombwell Diesel Company (Dealer), Wombwell, Yorkshire	05/69
RTL145	490869	5327	KGK809		
				Pickersgill & Laverick (Dealer), Cudworth, Yorkshire	05/69
RTL146	490923	4706	KGK810		
				Wombwell Diesel Company (Dealer), Wombwell, Yorkshire	10/69
RTL147	490867	4576	KGK811		
			23 sri 1057	Ceylon Transport Board, Colombo, Ceylon	04/64
RTL148	490920	5024	KGK812		
			23 sri 3252	Ceylon Transport Board, Colombo, Ceylon	07/68
RTL149	490970	4452	KGK813		
				A.H.Kearsey Limited, Cheltenham, Gloucestershire 69a	04/59
				Marchant's Coaches, Cheltenham, Gloucestershire upon takeover of Kearsey's business	01/68
RTL150	490921	4866	KGK814		
			23 sri 3260	Ceylon Transport Board, Colombo, Ceylon	07/68
RTL151	490967	4531	KGK815		
			CA 134 462	Golden Arrow Bus Service, Cape Town, South Africa 222	12/64
				Withdrawn and dismantled	05/70
RTL152	490971	4516	KGK816		
			SA 55 66	Gradeka Saobracaine Preduzece, Sarajevo, Yugoslavia 34	06/64
RTL153	490974	4563	KGK817		
			22 sri 3243	Ceylon Transport Board, Colombo, Ceylon	03/59
RTL154	490968	4451	KGK818		
			23 sri 1304	Ceylon Transport Board, Colombo, Ceylon	11/64
RTL155	491018	4438	KGK819		
			22 sri 2598	Ceylon Transport Board, Colombo, Ceylon	12/58
RTL156	491011	4522	KGK820		
				Gradeka Saobracaine Preduzece, Sarajevo, Yugoslavia	05/64
RTL157	491014	4814	KGK821		
				Pickersgill & Laverick (Dealer), Cudworth, Yorkshire	05/69
RTL158	490914	4586	KGK822		
			22 sri 2676	Ceylon Transport Board, Colombo, Ceylon	12/58
RTL159	491016	4524	KGK823		
			22 sri 3304	Ceylon Transport Board, Colombo, Ceylon	03/59
RTL160	491010	4498	KGK824		
			22 sri 2884	Ceylon Transport Board, Colombo, Ceylon	01/59
RTL161	491009	4852	KGK825		
				Pickersgill & Laverick (Dealer), Cudworth, Yorkshire	05/69

RTL162	490973	4571	KGK826		
			22 sri 2653	Ceylon Transport Board, Colombo, Ceylon	12/58
RTL163	490972	5049	KGK827		
				Pickersgill & Laverick (Dealer), Cudworth, Yorkshire	08/70
RTL164	491015	6322	KGK828		
				Pickersgill & Laverick (Dealer), Cudworth, Yorkshire	05/69
RTL165	491020	5206	KGK829		
			CA 119 168	City Tramways Co., Cape Town, South Africa 467	02/64
				Still in service	04/74
RTL166	491017	4609	KGK830		
			23 sri 3265	Ceylon Transport Board, Colombo, Ceylon	07/68
				Still in existence but withdrawn	02/77
RTL167	491012	4566	KGK831		
			22 sri 2948	Ceylon Transport Board, Colombo, Ceylon	01/59
RTL168	491013	4445	KGK832		
				Bird's Commercial Motors (Dealer), Stratford-upon-Avon, Warwickshire	12/58
				W.Stonier & Sons, Goldenhill, Stoke-on-Trent, Staffordshire	12/58
				Withdrawn	08/65
				Tiger Coaches (Dealer), Salsburgh, Lanarkshire and scrapped	09/65
RTL169	490919	4553	KGK833		
			CA 130 869	Golden Arrow Bus Service, Cape Town, South Africa 218	01/65
RTL170	490916	6379	KGK834		
			CA 80848	City Tramways Co., Cape Town, South Africa 707	09/64
				Golden Arrow Bus Service, Cape Town, South Africa 234	03/65
				Withdrawn and dismantled for spares	05/70
				Remains to S.A. Metal & Machinery Company (Breaker), Cape Town, South Africa	06/70
RTL171	490905	4674	KGK835		
			22 sri 2673	Ceylon Transport Board, Colombo, Ceylon	12/58
RTL172	490915	2084	KGK836		
				Wombwell Diesel Company (Dealer), Wombwell, Yorkshire after mechanical units had been removed at Stonebridge Garage for Ceylon Transport Board	04/69
RTL173	490917	4528	KGK837		
			CA 134 463	Golden Arrow Bus Service, Cape Town, South Africa 223	01/65
				Scrapped	10/70
RTL174	490904	4440	KGK838		
				Chassis dismantled at Aldenham	10/60
				Fire damaged body to G.Cohen	10/60
RTL175	490918	5071	KGK839		
				Pickersgill & Laverick (Dealer), Cudworth, Yorkshire after mechanical units had been removed at Stonebridge Garage for Ceylon Transport Board	06/69
RTL176	490873	5059	KGK840		
				Pickersgill & Laverick (Dealer), Cudworth, Yorkshire	06/69
RTL177	490872	5196	KGK841		
			23 sri 1614	Ceylon Transport Board, Colombo, Ceylon	04/65
RTL178	490907	4532	KGK842		
			23 sri 1128	Ceylon Transport Board, Colombo, Ceylon	05/64
RTL179	490922	4547	KGK843		
			23 sri 3255	Ceylon Transport Board, Colombo, Ceylon	07/68
RTL180	490906	5115	KGK844		
			23 sri 3284	Ceylon Transport Board, Colombo, Ceylon	08/68
RTL181	491082	5028	KGK845		
				Pickersgill & Laverick (Dealer), Cudworth, Yorkshire	05/69
RTL182	491083	4567	KGK846		
			23 sri 1058	Ceylon Transport Board, Colombo, Ceylon	04/64
RTL183	491077	5037	KGK847		
			23 sri 3385	Ceylon Transport Board, Colombo, Ceylon	12/68
				Still in existence but withdrawn	02/77
RTL184	491075	2410	KGK848		
				Bird's Commercial Motors (Dealer), Stratford-upon-Avon, Warwickshire	04/69
RTL185	491256	4583	KGK849		
			22 sri 2613	Ceylon Transport Board, Colombo, Ceylon	12/58
RTL186	491076	4621	KGK850		
			22 sri 2624	Ceylon Transport Board, Colombo, Ceylon	12/58
RTL187	491259	4670	KGK851		
			22 sri 2667	Ceylon Transport Board, Colombo, Ceylon	12/58
				Still in existence having been fitted with single deck bodywork	02/77
RTL188	491255	4559	KGK852		
			22 sri 2609	Ceylon Transport Board, Colombo, Ceylon	12/58
RTL189	491257	4617	KGK853		
			22 sri 2657	Ceylon Transport Board, Colombo, Ceylon	12/58
RTL190	491258	5192	KGK854		
				Wombwell Diesel Company (Dealer), Wombwell, Yorkshire	05/69

RTL191	491262	4693	KGK855		
			22 sri 2607	Ceylon Transport Board, Colombo, Ceylon	12/58
RTL192	491379	4506	KGK856		
			22 sri 3258	Ceylon Transport Board, Colombo, Ceylon	03/59
RTL193	491474	4594	KGK857		
			22 sri 2690	Ceylon Transport Board, Colombo, Ceylon	12/58
				Still in service	02/77
RTL194	491260	4523	KGK858		
			22 sri 2885	Ceylon Transport Board, Colombo, Ceylon	01/59
RTL195	491261	4690	KGK859		
			22 sri 2605	Ceylon Transport Board, Colombo, Ceylon	12/58
RTL196	491381	4622	KGK860		
			22 sri 2666	Ceylon Transport Board, Colombo, Ceylon	12/58
RTL197	491265	4478	KGK861		
			22 sri 2612	Ceylon Transport Board, Colombo, Ceylon	12/58
				Sold	05/72
				Still in existence as a private lorry having not been reregistered	02/77
RTL198	461264	4897	KGK862		
				Wombwell Diesel Company (Dealer), Wombwell, Yorkshire	01/70
RTL199	491472	4828	KGK863		
				Bird's Commercial Motors (Dealer), Stratford-upon-Avon, Warwickshire	12/67
RTL200	491473	3424	KGK864		
			SA 55 23	Gradeka Saobracaine Preduzece, Sarajevo, Yugoslavia 13	06/64
RTL201	491263	5187	KGK865		
			23 sri 3240	Ceylon Transport Board, Colombo, Ceylon	07/68
				Still in existence, having been fitted with CTB single deck bodywork but withdrawn	by 02/77
				Sold	01/79
RTL202	491378	4682	KGK866		
			22 sri 2878	Ceylon Transport Board, Colombo, Ceylon	01/59
RTL203	491377	4633	KGK867		
			22 sri 2604	Ceylon Transport Board, Colombo, Ceylon	12/58
				Still in existence but withdrawn	02/77
RTL204	491375	4488	KGK868		
			22 sri 2659	Ceylon Transport Board, Colombo, Ceylon	12/58
RTL205	491266	4517	KGK869		
			23 sri 1059	Ceylon Transport Board, Colombo, Ceylon	04/64
RTL206	491373	4669	KGK870		
			22 sri 2669	Ceylon Transport Board, Colombo, Ceylon	12/58
RTL207	491374	4755	KGK871		
			22 sri 2608	Ceylon Transport Board, Colombo, Ceylon	12/58
RTL208	491376	4454	KGK872		
			CA 134 464	Golden Arrow Bus Service, Cape Town, South Africa 224	01/65
				Withdrawn and dismantled	05/70
RTL209	491380	4689	KGK873		
			22 sri 2932	Ceylon Transport Board, Colombo, Ceylon	01/59
RTL210	491479	4637	KGK874		
			22 sri 2623	Ceylon Transport Board, Colombo, Ceylon	12/58
RTL211	491475	4624	KGK875		
			22 sri 2697	Ceylon Transport Board, Colombo, Ceylon	12/58
RTL212	491477	4691	KGK876		
			22 sri 3303	Ceylon Transport Board, Colombo, Ceylon	03/59
RTL213	491478	4668	KGK877		
			22 sri 2627	Ceylon Transport Board, Colombo, Ceylon	12/58
				Still in existence as a staff bus	02/77
				Sold	06/78
RTL214	491482	4495	KGK878		
			22 sri 2877	Ceylon Transport Board, Colombo, Ceylon	01/59
RTL215	491541	4686	KGK879		
			22 sri 3247	Ceylon Transport Board, Colombo, Ceylon	03/59
RTL216	491548	4598	KGK880		
			22 sri 2671	Ceylon Transport Board, Colombo, Ceylon	12/58
RTL217	491550	4497	KGK881		
			22 sri 2686	Ceylon Transport Board, Colombo, Ceylon	12/58
RTL218	491968	4520	KGK882		
			22 sri 2601	Ceylon Transport Board, Colombo, Ceylon	12/58
				Sold	03/77
				Converted to a private lorry, not reregistered and still in use	04/81
RTL219	492116	4486	KGK883		
			22 sri 3238	Ceylon Transport Board, Colombo, Ceylon	03/59
RTL220	491972	4436	KGK884		
			22 sri 2670	Ceylon Transport Board, Colombo, Ceylon	12/58
RTL221	491966	4688	KGK885		
			22 sri 2664	Ceylon Transport Board, Colombo, Ceylon	12/58

RTL222	491547	4525	KGK886		
				Gradeka Saobracaine Preduzece, Sarajevo, Yugoslavia	07/64
RTL223	491545	5026	KGK887		
				Wombwell Diesel Company (Dealer), Wombwell, Yorkshire after mechanical units had been removed at Stonebridge garage for Ceylon Transport Board	05/69
RTL224	491546	4663	KGK888		
			22 sri 2880	Ceylon Transport Board, Colombo, Ceylon	01/59
RTL225	491967	4692	KGK889		
			22 sri 3250	Ceylon Transport Board, Colombo, Ceylon	03/59
				Still in service	07/78
RTL226	491549	4476	KGK890		
			22 sri 2661	Ceylon Transport Board, Colombo, Ceylon	12/58
RTL227	491544	4491	KGK891		
			22 sri 2971	Ceylon Transport Board, Colombo, Ceylon	01/59
RTL228	491975	4585	KGK892		
			22 sri 2873	Ceylon Transport Board, Colombo, Ceylon	01/59
				Still in existence but withdrawn	02/77
RTL229	491963	5170	KGK893		
				Pickersgill & Laverick (Dealer), Cudworth, Yorkshire	05/69
RTL230	491962	4429	KGK894		
			22 sri 2603	Ceylon Transport Board, Colombo, Ceylon	12/58
				Still in existence but withdrawn	02/77
RTL231	492119	4512	KGK895		
			22 sri 2931	Ceylon Transport Board, Colombo, Ceylon	01/59
RTL232	492120	4483	KGK896		
			22 sri 2606	Ceylon Transport Board, Colombo, Ceylon	12/58
RTL233	492118	4474	KGK897		
			22 sri 2937	Ceylon Transport Board, Colombo, Ceylon	01/59
RTL234	492114	4473	KGK898		
			22 sri 2655	Ceylon Transport Board, Colombo, Ceylon	12/58
RTL235	491964	4687	KGK899		
			22 sri 2972	Ceylon Transport Board, Colombo, Ceylon	01/59
RTL236	491965	4753	KGK900		
			22 sri 2656	Ceylon Transport Board, Colombo, Ceylon	12/58
RTL237	492122	2239	KGK901		
			23 sri 1314	Ceylon Transport Board, Colombo, Ceylon	11/64
RTL238	492235	4804	KGK902		
				Pickersgill & Laverick (Dealer), Cudworth, Yorkshire	05/69
RTL239	492238	4592	KGK903		
			22 sri 2615	Ceylon Transport Board, Colombo, Ceylon	12/58
RTL240	492298	4584	KGK904		
			22 sri 3302	Ceylon Transport Board, Colombo, Ceylon	03/59

Cooke's Coaches of Dunstable RTL580 is seen on the 1st February 1969 in company with a further bus owned, which was Luton Corporation fleet number 136, one of a batch of five all Leyland PD2/10 which first entered services in 1954. Note the variation in livery applied to the two buses. (John G.S. Smith)

RTL241	492121	5019	KGK905		
			23 sri 3414	Ceylon Transport Board, Colombo, Ceylon	12/68
				Rebodied as a single decker, with CTB full front 33 seat bodywork	—/—
				Elk Arc, Colombo	01/80
				Nayona Travels	01/82
RTL242	492237	4573	KGK906		
			22 sri 2626	Ceylon Transport Board, Colombo, Ceylon	12/58
RTL243	492241	4685	KGK907		
			22 sri 3245	Ceylon Transport Board, Colombo, Ceylon	03/59
RTL244	492123	5062	KGK908		
				R. Doughty & Sons, Kings Lynn, Norfolk	03/69
				Withdrawn	06/72
				Bacon (Dealer), Bawsey, for scrap	06/72
RTL245	492240	4636	KGK909		
			22 sri 2689	Ceylon Transport Board, Colombo, Ceylon	12/58
RTL246	492236	2111	KGK910		
				Wombwell Diesel Company (Dealer), Wombwell, Yorkshire	05/69
RTL247	492244	2092	KGK911		
				R.C.Doughty & Sons, Kings Lynn, Norfolk	08/68
				Withdrawn	06/72
				G.Lister (Dealer), Bolton, Lancashire	06/72
				E.Brakell and T.Hornby, Cheam, Surrey for preservation	12/72
				Singapore Port Authority, Singapore as agent	06/75
			PB 50 E	Sentoza Development Corporation 30 and used on tourist services on Sentoza Island	09/75
				Placed on sea bed off the Island's lagoon for use as fish breeding grounds	by 12/80
RTL248	492243	4812	KGK912		
				Wombwell Diesel Company (Dealer), Wombwell, Yorkshire	05/69
RTL249	492318	4471	KGK913		
			22 sri 2883	Ceylon Transport Board, Colombo, Ceylon	01/59
RTL250	492313	4596	KGK914		
			22 sri 3261	Ceylon Transport Board, Colombo, Ceylon	03/59
RTL251	492314	4568	KGK915		
			22 sri 2947	Ceylon Transport Board, Colombo, Ceylon	01/59
RTL252	492242	4665	KGK916		
			22 sri 2611	Ceylon Transport Board, Colombo, Ceylon	12/58
RTL253	492387	4616	KGK929		
			22 sri 2886	Ceylon Transport Board, Colombo, Ceylon	01/59
RTL254	492321	4575	KGK930		
			22 sri 2668	Ceylon Transport Board, Colombo, Ceylon	12/58
				Still in existence but withdrawn	02/77
RTL255	492315	4475	KGU201		
			22 sri 2928	Ceylon Transport Board, Colombo, Ceylon	01/59
RTL256	492319	5073	KGU202		
				Pickersgill & Laverick (Dealer), Cudworth, Yorkshire	05/69
RTL257	492320	4504	KGU203		
			22 sri 2654	Ceylon Transport Board, Colombo, Ceylon	12/58
RTL258	492317	4676	KGU204		
			22 sri 2945	Ceylon Transport Board, Colombo, Ceylon	01/59
				Still in existence but withdrawn	02/77
RTL259	492239	4696	KGU205		
			22 sri 2688	Ceylon Transport Board, Colombo, Ceylon	12/58
RTL260	492316	4439	KGK206		
			J 34655	Jersey Motor Transport Co. Ltd, St. Helier, Jersey, Channel Islands 655	04/65
				Withdrawn	02/71
				Amos (Dealer), Ludlow, Shropshire	02/71
			VUJ375J	Harry's Coaches Limited, Cheltenham, Gloucestershire	09/71
				G.Lister (Dealer), Bolton	04/73
				Dunscroft Commercials (Breakers), Doncaster	01/74
RTL261	492322	4631	KGU207		
			22 sri 2927	Ceylon Transport Board, Colombo, Ceylon	01/59
RTL262	492555	4469	KGU208		
			22 sri 2875	Ceylon Transport Board, Colombo, Ceylon	01/59
RTL263	492553	4490	KGU209		
			22 sri 2695	Ceylon Transport Board, Colombo, Ceylon	12/58
RTL264	492544	4580	KGU210		
			22 sri 2674	Ceylon Transport Board, Colombo, Ceylon	12/58
				Still in existence, but withdrawn	02/77
RTL265	492554	4482	KGU211		
			22 sri 3237	Ceylon Transport Board, Colombo, Ceylon	03/59
RTL266	492551	5257	KGU212		
				Pickersgill & Laverick (Dealer), Cudworth, Yorkshire	06/69

From the 23rd January 1966 an overtime and rest day ban was imposed by the operating crews which in turn forced London Transport to withdraw a large number of routes from the 30th of the month. During the year the withdrawn routes were gradually reinstated but route 98 and 98B north of Ruislip and the 235 in its entirety were not again operated by the Board. Route 235, which operated between Richmond station and Richmond Hill, Friars Stile Road, was one of the victims but in this case Isleworth Coaches took over the route and here in sunny summer weather conditions their RTL633 is seen at the latter terminus. (John Gascoine)

Barton Transport limited built up a mixture of twenty five Leyland class buses and RTL837 as their fleet number, 1085 seen here was owned between March 1967 and March 1972. The radiator has been enhanced with the operator's name and notice proclaiming parcels are carried. (R.F. Mack)

RTL267	492552	4597	KGU213		
			22 sri 2881	Ceylon Transport Board, Colombo, Ceylon	01/59
				Still in existence, but withdrawn	02/77
RTL268	292545	4739	KGU214		
			22 sri 3299	Ceylon Transport Board, Colombo, Ceylon	03/59
RTL269	492546	4758	KGU215		
				Bird's Commercial Motors (Dealer), Stratford-upon-Avon, Warwickshire	07/59
				Walter Mills Tours Limited, Gornal Woods, Staffordshire	07/59
				Withdrawn	by 03/65
				Don Everall Limited (Dealer), Wolverhampton	03/65
				G.E.Martindale, Ferryhill, Co. Durham	03/65
				Withdrawn	08/66
RTL270	492547	4782	KGU216		
				Bird's Commercial Motors (Dealer), Stratford-upon-Avon, Warwickshire	10/59
				Stevenson's Bus Service, Spath, Uttoxeter, Staffordshire 29	11/59
				Fitted with platform doors	10/65
				Withdrawn	05/76
				Bloor (Dealer), Spath, in use as a green house on site	—/77
				Still there, derelict	09/94
				Body disintegrated and chassis remains to Messrs Hurst, Hammell, Lloyd and Thrower for spares	10/97
RTL271	492549	4741	KGU217		
			22 sri 3296	Ceylon Transport Board, Colombo, Ceylon	03/59
RTL272	492548	4627	KGU218		
			22 sri 2946	Ceylon Transport Board, Colombo, Ceylon	01/59
RTL273	493068	4481	KGU219		
			22 sri 2660	Ceylon Transport Board, Colombo, Ceylon	12/58
RTL274	493061	4728	KGU220		
			22 sri 3301	Ceylon Transport Board, Colombo, Ceylon	03/59
RTL275	493063	4731	KGU221		
			22 sri 2614	Ceylon Transport Board, Colombo, Ceylon	12/58
RTL276	493062	4777	KGU222		
				Bird's Commercial Motors (Dealer), Stratford-upon-Avon, Warwickshire	08/59
				Anderson Brothers t/a Blue Belle Services, Evenwood, Co. Durham	10/59
				OK Motor Services, (W.Emerson), Bishop Auckland, Co. Durham upon takeover of Anderson's business	01/60
				Morley (Dealer), Shildon, Co. Durham, for scrap	—/70
RTL:277	493064	5041	KGU223		
				Pickersgill & Laverick (Dealer), Cudworth, Yorkshire	02/70
RTL278	493069	4749	KGU224		
				Bird's Commercial Motors (Dealer), Stratford-upon-Avon, Warwickshire	08/59
				A1 Service, (McKinnon, Kilmarnock), Ardrossan, Ayrshire	—/59
				Delicenced	11/73
				Bering Cannibalised	11/73

RTL279	493066	4502	KGU225			
			22 sri 3300	Ceylon Transport Board, Colombo, Ceylon		03/59
RTL280	493065	4729	KGU226			
			22 sri 2602	Ceylon Transport Board, Colombo, Ceylon		12/58
RTL281	493130	4507	KGU227			
			22 sri 2949	Ceylon Transport Board, Colombo, Ceylon		01/59
				Still in existence now fitted with a Leyland Power Plus engine		02/77
				Still in use		12/81
				Back in service with subsidiary Ratmalana Peoplised Transport Co. Ratmalana, Sri Lanka		03/93
				Still in use		—/94
				Not seen		12/97
RTL282	493071	4595	KGU228			
			22 sri 2610	Ceylon Transport Board, Colombo, Ceylon		12/58
RTL283	493070	4626	KGU229			
			22 sri 2944	Ceylon Transport Board, Colombo, Ceylon		01/59
RTL284	493129	4508	KGU230			
			22 sri 3293	Ceylon Transport Board, Colombo, Ceylon		03/59
RTL285	493067	3416	KGU231			
				Pickersgill & Laverick (Dealer), Cudworth, Yorkshire		05/69
RTL286	493134	4632	KGU244			
			22 sri 3242	Ceylon Transport Board, Colombo, Ceylon		03/59
RTL287	493135	4736	KGU245			
			22 sri 2696	Ceylon Transport Board, Colombo, Ceylon		12/58
RTL288	493255	4732	KGU246			
			22 sri 2625	Ceylon Transport Board, Colombo, Ceylon		12/58
RTL289	493251	4533	KGU247			
				Pickersgill & Laverick (Dealer), Cudworth, Yorkshire		05/69
RTL290	493136	4470	KGU248			
			22 sri 3263	Ceylon Transport Board, Colombo, Ceylon		03/59
				Sold		08/75
				Converted to a private lorry, not reregistered and still in use		04/81
RTL291	493252	4677	KGU249			
			22 sri 3294	Ceylon Transport Board, Colombo, Ceylon		03/59
RTL292	493072	4635	KGU250			
			22 sri 3257	Ceylon Transport Board, Colombo, Ceylon		03/59
RTL293	493133	4762	KGU251			
				Wombwell Diesel Company (Dealer), Wombwell, Yorkshire		06/69

RTL960 was one of the last batch of three to arrive on the island of Jersey in 1967. Previous numbers had been purchased in 1959 (8) and 1965 (3) which made a total of fourteen to be operated by the Jersey Motor Transport. OMO single deck vehicles were to replace all double deck operation on the island from 1971 and these RTLs have now all gone their separate ways mostly being re-exported, some scrapped, while others can still be viewed to this present day at an occasional rally. (R.F. Mack)

RTL294	493132	5203	KGU252		
			22 sri 3275	Ceylon Transport Board, Colombo, Ceylon	08/68
				Still in existence having been fitted with CTB single deck bodywork, but withdrawn	by 02/77
				Still extant	04/87
RTL295	493256	4972	KGU253		
			22 sri 2670	Ceylon Transport Board, Colombo, Ceylon	12/66
RTL296	493137	4467	KGU254		
			23 sri 1505	Ceylon Transport Board, Colombo, Ceylon	02/65
RTL297	493257	4742	KGU255		
			22 sri 3244	Ceylon Transport Board, Colombo, Ceylon	03/59
				Still in existence but withdrawn	07/78
RTL298	493138	4484	KGU256		
			22 sri 3265	Ceylon Transport Board, Colombo, Ceylon	03/59
RTL299	493250	5176	KGU257		
				Pickersgill & Laverick (Dealer), Cudworth, Yorkshire	05/69
RTL300	4932588	4774	KGU258		
			22 sri 7927	Ceylon Transport Board, Colombo, Ceylon	01/61
RTL301	493254	4879	KGU259		
				Wombwell Diesel Company (Dealer), Wombwell, Yorkshire	05/69
RTL302	493265	4784	KGU260		
			22 sri 2935	Ceylon Transport Board, Colombo, Ceylon	01/59
RTL303	493253	4630	KGU261		
			22 sri 3298	Ceylon Transport Board, Colombo, Ceylon	03/59
RTL304	493262	4743	KGU262		
				W.North, Sherburn-in-Elmet, Yorks	02/66
				Broken up	03/66
RTL305	493260	4748	KGU263		
				Bird's Commercial Motors (Dealer), Stratford-upon-Avon, Warwickshire	08/59
				Silver Star, Porton Down, Salisbury, Wilts 36	09/59
				Wilts & Dorset Motor Services upon take over of Silver Star business, not used	06/63
				Passenger Vehicle Sales (London) Ltd (Dealer), Upminster, Essex	06/63
				Super Coaches (Upminster) Limited, Upminster, Essex	06/63
				Passenger Vehicle Sales (London) Ltd, Upminster, (Contracts fleet)	05/64
				Lesney Products, London E4 as a staff bus	06/64
				Passenger Vehicle Sales (London) Ltd (Dealer), Upminster, Essex	02/65
				Executors of S.Ledgard, Armley, Leeds	03/65
				West Yorkshire R.C.C. Harrogate, West Yorkshire upon take over of Ledgard business, not used	10/67
				Passenger Vehicle Sales (London) Ltd (Dealer), Canvey Island, Essex	10/67
				Broadway Coaches (Wickford) Limited, but not operated	06/68
				Passenger Vehicle Sales (London) Ltd (Dealer) Contracts, Ongar, Essex 60	09/68
				Passenger Vehicle Sales (London) Ltd (Dealer), Canvey Island, Essex	03/69
				E.Brakell, Cheam, Surrey for preservation	04/69
				Body gutted by fire, chassis restored	06/70
				Chassis scrapped at Cobham Bus Museum	c02/73
RTL306	493264	4496	KGU264		
			22 sri 3262	Ceylon Transport Board, Colombo, Ceylon	03/59
RTL307	493261	4746	KGU265		
			22 sri 3264	Ceylon Transport Board, Colombo, Ceylon	03/59
RTL308	493263	4734	KGU266		
				Pickersgill & Laverick (Dealer), Cudworth, Yorkshire	06/69
RTL309	493259	4500	KGU267		
			22 sri 3240	Ceylon Transport Board, Colombo, Ceylon	03/59
RTL310	493268	4811	KGU268		
				Wombwell Diesel Company (Dealer), Wombwell, Yorkshire	05/69
RTL311	493131	4485	KGU269		
			22 sri 3253	Ceylon Transport Board, Colombo, Ceylon	03/59
RTL312	493266	3429	KGU270		
				Wombwell Diesel Company (Dealer), Wombwell, Yorkshire	12/69
RTL313	493418	5035	KGU271		
				Stanley Donan Enterprises, London W2, for film work	08/68
				Used in film "La Faute Venee France" with registration 166 DWF 75	—/68
				Offered for sale	12/68
			166 DWF 75	Noted parked in a field at La Faute-Sur-Mer, Vendee, France	07/81
RTL314	493423	4795	KGU272		
				Wombwell Diesel Company (Dealer), Wombwell, Yorkshire	12/69
RTL315	493415	5151	KGU273		
				William Warne & Company Limited, Barking, Essex as a staff bus	08/68
				Still in use	06/73
				Westfield Exports (Dealer), Barking, Essex	12/74
				D.Miles, Clayhall	02/75
				B.Smith, Richmond, in LT livery but fitted out as a fruit and vegetable shop	10/76
				E.Brakell (Dealer), Cheam, Surrey	04/77
				W.R.Luft, Hamburg, Germany	03/78

From left to right RTL579, RTL531 (masquerading as RT531) and RTL1176 get together in far away Canada. For added interest an East Lancs bodied AEC Regent V which had initially entered service with West Bridgford UDC as their number 34 can be seen to the far left. All the buses appear in pristine condition with the addition of extra regulation light fittings and a bumper bar to RTL1176 and the AEC Regent V. Interesting to note also that a Leyland badge has been obtained and fitted to the center RTL while the other two await such adornment. (I MacDonald)

RTL316	493416	4750	KGU274

Passenger Vehicle Sales (London) Ltd (Dealer), Canvey Island, Essex — 07/68
Hylton Castle Coaches, Sunderland 29 — 08/68
Withdrawn — 08/71
Wombwell Diesel Company (Dealer), Wombwell, Yorkshire — 08/71

RTL317	493420	5188	KGU275

Bird's Commercial Motors (Dealer), Stratford-upon-Avon, Warwickshire — 09/67

RTL318	493425	4638	KGU276
		22 sri 3256	

Ceylon Transport Board, Colombo, Ceylon — 03/59
Still in existence as a staff bus — 02/77
Sold — 12/79

RTL319	493417	5178	KGU277
		23 sri 3381	

Ceylon Transport Board, Colombo, Ceylon — 12/68
Still in existence, but withdrawn — 02/77

		26 sri 9152	

Sold and rebuilt as a private lorry — by 01/78

RTL320	493422	4735	KGU278
		22 sri 7929	

Ceylon Transport Board, Colombo, Ceylon — 01/61
Still in existence but withdrawn — 07/78

RTL321	493421	4794	KGU279

Wombwell Diesel Company (Dealer), Wombwell, Yorkshire — 12/69

RTL322	493428	4891	KGU280

Wombwell Diesel Company (Dealer), Wombwell, Yorkshire — 09/67

RTL323	493426	4743	KGU281
		22 sri 3297	

Ceylon Transport Board, Colombo, Ceylon — 03/59

RTL324	493429	4976	KGU282
		23 sri 1951	

Ceylon Transport Board, Colombo, Ceylon — 10/65

RTL325	493431	4798	KGU283
		23 sri 2701	

Ceylon Transport Board, Colombo, Ceylon — 12/66

RTL326	493427	3419	KGU284

H & C Transport, Garston, Hertfordshire — 08/67
West Herts Coaches, Garston, Hertfordshire. — 05/68
Kirby's Coaches, Bushey Heath, upon take over of West Herts Coaches business and named "Bushey Lady" — 03/69
Withdrawn — 04/74
Donated to East London Traction Society, London E13 for preservation — 02/75
M.Hebbard (Dealer), Biggin Hill, Kent — 07/78
Kingston Plant Hire, Hanworth, Middlesex — c11/78
Kingston Plant Hire moved to Guildford, Surrey and later to Billingshurst, Sussex — —/—
D.L.Richards, Teddington, Middlesex for preservation — c01/92
Moved to Hampton, Middlesex — c07/94
Still owned but for sale — 04/98

RTL327	493419	4759	KGU285

Wombwell Diesel Company (Dealer), Wombwell, Yorkshire — 05/69

RTL328	494100	4733	KGU286
		22 sri 3295	

Ceylon Transport Board, Colombo, Ceylon — 03/59

RTL329	493430	4961	KGU287

Passenger Vehicle Sales (London) Ltd (Dealer), Canvey Island, Essex — 07/68
British Promotions (Dealer), Boston, Massachusetts, USA — 08/68
Hired to Antony's Pier 4 Restaurant, Boston, Massachusetts, USA amongst others — 09/68
De-roofed and converted to open-top — —/—
Holiday Transport, Virginia Beach, Virginia, USA — —/—
British Promotions (Dealer), Norfolk, Virgina for resale — 10/74

RTL330	493433	4805	KGU288

Pickersgill & Laverick (Dealer), Cudworth, Yorkshire — 04/70

RTL331	493424	5324	KGU289
		23 sri 1582	

Ceylon Transport Board, Colombo, Ceylon — 04/65

RTL332	494103	4744	KGU401
		22 sri 3241	

Ceylon Transport Board, Colombo, Ceylon — 03/59
Still in existence but withdrawn — 02/77

RTL333	493390	4789	KGU402

Pickersgill & Laverick (Dealer), Cudworth, Yorkshire — 08/70

RTL334	494102	5266	KGU403
		22 sri 1883	

Ceylon Transport Board, Colombo, Ceylon — 09/65

RTL335	494104	4965	KGU404
		23 sri 3027	

Ceylon Transport Board, Colombo, Ceylon — 08/67
Still in existence but withdrawn — 02/77

RTL336	494109	4754	KGU405

Bird's Commercial Motors (Dealer), Stratford-upon-Avon, Warwickshire — 10/59
J.Laurie t/a Chieftain, Burnbank, Hamilton, Lanarkshire 71 — 10/59
Central SMT, Motherwell, Lanarkshire HL200 upon take over of Laurie's business — 10/61
Withdrawn — —/64
Belshill & Mossend Scrap Metal Company (Dealer), Bellshill, Lanarkshire — —/64

Photographed in glorious sunshine at Victoria, B.C., Canada, RTL506 has only recently had a change of ownership as shown by the crudely amended fleet name. Other than this small blemish the bus appears to be in superb condition and a joy to view even though small cosmetic changes have been applied to its exterior. (I.MacDonald)

Standing at Victoria, B.C., Canada in 1981 these two RTLs carry enough information to allow identification. Nearer the camera is RTL579 with operator's fleet number 210 carried to the right of the rear destination box while the bottom half of its previous British registration shows beneath the smaller Canadian plate. The further bus for some reason has had its old London Transport fleet number RTL1076 added to the bottom of its rear panel. Patriotically, the owner uses the Canadian maple leaf within the paint scheme of the further bus while something approaching a British Union Jack adorns the second vehicle. (I.MacDonald)

Fleet No	Chassis	Body	Registration	History	Date
RTL337	494107	5177	KGU406		
				Pickersgill & Laverick (Dealer), Cudworth, Yorkshire	05/69
RTL338	494101	4934	KGU407		
				Pickersgill & Laverick (Dealer), Cudworth, Yorkshire	04/70
RTL339	494108	4902	KGU408		
				Wombwell Diesel Company (Dealer), Wombwell, Yorkshire	12/69
RTL340	494105	5242	KGU409		
				Wombwell Diesel Company (Dealer), Wombwell, Yorkshire	11/69
RTL341	494106	5279	KGU417		
				Wombwell Diesel Company (Dealer), Wombwell, Yorkshire	11/69
RTL342	494139	4830	KGU418		
				Pickersgill & Laverick (Dealer), Cudworth, Yorkshire	05/69
RTL343	494138	4817	KGU419		
				E.Brakell, Cheam, Surrey for preservation	08/70
				Friends Roadshow for use as mobile theatre	04/74
				Being converted to mobile theatre accommodation at Crystal Palace, London	06/74
				Still with Friends Roadshow	06/76
				Stage Space Theatre Company, London SE24 rebuilt to open top	09/78
				Unknown owner, Somerset	12/81
				Parked at Battersea, London	c05/83
				Snowball Events as mobile theatre, London SE5	by 07/87
				Burnt out and scrapped	c04/88
RTL344	494141	4509	KGU420		
			CA 134 466	Golden Arrow Bus Service, Cape Town, South Africa 226	01/65
				Withdrawn and scrapped	11/70
RTL345	494137	4887	KGU421		
				Wombwell Diesel Company (Dealer), Wombwell, Yorkshire	12/69
RTL346	494144	4816	KGU422		
				Pickersgill & Laverick (Dealer), Cudworth, Yorkshire	06/69
RTL347	493392	4813	KGU423		
				Pickersgill & Laverick (Dealer), Cudworth, Yorkshire	05/69
RTL348	494181	4851	KGU424		
				Wombwell Diesel Company (Dealer), Wombwell, Yorkshire	12/69
RTL349	494277	4654	KGU425		
			22 sri 7940	Ceylon Transport Board, Colombo, Ceylon	01/61
RTL350	494276	4787	KGU426		
				Wombwell Diesel Company (Dealer), Wombwell, Yorkshire	12/69
RTL351	494176	4802	KGU427		
				Wombwell Diesel Company (Dealer), Wombwell, Yorkshire	12/69
RTL352	494142	4836	KGU428		
				Wombwell Diesel Company (Dealer), Wombwell, Yorkshire	12/69
RTL353	494292	4881	KGU429		
				Wombwell Diesel Company (Dealer), Wombwell, Yorkshire	12/69
RTL354	494275	4867	KGU430		
				Pickersgill & Laverick (Dealer), Cudworth, Yorkshire	08/70
RTL355	494174	4752	KGU431		
			22 sri 7930	Ceylon Transport Board, Colombo, Ceylon	01/61
RTL356	494274	4899	KGU432		
			22 sri 7933	Ceylon Transport Board, Colombo, Ceylon	01/61
RTL357	494278	4781	KGU433		
				Bird's Commercial Motors (Dealer), Stratford-upon-Avon, Warwickshire	10/59
				J.Laurie t/a Chieftain, Burnbank, Hamilton, Lanarkshire 72	10/59
				Central SMT Motherwell, Lanarkshire HL201 upon take over of Laurie's business	10/61
				Withdrawn	—/64
				Bellshill & Mossend Scrap Metal Co. Bellshills, Lanarkshire	—/64
RTL358	494183	4785	KGU434		
				Bird's Commercial Motors (Dealer), Stratford-upon-Avon, Warwickshire	07/59
				Red Rover, Aylesbury, Buckinghamshire 9	07/59
				Transferred to associated Keith Coaches, Aylesbury 11	02/64
				Withdrawn	01/73
				F.A.Hewer, Leighton Buzzard, Bedfordshire for preservation	01/73
				Appeared in "Some Mothers Do 'Ave 'Em" on BBC1 television	12/73
				Hackney School Parent & Teachers Association	09/78
				E.Brakell (Dealer), Cheam, Surrey	10/81
				Stage Space Theatre Company, London SE24	12/81
				Group disbanded vehicle having never been used	—/82
				A.Witt, London E1	09/83
				P.Stanley, London NW10 for Church and Community Work and regarded as semi preserved	03/84
				Still owned	03/85
				Geoff Hills, Ilfracombe, Devon	by 06/97
RTL359	494282	4950	KGU435		
				Wombwell Diesel Company (Dealer), Wombwell, Yorkshire	09/67

The building housing RTL36 almost looks as if it has been especially adapted for the garaging of the bus by its new owners, Pulham & Sons of Bourton-on-the-Water. Luckily the radiator cover allows clear identification of the bus, whose body once carried a route number box at roof level. (Alan Mortimer)

RTL867 is seen on hire to London Transport while in use on a service provided for the Physics exhibition held at Alexandra Palace in late 1967. An Upminster and District service blind is fitted in the route via-box confirming the ownership of the bus with the organisation which included Passenger Vehicle Sales, the well known dealers, Super Coaches and City Line who have used various locations around Essex for their operations. (John G.S. Smith)

RTL360	494281	5248	KGU436		
				Pickersgill & Laverick (Dealer), Cudworth, Yorkshire	05/69
RTL361	494184	4984	KGU437		
			22 sri 7939	Ceylon Transport Board, Colombo, Ceylon	01/61
RTL362	494286	4772	KGU438		
				Bird's Commercial Motors (Dealer), Stratford-upon-Avon, Warwickshire	08/59
				H & C Transport Limited, Garston, Hertfordshire	08/59
				Used in film "The Day The Earth Caught Fire"	—/61
				Knightswood Coaches, Watford, Hertfordshire	12/65
				Withdrawn	04/69
RTL363	494287	4745	KGU439		
				Wombwell Diesel Company (Dealer), Wombwell, Yorkshire	11/69
RTL364	494296	4829	KGU451		
			22 sri 7921	Ceylon Transport Board, Colombo, Ceylon	01/61
				Still in existence but withdrawn	07/78
RTL365	494294	4975	KGU452		
				Wombwell Diesel Company (Dealer), Wombwell, Yorkshire	01/70
RTL366	494280	4453	KGU453		
			CA 130 871	Golden Arrow Bus Service, Cape Town, South Africa 220	01/65
				Withdrawn after accident and dismantled	04/70
RTL367	494288	4848	KGU454		
				Wombwell Diesel Company (Dealer), Wombwell, Yorkshire	12/69
RTL368	494284	4800	KGU455		
				Wombwell Diesel Company (Dealer), Wombwell, Yorkshire	12/69
RTL369	494291	4842	KGU456		
				Wombwell Diesel Company (Dealer), Wombwell, Yorkshire	05/69
RTL370	494293	4778	KGU457		
				Pickersgill & Laverick (Dealer), Cudworth, Yorkshire	05/69
RTL371	494285	4962	KGU458		
				Pickersgill & Laverick (Dealer), Cudworth, Yorkshire	01/70
RTL372	494298	5226	KGU459		
			23 sri 3422	Ceylon Transport Board, Colombo, Ceylon	12/68
				Still in service	02/77
RTL373	494299	4943	KGU460		
			CA 140 512	City Tramways Co., Cape Town, South Africa 740	08/65
				Still in service	04/74
RTL374	494279	4939	KGU461		
			CA 140 508	City Tramways Co., Cape Town, South Africa 736	08/65
				Still in service	04/74
				Stored for preservation after withdrawal by City Tramways	—/77
RTL375	494302	4946	KGU462		
				Pickersgill & Laverick (Dealer), Cudworth, Yorkshire	05/69
RTL376	494177	4966	KGU463		
				Wombwell Diesel Company (Dealer), Wombwell, Yorkshire	12/69
RTL377	494297	4845	KGU464		
			23 sri 1572	Ceylon Transport Board, Colombo, Ceylon	04/65
RTL378	494300	4844	KGU465		
				Pickersgill & Laverick (Dealer), Cudworth, Yorkshire	05/69
RTL379	494289	4809	KGU466		
				Pickersgill & Laverick (Dealer), Cudworth, Yorkshire	06/69
RTL380	494295	4940	KGU467		
				W.North (Dealer), Sherburn-in-Elmet, Yorkshire	01/67
				P.V.S. (Dealer), Upminster, Essex	01/67
				Barton Transport, Chilwell, Nottinghamshire, for spares	01/67
				Broken up	07/69
RTL381	494301	4863	KGU468		
				Pickersgill & Laverick (Dealer), Cudworth, Yorkshire	05/69
RTL382	494488	2119	KGU469		
				Pickersgill & Laverick (Dealer), Cudworth, Yorkshire	05/69
RTL383	494140	5174	KGU470		
				Wombwell Diesel Company (Dealer), Wombwell, Yorkshire	11/69
RTL384	494499	2129	KGU471		
				Pickersgill & Laverick (Dealer), Cudworth, Yorkshire	05/69
RTL385	494491	4898	KGU472		
			23 sri 1610	Ceylon Transport Board, Colombo, Ceylon	04/65
RTL386	494369	4768	KGU473		
				Pickersgill & Laverick (Dealer), Cudworth, Yorkshire, after mechanical units had been removed at Stonebridge garage for Ceylon Transport Board	06/69
RTL387	494493	5171	KGU474		
				Pickersgill & Laverick (Dealer), Cudworth, Yorkshire	06/69
RTL388	494492	5259	KGU475		
				Pickersgill & Laverick (Dealer), Cudworth, Yorkshire	05/69

Initially exported to South Africa for operation by City Tramways in January 1964, Park Royal bodied RTL1394 is now owned by Elwierda Tours and is still used in passenger service. It had been rebuilt to open top condition by City Tramways who then transferred it to their Sprinbok Atlas tourism division. After a further change of ownership it was eventually acquired by David Munton in 1993, though by then it had suffered the effects of many years alternating rain and sun. The fine condition the bus is now seen in was accomplished by a total rebuild by David, who for a number of years operated open top tourist buses in Cape Town using six Daimler Fleetlines. (D.Munton)

The tarmacadam roadway, telephone lines and street lighting appear to be the only contribution made by the authorities to Factreton a coloured suburb and factory area on the outskirts of Cape Town. RTW186 with additional side lights, bumper, rebuilt route aperture boxes and additional notice panel under the canopy still commands the air of once having been London Transport property. A Volkswagen saloon, gas guzzling American imported car and lorry departing in the opposite direction add interest to the general view taken in April 1970.

Red liveried RTL1515 is seen parked at the ferry terminus on Sentosa Island being used on the red bus service as opposed to the Green Coach Tour, which the green liveried RT and RTL were used on. Note the legal ownership black painted panel with reads, 'Sentosa Developments Corporation, Jetty Road, Sentosa, Singapore 2 and legal weight of 4980 kgs'. The nearside equivalent panel carried similar information except that the seating capacity replaced the weight information. (Alan Mortimer)

In top gear, causing RTW412 to lean over, the driver negotiates the roundabout at Galle Face, in the vicinity of Parliament House, central Colombo. A Jurassic Park monster appears to have taken a liking to the front nearside mudguard. Inadequate maintenance and repair facilities have taken their toll and show in the severe front nearside dome damage, panel beading coming adrift and an inoperative opening window. Add to this the clumsy repanelling to the route aperture box above the platform and it all adds up to a sorry state for this all Leyland product to have deteriated into, when seen in October 1972. (Alan Mortimer)

The crew in Colombo must be commended for the way they have looked after RTL1282. Obviously they cannot do anything about the roof damage but with a little bit of ingenuity they have certainly made the bus stand out from the others of the class still in operation in October 1972. The radiator and bumper area, life guard and London Transport fleet number panel have all received extra attention. With the additional width marker lights fixed beneath the front upper deck windows and air horn carried beneath the canopy, route 100 passengers to Panadura are certainly carried to their destination in style. (Alan Mortimer)

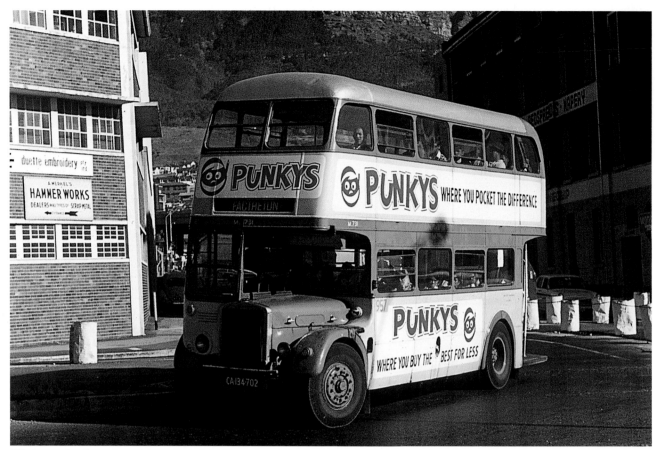

RTL1260 carries fleet number 731 and garage identification M for Maitland when seen in service for coloured passengers in a factory suburb of Cape Town in April 1970. The lower parts of Table Mountain are visible in the background while use of a number of white painted oil drums make effective road barriers. (Bruce Harris)

RTL506 together with RT1849 parked a little further along the road stand outside the upmarket B.C. Hydro Hotel in Victoria, British Columbia, Canada in June 1975, when operated by the London Omnibus Tours. Note that this nearside view shows the RTL masquerading as an RT while carrying its operator's fleet number 660 and local registration plate 732.806. The direction indicators have been moved to either side of the radiator while width marker lights have been added at roof height. Except for the cage to the rear platform deletion of the life guard and the fitting of an additional rear view mirror to the nearside front wheel arch, the bus looks very much as it did when in use in London. (Alan Mortimer)

The Jursassic park monsters have been at it again this time with RTL844, devouring even more of the front mudguard in this instance. Though one must be thankful that the bus has been left in a useable state and in this October 1972 view it is seen on route 173 to Thotalanga. After nearly five years service in Ceylon the still carries its London Transport Badge at the top of the radiator shell together with the BESI plate holders between decks. (Alan Mortimer)

In 1965 Park Royal bodied RTL477, with faded London Transport fleet number, is seen in use on service 173 while in the ownership of the Ceylon Transport Board. Originally exported to the island in 1958 the bus has received little attention to its overall exterior condition except for some newer window panes, which clearly emphasizes the fact why the lowest fare on earth could be charged by the operator. (A.R. Packer Collection)

In August 1977 RTL411 is seen on the holiday and relaxation island of Sentosa which came to prominence in 1975 when a number of London Transport RT and RTL buses were acquired with the tourist in mind. The saloon windows and panels beneath have been replaced by one piece longitudinal grab rails with opaque panels below to help combat the extremely high temperatures and humidity. To the upper line of the erstwhile windows has been added a frilly decorative sunshade. (Alan Mortimer)

RTL875 operates on a short working to the Fort within the capital city, Colombo, by way of service 100 in October 1972. Why the nearside mudguard, like so many others operated by the CTB, has got in such a condition raises the question as to whether this was some crude way of obtaining extra air flow to the breaking system. With the usual roof damage in evidence and a nasty tear to the corner panelling between decks one can only assume it soldiered on in this condition or worse until withdrawn from service. (Alan Mortimer)

In Autumn sunshine 1973 RTL28, named 'Betsy' is pictured parked in the grounds of the cattle market car park at Northampton. It was owned by the Co-operative Wholesale Society and used as a staff bus at the time. (John A.S. Hambley)

RTL1516 in use on a whites only service stands at what was the main terminus in Cape Town. Note the illuminated indicator beneath the canopy announcing whites only, not coloureds, while an appropriate driver waits for departure time. With rebuilt front route apertures and some carefully planned advertising of suitable dimensions is incorporated covering the full width of the bus. The Pepsi advertisement along the whole length of the between deck space gives a much neater appearance than the British fashion. (Alan Mortimer)

This close up view of the platform area of RTL506 clearly shows the fitting of the cage. Permanently fixed to the side of the bulkhead it hinged at the rear with the intention of leading alighting passengers towards the kerb. Two reflectors also adorn, one at the front the other to the rear of the bus as Canadian regulations require. (Alan Mortimer)

RTL389	494671	4960	KGU476		
			23 sri 1564	Ceylon Transport Board, Colombo, Ceylon	04/65
				Still in existence but withdrawn	02/77
RTL390	494672	5260	KGU477		
				Pickersgill & Laverick (Dealer), Cudworth, Yorkshire	05/69
RTL391	494677	3423	KGU478		
			23 sri 2992	Ceylon Transport Board, Colombo, Ceylon	09/67
				Fitted with CTB single deck bodywork but withdrawn	by 02/77
				Still extant	04/81
RTL392	494674	4773	KGU479		
				Pickersgill & Laverick (Dealer), Cudworth, Yorkshire	06/69
RTL393	494673	4967	KGU480		
			22 sri 7926	Ceylon Transport Board, Colombo, Ceylon	01/61
RTL394	494670	4937	KGU481		
				Wombwell Diesel Company (Dealer), Wombwell, Yorkshire	12/69
RTL395	494676	4818	KGU482		
			23 sri 3231	Ceylon Transport Board, Colombo, Ceylon	07/68
RTL396	494675	4862	KGU483		
			CA 134 700	City Tramways Co., Cape Town, South Africa 729	05/65
				Converted to front entrance retaining rear staircase	by 04/74
				Still in service	02/76
RTL397	494680	4959	KGU484		
			22 sri 7937	Ceylon Transport Board, Colombo, Ceylon	01/61
RTL398	494682	4880	KGU485		
				Bird's Commercial Motors (Dealer), Stratford-upon-Avon, Warwickshire	03/64
				Scrapped	c04/65
RTL399	494678	4969	KGU486		
				Pickersgill & Laverick (Dealer), Cudworth, Yorkshire	02/70
RTL400	494688	4859	KGU487		
				Pickersgill & Laverick (Dealer), Cudworth, Yorkshire	02/70
RTL401	494684	4776	KGU488		
				F.Wrighton & Sos Limited, (Furniture Manufacturers), London E17 as staff transport	07/59
				Slade Green Autos, (Dealer), Erith, Kent	08/70
				Broken up	09/70
RTL402	494683	4895	KGU489		
			23 sri 1879	Ceylon Transport Board, Colombo, Ceylon	09/65

Hills Patents Limited, Staines used RTL918 for a little over eighteen months as a promotion vehicle in their business of motorway sign production. Why the bus lasted such a short time with its new owners is unknown at present but the exterior of the bodywork appears to be in good condition. The barrier against unwelcome intruders but not the weather reminds one of the problems shared by many enthusiasts of a vehicle with open platform. (Kevin Lane)

RTL403	494679	4797	KGU490		
			23 sri 3364	Ceylon Transport Board, Colombo, Ceylon	12/68
				Still in existence but withdrawn	02/77
RTL404	494765	5335	KGU491		
			22 sri 7924	Ceylon Transport Board, Colombo, Ceylon	01/61
RTL405	494689	4971	KGU492		
			23 sri 2009	Ceylon Transport Board, Colombo, Ceylon	12/65
				Still in existence but withdrawn	02/77
RTL406	494764	4790	KGU493		
				W.North (Dealer), Sherburn-in-Elmet, Yorkshire	01/67
				B.Johnson (Breakers), South Elmsall, Yorkshire	07/67
RTL407	494762	4841	KGU494		
				Wombwell Diesel Company (Dealer), Wombwell, Yorkshire	11/69
RTL408	494687	4945	KGU495		
			23 sri 2074	Ceylon Transport Board, Colombo, Ceylon	01/66
RTL409	494763	2034	KGU496		
				Pickersgill & Laverick (Dealer), Cudworth, Yorkshire	05/69
RTL410	494767	4857	KGU497		
			23 sri 2747	Ceylon Transport Board, Colombo, Ceylon	01/67
RTL411	494768	3522	KGU498		
			J 8774	Jersey Motor Transport Co. Ltd., St. Helier, Jersey, Channel Islands 3	03/59
				Out of use and in store	—/74
				E.Brakell (Dealer), Cheam, Surrey	02/75
				Singapore Port Authority, Singapore as agent	06/75
			PB 51 C	Sentoza Development Corporation 28 and used on tourist services on Sentoza Island	09/75
				Placed on the sea bed off the Island's lagoon for use as fish breeding grounds	by 12/80
RTL412	494766	4885	KGU499		
				Pickersgill & Laverick (Dealer), Cudworth, Yorkshire	06/69
RTL413	494686	3599	KGU500		
			22 sri 1440	Ceylon Transport Board, Colombo, Ceylon	02/58
RTL414	494681	4854	KLB601		
				Wombwell Diesel Company (Dealer), Wombwell, Yorkshire	11/69
RTL415	494685	4757	KLB602		
				Pickersgill & Laverick (Dealer), Cudworth, Yorkshire	06/69
RTL416	494761	5200	KLB603		
				Wombwell Diesel Company (Dealer), Wombwell, Yorkshire	05/69
RTL417	494911	4709	KLB604		
				Wombwell Diesel Company (Dealer), Wombwell, Yorkshire after mechanical units had been removed at Stonebridge garage for Ceylon Transport Board	04/69
RTL418	494912	4876	KLB605		
				Pickersgill & Laverick (Dealer), Cudworth, Yorkshire, after mechanical units had been removed at Stonebridge garage for Ceylon Transport Board	06/69
RTL419	494769	4886	KLB606		
			23 sri 2335	Ceylon Transport Board, Colombo, Ceylon	06/66
RTL420	494771	4831	KLB607		
				Pickersgill & Laverick (Dealer), Cudworth, Yorkshire	05/69
RTL421	494987	3509	KLB608		
			23 sri 2096	Ceylon Transport Board, Colombo, Ceylon	01/66
RTL422	494985	4702	KLB609		
				Bird's Commercial Motors (Dealer), Stratford-upon-Avon, Warwickshire	05/69
RTL423	494986	4952	KLB610		
			22 sri 7938	Ceylon Transport Board, Colombo, Ceylon	01/61
RTL424	494995	4896	KLB611		
				Wombwell Diesel Company (Dealer), Wombwell, Yorkshire	06/69
RTL425	494988	4935	KLB612		
				Pickersgill & Laverick (Dealer), Cudworth, Yorkshire	07/70
RTL426	494992	4837	KLB613		
			23 sri 2061	Ceylon Transport Board, Colombo, Ceylon	01/66
RTL427	494989	4877	KLB614		
				Pickersgill & Laverick (Dealer), Cudworth, Yorkshire	06/69
RTL428	494994	5172	KLB615		
				Pickersgill & Laverick (Dealer), Cudworth, Yorkshire	05/69
RTL429	494770	5205	KLB616		
				Pickersgill & Laverick (Dealer), Cudworth, Yorkshire, after mechanical units had been removed at Stonebridge garage for Ceylon Transport Board	06/69
RTL430	494993	5204	KLB617		
				Pickersgill & Laverick (Dealer), Cudworth, Yorkshire	06/69
RTL431	494997	5217	KLB618		
				Riverway Enterprises t/a Riverway Coaches, Harlow, Essex	02/69
				Withdrawn	12/71
RTL432	494996	4944	KLB619		
				Pickersgill & Laverick (Dealer), Cudworth, Yorkshire	02/70

RTL	Chassis	Body	Reg	Operator/Disposal	Date
RTL433	494991	5323	KLB620		
			22 sri 7922	Ceylon Transport Board, Colombo, Ceylon	01/61
RTL434	494990	4832	KLB621		
				Wombwell Diesel Company (Dealer), Wombwell, Yorkshire	01/70
RTL435	494998	4864	KLB622		
				Pickersgill & Laverick (Dealer), Cudworth, Yorkshire	06/69
RTL436	495000	4963	KLB623		
				Wombwell Diesel Company (Dealer), Wombwell, Yorkshire	04/70
RTL437	495503	4853	KLB624		
				Pickersgill & Laverick (Dealer), Cudworth, Yorkshire	05/69
RTL438	495502	4890	KLB625		
				Wombwell Diesel Company (Dealer), Wombwell, Yorkshire after mechanical units had been removed at Stonebridge Garage for Ceylon Transport Board	04/69
RTL439	494999	5238	KLB626		
				Pickersgill & Laverick (Dealer), Cudworth, Yorkshire, after mechanical units had been removed at Stonebridge Garage for Ceylon Transport Board	06/69
RTL440	495505	4860	KLB627		
				Pickersgill & Laverick (Dealer), Cudworth, Yorkshire	08/70
RTL441	495504	5297	KLB628		
			23 sri 3291	Ceylon Transport Board, Colombo, Ceylon	08/68
RTL442	495501	3447	KLB629		
				Pickersgill & Laverick (Dealer), Cudworth, Yorkshire, after mechanical units had been removed at Stonebridge Garage for Ceylon Transport Board	06/69
RTL443	495507	4884	KLB630		
				H & C Transport, Garston, Hertfordshire	08/66
				A1 Service, (Stewart, Stevenston), Ardrossan, Ayrshire	12/69
				Withdrawn and used for spares	12/70
				Remains to Keenan, Coalhall, Ayrshire	12/70
				Derelict on site	11/72
RTL444	495513	4882	KLB639		
			CA 134 699	City Tramways Co., Cape Town, South Africa 728	05/65
		4097		Still in service, now with body ex RTL600	04/74
RTL445	495517	4953	KLB640		
				Bird's Commercial Motors (Dealer), Stratford-upon-Avon, Warwickshire	03/64
				Scrapped	c04/65

S. Eynon & Sons, Trimsaran owned RTL1114 from October 1963 through to August 1971 when it was despatched to a dealer for scrap. It is seen in use on a service between its operator's home town and, three miles further along the B4308, Kidwelly with its castle. Interestingly both the advertising hoarding and side advert carried by the bus are for the best bitter in Wales, Felinfoel. No alterations have been made to the Park Royal bodywork save for a new livery which has included painting over the route number destination apertures. (R. F. Mack)

RTL446	495515	4986	KLB641		
			22 sri 7932	Ceylon Transport Board, Colombo, Ceylon	01/61
RTL447	495516	3441	KLB642		
			23 sri 1571	Ceylon Transport Board, Colombo, Ceylon	04/65
RTL448	495524	5328	KLB643		
			23 sri 1902	Ceylon Transport Board, Colombo, Ceylon	09/65
				Still in existence, fitted with CTB single deck 33 seat bodywork	02/77
				Withdrawn	01/79
				Elk Arc, Colombo	—/80
RTL449	495913	4985	KLB644		
			22 sri 7935	Ceylon Transport Board, Colombo, Ceylon	01/61
RTL450	495920	5263	KLB645		
			23 sri 1609	Ceylon Transport Board, Colombo, Ceylon	04/65
RTL451	495916	4680	KLB646		
				Pickersgill & Laverick (Dealer), Cudworth, Yorkshire	05/69
RTL452	495523	3854	KLB647		
			23 sri 3084	Ceylon Transport Board, Colombo, Ceylon	10/67
				Still in existence but withdrawn	02/77
RTL453	495918	2124	KLB648		
				M.R. Underhill (RTL453 Group), Grays, Thurrock, Essex preserved	02/70
				RTL453 Group, secretary D.Yates, Ilford, Essex for continued preservation	by 09/73
				RT10 Group, London N1 for continued preservation	by 06/77
				Still owned	08/95
RTL454	495915	4987	KLB649		
				Gradeka Saobracaine Preduzece, Sarajevo, Yugoslavia	05/64
RTL455	495511	5184	KLB650		
			23 sri 1900	Ceylon Transport Board, Colombo, Ceylon	09/65
RTL456	495923	4649	KLB651		
				Wombwell Diesel Company (Dealer), Wombwell, Yorkshire	05/69
RTL457	495510	6891	KLB652		
			23 sri 3162	Ceylon Transport Board, Colombo, Ceylon	12/67
				Still in existence but withdrawn	02/77
RTL458	495917	3511	KLB653		
			CA 147 368	Golden Arrow Bus Service, Cape Town, South Africa 286	09/66
				Withdrawn and dismantled	05/70
RTL459	495921	3717	KLB654		
				Wombwell Diesel Company (Dealer), Wombwell, Yorkshire	12/69
RTL460	495521	3598	KLB679		
			J 8804	Jersey Motor Transport Co. Ltd., St. Helier, Jersey, Channel Islands 4	03/59
				Out of use and in store	—/74
				E.Brakell (Dealer), Cheam, Surrey	12/74
				D.Gomm, London W5 for preservation	by 05/75
				E.Brakell (Dealer), Cheam, Surrey	05/75
				Singapore Port Authority, Singapore as agent	06/75
			PB 31 K	Sentoza Development Corporation 20 and used on tourist services on Sentoza Island	06/75
				Withdrawn and placed on the sea bed off the Island's lagoon for use as fish breeding grounds	by 12/80
RTL461	496154	4893	KLB680		
			23 sri 2698	Ceylon Transport Board, Colombo, Ceylon	12/66
RTL462	496155	5262	KLB681		
			23 sri 1888	Ceylon Transport Board, Colombo, Ceylon	09/65
RTL463	496151	3431	KLB682		
			22 sri 1463	Ceylon Transport Board, Colombo, Ceylon	02/58
RTL464	496152	4628	KLB683		
			22 sri 3246	Ceylon Transport Board, Colombo, Ceylon	03/59
RTL465	496480	5152	KLB684		
			23 sri 1884	Ceylon Transport Board, Colombo, Ceylon	09/65
RTL466	496479	3707	KLB685		
			23 sri 2101	Ceylon Transport Board, Colombo, Ceylon	01/66
RTL467	496486	3471	KLB686		
			23 sri 1615	Ceylon Transport Board, Colombo, Ceylon	04/65
RTL468	496487	5273	KLB687		
			23 sri 1581	Ceylon Transport Board, Colombo, Ceylon	04/65
RTL469	496482	4903	KLB688		
			23 sri 2170	Ceylon Transport Board, Colombo, Ceylon	03/66
				Still in existence but withdrawn	02/77
RTL470	496157	5307	KLB689		
				Leyland Motors Limited (Dealer), London W1	07/66
			PCB 142	Wascana Centre Authority, Regina, Saskatchewan, Canada	07/66
				Still owned	11/85
				Bus Stop restaurant, Saskatoon, Saskatchewan	10/89
				Still owned	07/91
RTL471	496481	3609	KLB690		
			23 sri 2010	Ceylon Transport Board, Colombo, Ceylon	12/65

RTL472	496478	4964	KLB691		
			23 sri 2011	Ceylon Transport Board, Colombo, Ceylon	12/65
RTL473	496496	5190	KLB692		
				Wombwell Diesel Company (Dealer), Wombwell, Yorkshire after mechanical units had been removed at Stonebridge Garage for Ceylon Transport Board	04/69
RTL474	496502	5255	KLB693		
			23 sri 1580	Ceylon Transport Board, Colombo, Ceylon	04/65
RTL475	496503	3426	KLB694		
			23 sri 2012	Ceylon Transport Board, Colombo, Ceylon	12/65
RTL476	496504	3402	KLB695		
				Wombwell Diesel Company (Dealer), Wombwell, Yorkshire	01/70
RTL477	496130	3433	KLB696		
			22 sri 1599	Ceylon Transport Board, Colombo, Ceylon	04/58
RTL478	496129	3467	KLB697		
			23 sri 1889	Ceylon Transport Board, Colombo, Ceylon	09/65
RTL479	496493	2382	KLB698		
			23 sri 1412	Ceylon Transport Board, Colombo, Ceylon	12/64
RTL480	496491	3517	KLB699		
			23 sri 3404	Ceylon Transport Board, Colombo, Ceylon	12/68
RTL481	496514	3600	KLB700		
			22 sri 1603	Ceylon Transport Board, Colombo, Ceylon	04/58
RTL482	496509	4979	KLB701		
			23 sri 2675	Ceylon Transport Board, Colombo, Ceylon	12/66
RTL483	496513	5334	KLB702		
			23 sri 1901	Ceylon Transport Board, Colombo, Ceylon	09/65
				Still in existence but withdrawn	02/77
RTL484	496511	5305	KLB703		
			23 sri 1999	Ceylon Transport Board, Colombo, Ceylon	11/65
				Still in existence but withdrawn	02/77
RTL485	496501	3608	KLB704		
			J 8853	Jersey Motor Transport Co. Ltd., St. Helier, Jersey, Channel Islands 12	03/59
				Donated by United Nations to Sisters of Immaculate Conception, St. Meen Le Grand, Ille Et Vilaine, France for work with children in and around Paris, as a library and art centre	—/74
				Not used as at 01/80 when with M.Vinot, 78500 Sactrouville in well maintained condition and was to be used as a mobile library	01/80

Seen at rest in Perth city RTL1133 of A & C McLennan looks extremely tidy and clean on the 30th May 1964. Now with an enclosed platform it was to continue in passenger service until 1972 when disposed of to a fruit farm for transport of pickers on his fields.

RTL486	496492	3476	KLB705		
			23 sri 1958	Ceylon Transport Board, Colombo, Ceylon	10/65
RTL487	496507	3442	KLB706		
			23 sri 1893	Ceylon Transport Board, Colombo, Ceylon	09/65
			24 sri 8217	Rebuilt as service lorry	—/—
				Noted derelict at CTB Werchera workshops	04/81
RTL488	496516	3512	KLB707		
			23 sri 2049	Ceylon Transport Board, Colombo, Ceylon	12/65
RTL489	496497	3418	KLB708		
			23 sri 1899	Ceylon Transport Board, Colombo, Ceylon	09/65
RTL490	496490	3710	KLB709		
			22 sri 1598	Ceylon Transport Board, Colombo, Ceylon	04/58
RTL491	496499	3505	KLB710		
			22 sri 1449	Ceylon Transport Board, Colombo, Ceylon	02/58
RTL492	496498	5319	KLB711		
			23 sri 1908	Ceylon Transport Board, Colombo, Ceylon	09/65
				Still in existence but withdrawn	02/77
RTL493	500053	4321	KXW277		
				Wombwell Diesel Company (Dealer), Wombwell, Yorkshire	12/69
RTL494	497089	5941	KXW278		
				Bird's Commercial Motors (Dealer), Stratford-upon-Avon, Warwickshire	01/70
RTL495	500001	5353	KXW279		
				Pickersgill & Laverick (Dealer), Cudworth, Yorkshire	05/69
RTL496	500038	3621	KXW280		
			CA 147 370	Golden Arrow Bus Service, Cape Town, South Africa 288	10/66
RTL497	500036	3514	KXW281		
			23 sri 2672	Ceylon Transport Board, Colombo, Ceylon	12/66
RTL498	496524	9142	KXW282		
			23 sri 3209	Ceylon Transport Board, Colombo, Ceylon	04/68
RTL499	500035	3611	KXW283		
				Wombwell Diesel Company (Dealer), Wombwell, Yorkshire	11/69
RTL500	496521	5214	KXW284		
				Harper Bros., Heath Hayes, Cannock, Staffordshire 4	04/65
				Harper Bros. taken over by Midland Red and now bus is operating on hire to Midland Red	07/74
				Midland Red 2204	09/74
				Withdrawn never operated by Midland Red	09/74
				Longbridge Engineering (Dealer), Longbridge	—/75
RTL501	472471	1936	JXC20		
				Bird's Commercial Motors (Dealer), Stratford-upon-Avon, Warwickshire	07/58
				A1 Services (Reid, Saltcoats), Ardrossan, Ayrshire	—/59
				Clyde Coast Services (W.Shields, Saltcoats), Saltcoats, Ayrshire	09/63
				Still in service	09/69
				Reported scrapped	by 01/70
RTL502	500002	5352	KXW285		
				Wombwell Diesel Company (Dealer), Wombwell, Yorkshire	11/69
RTL503	500003	5946	KXW286		
			23 sri 2164	Ceylon Transport Board, Colombo, Ceylon	03/66
RTL504	500403	3602	KXW287		
				Wombwell Diesel Company (Dealer), Wombwell, Yorkshire	05/69
RTL505	496527	3681	KXW288		
				Pickersgill & Laverick (Dealer), Cudworth, Yorkshire	05/69
RTL506	500063	5365	KXW289		
				London Omnibus Tours Limited, Victoria, Vancouver Island, British Columbia, Canada	02/70
			732 806	British Columbia Hydro and Power Authority t/a Royal Blue Motor Tours, Victoria, Vancouver Island, 660	01/73
				London Transport Limited, Victoria, Vancouver Island, British Columbia 207	09/79
				Gray Line of Victoria Ltd, Victoria, Vancouver Island, British Columbia 207	c09/83
				Charity Plus Society, Victoria, Vancouver Island, British Columbia for intended museum project	c—/94
				Still owned	09/97
RTL507	496525	5278	KXW290		
				Pickersgill & Laverick (Dealer), Cudworth, Yorkshire	02/70
RTL508	496522	5937	KXW291		
			CA 140 513	City Tramways Co., Cape Town, South Africa 741	08/65
				Rebuilt to front entrance retaining rear staircase and renumbered 0741	by 09/75
				Still in service	02/76
RTL509	500406	3566	KXW292		
				Wombwell Diesel Company (Dealer), Wombwell, Yorkshire	05/69
RTL510	496526	4901	KXW293		
			23 sri 2099	Ceylon Transport Board, Colombo, Ceylon	01/66
RTL511	500054	3606	KXW294		
			22 sri 1454	Ceylon Transport Board, Colombo, Ceylon	02/58
RTL512	500044	4715	KXW295		
			23 sri 1966	Ceylon Transport Board, Colombo, Ceylon	10/65

RTL30 disgorges passengers at the Hamilton post office on the 29th July 1959 having now completed nearly eighteen months service with J. Laurie. Sales of the RTL class commenced in 1958, still some time before trafficator 'ears were added to the London Transport fleet and inconsequence direction indictors of a different style have been fitted. (A.R. Packer)

RTL1258 with its new owners Gradeka Saobracaine Preduzece is seen while in passenger use at Sarajevo, Yugoslavia on the 28th June 1965. Fleet number 23, with Sarajevo (SA) registration identification followed by a four digit serial number are clearly visible on the rebuilt platform and staircase area. (John G.S. Smith)

RTL513	500418	3519	KXW296		
			22 sri 1437	Ceylon Transport Board, Colombo, Ceylon	02/58
RTL514	500416	5235	KXW297		
			CA 9765	City Tramways Co., Cape Town, South Africa 746	08/65
				Converted to front entrance retaining rear staircase and renumbered 0746	by 04/74
				Still in service	02/76
RTL515	500419	3596	KXW298		
			22 sri 1597	Ceylon Transport Board, Colombo, Ceylon	04/58
				Still in existence but withdrawn	02/77
RTL516	500417	3518	KXW299		
			22 sri 1442	Ceylon Transport Board, Colombo, Ceylon	02/58
RTL517	500420	3664	KXW300		
			23 sri 2995	Ceylon Transport Board, Colombo, Ceylon	08/67
RTL518	501226	4981	KXW344		
			23 sri 2013	Ceylon Transport Board, Colombo, Ceylon	12/65
RTL519	501215	3669	KXW345		
			22 sri 1450	Ceylon Transport Board, Colombo, Ceylon	02/58
RTL520	501096	3521	KXW346		
			22 sri 1425	Ceylon Transport Board, Colombo, Ceylon	02/58
RTL521	501224	9157	KXW347		
				Bird's Commercial Motors (Dealer), Stratford-upon-Avon, Warwickshire	09/67
RTL522	501103	3432	KXW348		
			23 sri 2087	Ceylon Transport Board, Colombo, Ceylon	01/66
RTL523	501214	3603	KXW349		
			J 8873	Jersey Motor Transport Co. Ltd., St Helier, Jersey, Channel Island 2	03/59
				Broken up on island by Picot and Rouille (Scrap Dealer), Mont Mado, St. John	11/71
RTL524	501089	3575	KXW350		
				Pickersgill & Laverick (Dealer), Cudworth, Yorkshire	02/70
RTL525	501091	3595	KYY521		
			J 8746	Jersey Motor Transport Co. Ltd., St Helier, Jersey, Channel Island 1	03/59
				Out of use and in store	—/74
				E.Brakell (Dealer,) Cheam, Surrey.	02/75
				Fully restored to L.T. Livery for promotional work	by 05/75
				Reregistered MGPIIP	by 11/75
				Hired to London Transport for driver training, being returned the following month	06/78
				D.Charnley, Ashford, Kent	05/82
				E.Brakell (Dealer), Cheam, Surrey	09/82
				Crelland (Milo Audio), London SW6 as agent	09/82
			B 4482 VE	Unknown, Barcelona, Spain and used as a campaign vehicle in elections	09/82
				Promobus SA, Torrejon de Ardoz, Spain and used for promotional hire	by —/86
				Still owned	02/96
RTL526	501092	5985	KYY522		
				Wombwell Diesel Company (Dealer), Wombwell, Yorkshire	06/69
RTL527	501104	3648	KYY523		
				Bird's Commercial Motors (Dealer), Stratford-upon-Avon, Warwickshire	04/69
RTL528	501225	5267	KYY524		
			23 sri 2003	Ceylon Transport Board, Colombo, Ceylon	11/65
RTL529	501506	3695	KYY558		
				Pickersgill & Laverick (Dealer), Cudworth, Yorkshire	02/70
RTL530	501507	3667	KYY559		
			22 sri 1605	Ceylon Transport Board, Colombo, Ceylon	04/58
RTL531	501497	3516	KYY560		
			4490 JE	London Omnibus Tours Limited, Victoria, Vancouver Island, British Columbia, Canada 209	02/70
				British Columbia Hydro and Power Authority t/a Royal Blue Motor Tours, Victoria, Vancouver Island 659	01/73
				London Transport Limited, Victoria, Vancouver Island, British Columbia 209	09/79
				Gray Line of Victoria Ltd, Victoria, Vancouver Island, British Columbia 209	c09/83
				D.J.Walker, Ladysmith used as food bar named 'Nibbles', painted red/green	by 09/93
				To unknown Ski Resort, Coeur d'Alene, Idaho, USA	by 09/96
RTL532	501397	5304	KYY561		
			23 sri 2000	Ceylon Transport Board, Colombo, Ceylon	11/65
RTL533	501392	5965	KYY562		
				Bird's Commercial Motors (Dealer), Stratford-upon-Avon, Warwickshire	01/70
RTL534	501391	9138	KYY563		
			23 sri 3261	Ceylon Transport Board, Colombo, Ceylon	07/68
RTL535	501393	5251	KYY564		
			23 sri 1886	Ceylon Transport Board, Colombo, Ceylon	09/65
RTL536	501389	9224	KYY565		
			23 sri 3179	Ceylon Transport Board, Colombo, Ceylon	04/68
				Still in existence but withdrawn	02/77
RTL537	501515	3523	KYY566		
			22 sri 1602	Ceylon Transport Board, Colombo, Ceylon	04/58

RTL			Reg	History	Date
RTL538	501542	9152	KYY567		
				S. Miller, 427 Main Street, Bangor, Maine, USA	05/69
				Used at Bangor State Fair, Bangor	by 07/80
				Still owned by S.Miller	08/81
				Auctioned by Bangor State Fairgrounds	—/86
				Real Thing Fish & Chips, South Penobscot, Maine as mobile shop and restaurant	by 11/91
RTL539	501539	6295	KYY568		
			23 sri 3122	Ceylon Transport Board, Colombo, Ceylon	11/67
RTL540	501722	9159	KYY633		
			23 sri 3182	Ceylon Transport Board, Colombo, Ceylon	04/68
				Still in existence but withdrawn	02/77
RTL541	501723	3705	KYY634		
			22 sri 7923	Ceylon Transport Board, Colombo, Ceylon	01/61
RTL542	501552	3550	KYY635		
				Wombwell Diesel Company (Dealer), Wombwell, Yorkshire	12/69
RTL543	501554	5978	KYY636		
				Wombwell Diesel Company (Dealer), Wombwell, Yorkshire	11/69
RTL544	501553	3751	KYY637		
				Pickersgill & Laverick (Dealer), Cudworth, Yorkshire	02/70
RTL545	501548	3907	KYY638		
			22 sri 7934	Ceylon Transport Board, Colombo, Ceylon	01/61
RTL546	501545	6297	KYY639		
				Pickersgill & Laverick (Dealer), Cudworth, Yorkshire	02/70
RTL547	501732	5948	KYY640		
				P.W.Marlsham, Antique Auto Museum,. Wembley, Australia but damaged in transit and not used	04/69
				Donated to Western Australia Transport Museum, Perth, Western Australia	04/69
			Y 1650	Used weekends in Wanneroo Lion Park, Perth, Western Australia	11/74
			TC 429	Still owned by bus Museum of Western Australia	—/—
			UBH 698	Museum moved to Whiteman Park, still owned	09/96
RTL548	501907	3780	KYY641		
			23 sri 3120	Ceylon Transport Board, Colombo, Ceylon	11/67
				Still in existence as a CTB Welfare bus	02/77
				Still in use	04/81
RTL549	501913	5367	KYY642		
				Bird's Commercial Motors (Dealer), Stratford-upon-Avon, Warwickshire	12/69
RTL550	501925	4956	KYY643		
				Walsall Corporation Transport, Walsall 201	08/59
				West Midlands PTE (Northern Division) numbered 201L	10/69
				Withdrawn	02/71
				Sykes (Dealer), Blackerhill for scrap	09/71
RTL551	490870	3971	KGU1		
				Leyland Motors Limited (Dealer), London W1	05/66
				Exported to USA, owner unknown	05/66
RTL552	490969	3966	KGU2		
				A1 Service, (T.Docherty Irvine), Ardrossan, Ayrshire for spares	12/64
				Still owned	09/65
RTL553	491019	3954	KGU3		
				W.North (Dealer), Sherburn-in-Elmet, Yorkshire	01/67
				B.Johnson (Breakers) South Elmsall, Yorks	by 07/67
RTL554	491072	4368	KGU4		
				Acrow Engineers Limited, London W2 and used as a staff bus at their Harefield, Middlesex depot	04/67
				E.Brakell , Cheam, Surrey for preservation	by 05/72
				N.Syrett, Bromley for continued preservation	04/74
				E.Brakell (Dealer), Cheam, Surrey	11/75
				N.Pomeroy, Croydon, Surrey for preservation	08/76
				D.Thrower and J.Fozard, Baildon, near Shipley, Yorkshire for continued preservation	10/77
				Still owned by J. Fozard	10/95
RTL555	491073	3958	KGU5		
				W.North (Dealer), Sherburn-in-Elmet, Yorkshire	01/67
				Johnson (Breakers), South Elmsall, Yorks	10/67
RTL556	491074	4358	KGU6		
			23 sri 3288	Ceylon Transport Board, Colombo, Ceylon	08/68
				Still in existence but withdrawn	02/77
RTL557	491078	3973	KGU7		
			23 sri 2073	Ceylon Transport Board, Colombo, Ceylon	01/66
RTL558	491079	3952	KGU8		
			23 sri 2054	Ceylon Transport Board, Colombo, Ceylon	12/65
RTL559	491080	4385	KGU9		
			23 sri 3279	Ceylon Transport Board, Colombo, Ceylon	08/68
				Still in service	02/77
RTL560	491081	4362	KGU10		
			23 sri 3365	Ceylon Transport Board, Colombo, Ceylon	12/68

RTL561	491382	3960	KGU11		
			23 sri 2699	Ceylon Transport Board, Colombo, Ceylon	12/66
				Still in service	02/77
RTL562	491383	4348	KGU12		
				Wombwell Diesel Company (Dealer), Wombwell, Yorkshire	10/69
RTL563	491384	4355	KGU13		
				Pickersgill & Laverick (Dealer), Cudworth, Yorkshire	06/69
RTL564	491476	4339	KGU14		
			E 535399	Long Beach Public Transport Corporation, Long Beach, California USA 4 used on services to and from the "Queen Mary" liner at Long Beach	07/68
				Long Beach City College, Long Beach, California	04/75
RTL565	491480	4341	KGU15		
			23 sri 3065	Ceylon Transport Board, Colombo, Ceylon	10/67
RTL566	491481	4283	KGU16		
			23 sri 3068	Ceylon Transport Board, Colombo, Ceylon	10/67
				Still in existence but withdrawn	02/77
RTL567	491483	4350	KGU17		
				Lowdes Leasing & Finance Limited, London SW1	11/67
				Noted with Wendall Mobile Showrooms, demonstrating sack sewing machines near Turners Hill, Sussex	08/68
				Winlon Autos (Dealer), Kew Bridge station yard	11/71
				Being repainted	12/71
				Noted in use as mobile showroom for Western Waterbeds International Limited, in London and Nottingham	07/72
				Children of God, London W9	c07/73
				Winlon Autos (Dealer), Kew Bridge station yard as an office	c08/73
				Dovery Car Sales, Brentford, Middlesex	by 10/74
RTL568	491539	4399	KGU18		
			23 sri 3105	Ceylon Transport Board, Colombo, Ceylon	11/67
				Still in existence but withdrawn	02/77
RTL569	491540	4343	KGU19		
			23 sri 3215	Ceylon Transport Board, Colombo, Ceylon	05/68
				Still in existence but withdrawn	02/77
RTL570	491542	4037	KGU20		
			23 sri 3207	Ceylon Transport Board, Colombo, Ceylon	04/68
				Still in existence but withdrawn	02/77
RTL571	491543	4337	KGU21		
			23 sri 3419	Ceylon Transport Board, Colombo, Ceylon	12/68
RTL572	491969	3968	KGU22		
			23 sri 2176	Ceylon Transport Board, Colombo, Ceylon	03/66
RTL573	491970	4229	KGU23		
			23 sri 3113	Ceylon Transport Board, Colombo, Ceylon	11/67
RTL574	491971	4069	KGU24		
				Bird's Commercial Motors (Dealer), Stratford-upon-Avon, Warwickshire	08/67
RTL575	492115	4393	KGU25		
				Passenger Vehicle Sales (London) Ltd (Dealer), Upminster, Essex	04/67
				R.Duncan, Motherwell, Lanarkshire	04/67
				Withdrawn	—/—
				Allen Grey (Dealer), Braidwood, Lanarkshire	04/72
				Still on site	10/73
RTL576	492117	3967	KGU26		
			23 sri 2015	Ceylon Transport Board, Colombo, Ceylon	12/65
RTL577	492550	4391	KGU27		
				Wombwell Diesel Company (Dealer), Wombwell, Yorkshire	10/69
RTL578	493267	4366	KGU28		
				Wombwell Diesel Company (Dealer), Wombwell, Yorkshire	09/67
RTL579	493269	4398	KGU29		
				Robertson Buckley, (Shipping Agents), London EC3	11/66
				Shipped to Montreal, Canada for use in Montreal during Canada's Centennial Year	11/66
			732 802	London Omnibus Tours Limited, Victoria, Vancouver Island, British Columbia, Canada	by 01/73
				British Columbia Hydro and Power Authority t/a Royal Blue Motor Tours, Victoria, Vancouver Island 657	01/73
				London Transport Limited, Victoria, Vancouver Island, British Columbia, Canada 210	09/79
				Gray Line of Victoria Limited, Victoria, Vancouver Island, British Columbia, Canada	c09/83
				Largely cannibalised	by 07/85
				Scrapped	07/85
RTL580	493384	4397	KGU30		
				Stringer t/a Prince of Wales Coaches, Ampthill, Bedfordshire as agent	06/67
				B.G.Cooke, t/a Cooke's Coaches, Dunstable, Bedfordshire	06/67
				Luton Commercial Motors (Dealer), Dunstable, Bedfordshire	12/69
				Bylands Service Station (Dealer), Redbourne	—/70
				Johnson (Breakers), Royston, Yorkshire	by 04/70

Alder Valley found itself short of vehicles coupled to a spares problem in 1973 and 1974, being forced to borrow a motley collection of RT family buses, mostly from LCBS. RTL1298 then owned by G.Ward t/a Wards Coaches was also on hire between September and December 1974 and is seen in Reading town centre on the 12th October 1974 near the bus station on service and heading for Baughurst. An on hire sticker can just be made out affixed to the upper corner of the forward facing lower deck saloon window. (John G.S. Smith)

RTL581	493385	4372	KGU31		
			23 sri 3392	Ceylon Transport Board, Colombo, Ceylon	12/68
				Still in service	02/77
RTL582	493386	4331	KGU32		
				Pickersgill & Laverick (Dealer), Cudworth, Yorkshire	06/69
RTL583	493387	4346	KGU33		
			23 sri 3238	Ceylon Transport Board, Colombo, Ceylon	07/68
				Still in existence but withdrawn	02/77
RTL584	493388	4019	KGU34		
				Passenger Vehicle Sales (London) Ltd (Dealer), Upminster, Essex	02/67
				P.Irvine t/a Golden Eagle, Salsburgh, Lanarkshire	02/67
				Still in service	01/72
				Tiger Coaches (Dealer), Salsburgh, Lanarkshire	by 04/72
				Still on site	12/72
				Gone	by 05/73
RTL585	493389	3972	KGU35		
			23 sri 2039	Ceylon Transport Board, Colombo, Ceylon	12/65
RTL586	493391	3976	KGU36		
			23 sri 3109	Ceylon Transport Board, Colombo, Ceylon	11/67
				Still in existence but withdrawn	02/77
				Sold	12/78
			27 sri 7886	Rebuilt as a private lorry	01/81
RTL587	493393	3957	KGU37		
				Wombwell Diesel Company (Dealer), Wombwell, Yorkshire	09/67
RTL588	493414	3956	KGU38		
			23 sri 2350	Ceylon Transport Board, Colombo, Ceylon	06/66
RTL589	493432	4359	KGU39		
			23 sri 3142	Ceylon Transport Board, Colombo, Ceylon	12/67
				Still in existence but withdrawn	02/77
RTL590	494133	3996	KGU40		
				Bird's Commercial Motors (Dealer), Stratford-upon-Avon, Warwickshire	08/67
RTL591	494134	4020	KGU41		
				F.Wilde, t/a Wimbledon Coaches, London SW19	10/66
				Fisher & Ford (Dealer), Barnsley, Yorkshire for scrap	03/69

RTL592	494135	4351	KGU42			
					Passenger Vehicle Sales (London) Ltd (Dealer), Upminster, Essex	10/65
					A1 Service, (Kerr & Linney), Ardrossan, Ayrshire	10/65
					Sold within group to Duff, Ardrossan, Ayrshire	04/68
					Sold within group to Brown, Dreghorn	11/69
					The Round Table movement, Irvine, Ayrshire	c01/72
					Derelict at Brown, Dreghorn garage	—/74
					Wombwell Diesel Company (Dealer), Wombwell, Yorkshire	—/79
RTL593	494136	4321	KGU43			
					Wombwell Diesel Company (Dealer), Wombwell, Yorkshire after mechanical units had been removed at Stonebridge Garage for Ceylon Transport Board	04/69
RTL594	494143	4013	KGU44			
				23 sri 2342	Ceylon Transport Board, Colombo, Ceylon	06/66
RTL595	494173	4073	KGU45			
					Bird's Commercial Motors (Dealer), Stratford-upon-Avon, Warwickshire	09/67
RTL596	494175	4377	KGU46			
					Passenger Vehicle Sales (London) Ltd (Dealer), Upminster, Essex	05/67
					Used for filmwork	05/67 to 07/67
					Broadway Coaches, Wickford, Essex and fitted with platform doors	07/67
					Hall, Wickford, Essex	09/68
					Passenger Vehicle Sales (London) Ltd (Dealer), Silver End, Essex	10/71
					Blue Line Coaches, Upminster, Essex	10/71
					Scrapped by Blue Line	10/72
					Remains to Romford Scrap & Salvage Company, Collier Row, Essex	12/72
RTL597	494178	3961	KGU47			
				CA 147 374	Golden Arrow Bus Service, Cape Town, South Africa 292	10/66
RTL598	494179	3974	KGU48			
					Milk Marketing Board, London EC3	08/66
					Exported to Canada on behalf of Milk Marketing Board and used in cheese products advertising campaign	08/66
					Double Deck Tours Limited, Niagara, Ontario, Canada	by 10/73
				BD6 697	Toronto Double Deck Services, Toronto, Ontario, Canada	—/—
					Fuhrman Auto Centre (Dealer), Toronto, Ontario, Canada	by 12/87
					Beaton's, Havelock	c—/90
				HVN 682	Central Ontario Automotive Historical Society, Belleville, Ontario, Canada for preservation	by 09/95
					Still owned	09/97
RTL599	494180	3993	KGU49			
				23 sri 3130	Ceylon Transport Board, Colombo, Ceylon	11/67
					Still in service	02/77
RTL600	494182	4097	KGU50			
				CA 59121	City Tramways Co., Cape Town, South Africa 754	10/65
					Still in service	04/74
					At sometime body transferred to RTL444 (City Tramways 728)	—/—
RTL601	494273	3977	KGU51			
					Leyland Motors Limited (Dealer), London WC1	01/67
					Exported to USA unknown owner	01/67
RTL602	494283	4363	KGU52			
					Pickersgill & Laverick (Dealer), Cudworth, Yorkshire	06/69
RTL603	494290	3962	KGU53			
				23 sri 2702	Ceylon Transport Board, Colombo, Ceylon	12/66
					Withdrawn and scrapped by Ceylon Transport Board	by 04/81
RTL604	494365	4011	KGU54			
					Wombwell Diesel Company (Dealer), Wombwell, Yorkshire	09/67
RTL605	494366	4396	KGU55			
					A1 Service, (Brown, Dreghorn), Ardrossan, Ayrshire	07/67
					Delicenced	12/70
					Remains on site after being cannibalised	11/73
RTL606	494367	4165	KGU56			
				CA 147 369	Golden Arrow Service, Cape Town, South Africa 287	10/66
RTL607	494368	3953	KGU57			
					F.Widle t/a Wimbledon Coaches, London SW19	09/65
					Clarke, London W12 and broken up	03/68
RTL608	494370	3955	KGU58			
					Leyland Motors Limited (Dealer), London W1	09/65
				2754	Grand Bahama Port Authority, Freeport, Grand Bahama, Bahamas, used on sightseeing Tours in L.T. Livery	09/65
RTL609	494371	4394	KGU59			
				23 sri 3262	Ceylon Transport Board, Colombo, Ceylon	07/68
					Still in existence having been fitted with CTB single deck bodywork	02/77
					Withdrawn	01/80
RTL610	494487	4005	KGU60			
					R.Armstrong t/a Moordale Bus Service, Newcastle-upon-Tyne	11/65
					Withdrawn	01/72

RTL611	494489	3989	KGU61		
			23 sri 2671	Ceylon Transport Board, Colombo, Ceylon	12/66
RTL612	494490	3964	KGU62		
			23 sri 2050	Ceylon Transport Board, Colombo, Ceylon	12/65
				Still in existence but withdrawn	02/77
RTL613	494494	4392	KGU63		
				W.North (Dealer), Sherburn-in-Elmet, Yorkshire	01/67
				Johnson, (Breakers), South Elmsall, Yorkshire	10/67
RTL614	494495	4021	KGU64		
			23 sri 3062	Ceylon Transport Board, Colombo, Ceylon	10/67
RTL615	494496	3998	KGU65		
			CA 28067	City Tramways Co., Cape Town, South Africa 751	10/65
				Still in service	04/74
RTL616	494497	3990	KGU66		
			23 sri 3382	Ceylon Transport Board, Colombo, Ceylon	12/68
				Still in existence but withdrawn	02/77
RTL617	494498	4063	KGU67		
			23 sri 2703	Ceylon Transport Board, Colombo, Ceylon	12/66
				Still in existence but withdrawn	02/77
RTL618	494772	3992	KGU68		
			23 sri 2044	Ceylon Transport Board, Colombo, Ceylon	12/65
RTL619	494902	4395	KGU69		
				J.Stevenson, Spath, Uttoxeter, Staffordshire 15	06/67
				Withdrawn after accident, stripped for spares	10/68
				Remains broken up on site and sold	—/72
RTL620	494903	3963	KGU70		
			23 sri 3263	Ceylon Transport Board, Colombo, Ceylon	07/68
RTL621	494904	3983	KGU71		
			23 sri 2016	Ceylon Transport Board, Colombo, Ceylon	12/65
RTL622	494905	3994	KGU72		
				W.North (Dealer), Sherburn-in-Elmet, Yorkshire	01/67
				Jackson (Breakers), Bradford, Yorkshire	02/67
				Finally scrapped	10/67

RTL988 now carries a further unfamiliar registration number when seen parked within Ilford, Essex on the 30th June 1989. This was the fourth registration to be carried by the bus which at one time had been operated by Jersey Motor Services. The professional conversion to open top condition had been carried out since its return to the mainland in 1974 but probably would have been more suitable for its use on the Island of Jersey. (John G. S. Smith)

RTL623	494906	4065	KGU73		
				F.Wilde t/a Wimbledon Coaches, London SW19, not used	10/65
				Shaw & Kilburn (Dealer), London W5	10/65
				E.H.Smith t/a/ Eddie's Coaches, Dunstable, Bedfordshire	10/65
				Withdrawn	03/67
				Luton Commercial Motors (Dealer), Dunstable, Bedfordshire	04/67
				Stevenage Travel	by 06/67
				Withdrawn and broken up	09/68
RTL624	494907	3978	KGU74		
				Wombwell Diesel Company (Dealer), Wombwell, Yorkshire	09/67
RTL625	494908	4003	KGU75		
				W.North (Dealer), Sherburn-in-Elmet, Yorkshire	01/67
				Johnson (Breakers), South Elmsall, Yorks	09/67
RTL626	494909	5943	KGU76		
				W.E.G. Mahy, Ghent, Brussels, Belgium (motor vehicle collector)	05/69
				Still owned	05/98
RTL627	494910	3999	KGU77		
			23 sri 3208	Ceylon Transport Board, Colombo, Ceylon	04/68
RTL628	494913	3986	KGU78		
			23 sri 2994	Ceylon Transport Board, Colombo, Ceylon	08/67
RTL629	495506	3987	KGU79		
				W.North (Dealer), Sherburn-in-Elmet, Yorkshire	01/67
				Johnson, (Breakers), South Elmsall, Yorks	08/67
RTL630	495509	4009	KGU80		
			23 sri 2669	Ceylon Transport Board, Colombo, Ceylon	12/66
				Still in existence but withdrawn	02/77
RTL631	495514	4000	KGU81		
			23 sri 3072	Ceylon Transport Board, Colombo, Ceylon	10/67
				Still in existence but withdrawn	02/77
RTL632	495512	3975	KGU82		
			23 sri 2168	Ceylon Transport Board, Colombo, Ceylon	03/66
				Withdrawn and scrapped by Ceylon Transport Board for spares	03/77
RTL633	495518	4267	KGU83		
				Passenger Vehicle Sales (London) Ltd (Dealer), Upminster, Essex	10/65
				D.C.Blackford t/a Isleworth Coaches, Isleworth, Middlesex	10/65
				J.Dreelan t/a Langley Coaches, Slough, Buckinghamshire	04/68
				Scrapped	09/70
RTL634	495519	3984	KGU84		
			23 sri 3086	Ceylon Transport Board, Colombo, Ceylon	10/67
RTL635	495925	4045	KGU85		
				Hollis Coaches Limited, Queensferry, Chester	10/65
				Withdrawn	04/69
RTL636	495930	3959	KGU86		
				Bird's Commercial Motors (Dealer), Stratford-upon-Avon, Warwickshire	09/67
				Used as internal transport at their Long Marston yard	01/68
RTL637	495924	4285	KGU87		
				W.North (Dealer), Sherburn-in-Elmet, Yorkshire	01/67
				Unknown dealer, South Kirkby, Yorkshire	10/67
RTL638	495926	4142	KGU88		
				W.North (Dealer), Sherburn-in-Elmet, Yorkshire	05/67
				Jackson (Breakers), Bradford, Yorkshire	06/67
RTL639	495911	4027	KGU89		
				Leyland Motors Limited (Dealer), London W1	09/65
				Grand Bahama Port Authority, Freeport, Bahamas and used on Sightseeing tours in L.T. Livery	09/65
RTL640	495914	4024	KGU90		
			CA 147 371	Golden Arrow Bus Service, Cape Town, South Africa 289	10/66
RTL641	495919	4031	KGU91		
				Passenger Vehicle Sales (London) Ltd (Dealer), Upminster, Essex	10/65
				A1 Service, (Kerr & Linney Ardrossan), Ardrossan, Ayrshire	11/65
				Sold within Group to Duff, Ardrossan, Ayrshire	04/68
				Still in service	01/71
				Keenan, Coalhall, for spares	—/71
RTL642	495520	3995	KGU92		
				W.North (Dealer), Sherburn-in-Elmet, Yorkshire	01/67
				Johnson, (Breakers), South Elmsall, Yorks	02/67
RTL643	495928	4032	KGU93		
			23 sri 2057	Ceylon Transport Board, Colombo, Ceylon	01/66
RTL644	495931	4015	KGU94		
				Wombwell Diesel Company (Dealer), Wombwell, Yorkshire , after mechanical units had been removed at Stonebridge Garage for Ceylon Transport Board	04/69
RTL645	495932	3980	KGU95		
			23 sri 3069	Ceylon Transport Board, Colombo, Ceylon	10/67
				Still in existence but withdrawn	02/77

RTL21 is seen here on the 11th September 1966 having already completed some eight years within the ownership of the Clyde Coast Services. Rather remarkable is the fact that London Transport garage duty plate holders are still in place together with the complete route detail aperture boxes which in this instance could have been put to better use. The route information box once carried above the rear platform has been panelled over while the inevitable direction indicator has been fixed on the front lower bulkhead corner. (V. C. Jones)

A. Hornsby of Scunthorpe traded as Primrose Coaches and at their garage RTL1444 is kept company by two of their coaches the most prominent being registered 3855HP. A nicely produced set of route blinds show for a service to Foxhills Rd via Brumby Corner and Rly Station. (John Gascoine)

RTL646	495933	4040	KGU96		
				Passenger Vehicle Sales (London) Ltd (Dealer), Upminster, Essex	10/65
				D.Blackford t/a Isleworth Coaches, Isleworth, Middlesex	10/65
				J.Dreelan, t/a Langley Coaches, Slough, Buckinghamshire	04/68
				Noted derelict at rear of Lewis (Scrap Dealer and Crane Hire), Maidenhead, Berkshire	c10/72
RTL647	495927	4104	KGU97		
			CA 143 803	City Tramways Co., Cape Town, South Africa 764	12/66
				Still in service	04/74
RTL648	495929	3982	KGU98		
			23 sri 2760	Ceylon Transport Board, Colombo, Ceylon	01/67
RTL649	496133	4017	KGU99		
			23 sri 2014	Ceylon Transport Board, Colombo, Ceylon	12/65
RTL650	496134	4001	KGU100		
			23 sri 2705	Ceylon Transport Board, Colombo, Ceylon	12/66
RTL651	495522	4044	KXW1		
				W.North (Dealer), Sherburn-in-Elmet, Yorkshire	01/67
				Johnson, (Breakers), South Elmsall, Yorkshire and broken up the following month	08/67
RTL652	495912	4093	KXW2		
				Wombwell Diesel Company (Dealer), Wombwell, Yorkshire	09/67
RTL653	495922	4060	KXW3		
				W.North (Dealer), Sherburn-in-Elmet, Yorkshire	01/67
				Johnson, (Breakers), South Elmsall, Yorkshire	10/67
RTL654	495508	4101	KXW4		
				Passenger Vehicle Sales (London) Ltd, Upminster, Essex	10/65
				Garelochhead Coach Services, Garelochhead, Dunbartonshire 47	10/65
				Into service	11/65
				Garelochhead ceased operations and vehicle not traced	08/80
RTL655	495934	4061	KXW5		
				T.Hollis Coaches Limited, Queensferry, Chester	10/65
				Wilcock, Buckley	03/68
				Withdrawn	04/69
RTL656	495935	4018	KXW6		
				W.North (Dealer), Sherburn-in-Elmet, Yorkshire	01/67
				Johnson, (Breakers), South Elmsall, Yorkshire	09/67
RTL657	495936	4025	KXW7		
			23 sri 3420	Ceylon Transport Board, Colombo, Ceylon	12/68
				Still in service	02/77
RTL658	495937	3991	KXW8		
			23 sri 2744	Ceylon Transport Board, Colombo, Ceylon	01/67
				Still in existence but withdrawn	02/77
			27 sri 6466	Sold and rebuilt as a private lorry	06/78
RTL659	495938	4058	KXW9		
				F.Widle, t/a/ Wimbledon Coaches, London SW19	09/65
				Withdrawn	by 10/70
RTL660	495939	4084	KXW10		
				Passenger Vehicle Sales (London) Ltd (Dealer), Upminster, Essex	02/66
				A1 Service, (McKinnon, Kilmarnock), Ardrossan, Ayrshire	02/66
				Still in service	11/73
				Out of use	—/74
				To service	05/75
				T.Rowe (Dealer), Muirkirk	—/78
				Unknown breaker and broken up	c07/79
RTL661	495940	4141	KXW11		
				Bird's Commercial Motors (Dealer), Stratford-upon-Avon, Warwickshire	09/67
RTL662	496128	4102	KXW12		
				W.North, Sherburn-in-Elmet, Yorkshire	08/66
				Johnson, (Breakers), South Elmsall, Yorkshire	02/67
RTL663	496132	4049	KXW13		
			23 sri 2756	Ceylon Transport Board, Colombo, Ceylon	01/67
RTL664	496135	4298	KXW14		
				Wombwell Diesel Company (Dealer), Wombwell, Yorkshire	05/69
RTL665	496136	4014	KXW15		
				W.North (Dealer), Sherburn-in-Elmet, Yorkshire	01/67
				Unknown breaker	06/67
RTL666	496137	4057	KXW16		
			23 sri 2154	Ceylon Transport Board, Colombo, Ceylon	03/66
				Still in existence but withdrawn	02/77
RTL667	496138	4075	KXW17		
			23 sri 2999	Ceylon Transport Board, Colombo, Ceylon	08/67
RTL668	496139	4081	KXW18		
			CA 147 381	Golden Arrow Bus Service, Cape Town, South Africa 299	12/66

RTL669	496140	3965	KXW19		
				R.Armstrong t/a Moordale Bus Service , Newcastle-upon-Tyne	11/65
				Fleet of Armstrong sold to Tyne & Wear PTE 84	08/73
				Withdrawn	10/74
				W.North (Dealer), Sherburn-in-Elmet, Yorkshire	12/74
				Broken up by Barraclough	03/76
RTL670	496141	4034	KXW20		
				Wombwell Diesel Company (Dealer), Wombwell, Yorkshire	09/67
RTL671	496142	4004	KXW21		
				W.North (Dealer), Sherburn-in-Elmet, Yorkshire	01/67
				Johnson, (Breakers), South Elmsall, Yorkshire	08/67
				Broken up	09/67
RTL672	496143	4046	KXW22		
				Astill & Jordan Limited, Ratby, Leicestershire	10/65
				Withdrawn	06/72
				D.Thorne, Nuneaton, Warwickshire, later to Ashwell, Cambridgeshire as a hospitality unit	06/72
				Wombwell Diesel Company (Dealer), Wombwell, Yorkshire for continued use as a hospitality unit	07/92
				R.Wright t/a Blue Triangle, Rainham, Essex	03/94
				Still owned	05/98
RTL673	496144	4026	KXW23		
			23 sri 2700	Ceylon Transport Board, Colombo, Ceylon	12/66
RTL674	496145	4043	KXW24		
				Leyland Motors Limited (Dealer), London WC1	12/66
				Grand Bahama Port Authority, Freeport, Bahamas 6 and used on sightseeing tours	01/67
				To unknown dealer in Florida, USA	by 11/79
				Noted at Fort Lauderdale International Airport, Florida, USA	11/79
				Later owned/used by a Church/religious group in Fort Lauderdale seen semi derelict in Fort Lauderdale	08/82
RTL675	496146	4012	KXW25		
			CA 147 367	Golden Arrow Bus Service, Cape Town, South Africa 285	09/66
RTL676	496147	4078	KXW26		
				W.North (Dealer), Sherburn-in-Elmet, Yorkshire	01/67
				Body mounted onto RTL958 by North's, chassis scrapped	03/67
RTL677	496148	4033	KXW27		
				Wombwell Diesel Company (Dealer), Wombwell, Yorkshire	05/69
RTL678	496149	3997	KXW28		
			23 sri 2761	Ceylon Transport Board, Colombo, Ceylon	01/67
				Still in existence having had chassis shortened and fitted with single deck body, now withdrawn	02/77
RTL679	496150	4048	KXW29		
			CA 58703	City Tramways Co., Cape Town, South Africa 752	10/65
RTL680	496153	4144	KXW30		
			CA 10376	Golden Arrow Bus Service , Cape Town, South Africa 265	11/65
RTL681	496131	4071	KXW31		
			23 sri 3218	Ceylon Transport Board, Colombo, Ceylon	07/68
				Still in existence but withdrawn	02/77
RTL682	496156	4028	KXW32		
			23 sri 3104	Ceylon Transport Board, Colombo, Ceylon	11/67
				Fitted with CTB single deck bodywork	—/—
				Withdrawn	01/80
			27 sri 4723	Sold and rebuilt as a private lorry	—/—
RTL683	496483	4074	KXW33		
			23 sri 3017	Ceylon Transport Board, Colombo, Ceylon	08/67
RTL684	496484	4098	KXW34		
				Wombwell Diesel Company (Dealer), Wombwell, Yorkshire	05/69
RTL685	496485	4086	KXW35		
				Wombwell Diesel Company (Dealer), Wombwell, Yorkshire	11/67
RTL686	496488	4079	KXW36		
			23 sri 3154	Ceylon Transport Board, Colombo, Ceylon	12/67
				Still in service numbered RL29	12/81
RTL687	496489	4067	KXW37		
			23 sri 3228	Ceylon Transport Board, Colombo, Ceylon	07/68
				Still in service but withdrawn	02/77
RTL688	496494	4080	KXW38		
				W.North (Dealer), Sherburn-in-Elmet, Yorkshire	01/67
				Johnson, (Breakers), South Elmsall, Yorkshire	10/67
RTL689	496495	4041	KXW39		
			23 sri 3153	Ceylon Transport Board, Colombo, Ceylon	12/67
RTL690	496500	4108	KXW40		
				Passenger Vehicle Sales (London) Ltd (Dealer), Upminster, Essex	10/65
				A1 Service, (T.Hunter, Kilmarnock), Ardrossan, Ayrshire	10/65
				Withdrawn	03/70
				Tiger Coaches (Dealer), Salsburgh, Lanarkshire	by 04/70

RTL691	496505	4094	KXW41		
				W.North (Dealer), Sherburn-in-Elmet, Yorkshire	01/67
				Johnson, (Breakers), South Elmsall, Yorkshire	09/67
RTL692	496506	4137	KXW42		
			23 sri 2748	Ceylon Transport Board, Colombo, Ceylon	01/67
RTL693	496508	3981	KXW43		
			23 sri 2758	Ceylon Transport Board, Colombo, Ceylon	01/67
RTL694	496510	4099	KXW44		
			CA 59122	City Tramways Co., Cape Town, South Africa 755	10/65
				Still in service	04/74
RTL695	496512	4029	KXW45		
				The Agent General, Canadian Atlantic Provinces, London WC2 as agent	04/67
				Fredericton Board of Trade, Fredericton, New Brunswick, Canada	04/67
				Subsequently sold, not traced further	—/—
RTL696	496515	4128	KXW46		
			23 sri 2991	Ceylon Transport Board, Colombo, Ceylon	09/67
				Still in existence having had been fitted with CTB single deck bodywork	02/77
				Withdrawn	01/80
			27 sri 1339	Sold and rebuilt as a private lorry	—/—
RTL697	496517	3951	KXW47		
			23 sri 2017	Ceylon Transport Board, Colombo, Ceylon	12/65
RTL698	496518	4016	KXW48		
			23 sri 2674	Ceylon Transport Board, Colombo, Ceylon	12/66
				Still in existence but withdrawn	02/77
RTL699	496519	4006	KXW49		
				Bird's Commercial Motors (Dealer), Stratford-upon-Avon, Warwickshire	09/67
RTL700	496520	4126	KXW50		
			23 sri 2704	Ceylon Transport Board, Colombo, Ceylon	12/66
RTL701	496523	4007	KXW51		
			23 sri2743	Ceylon Transport Board, Colombo, Ceylon	01/67
				Fitted with CTB 33 seat single deck bodywork	between 1973-75
				Still in existence now withdrawn	02/77
RTL702	497068	3985	KXW52		
				W.North (Dealer), Sherburn-in-Elmet, Yorkshire	01/67
				Johnson, (Breakers), South Elmsall, Yorkshire	10/67
RTL703	497069	4051	KXW53		
				J.Berger, London NW2	07/67
RTL704	497070	4138	KXW54		
			23 sri 2745	Ceylon Transport Board, Colombo, Ceylon	01/67
RTL705	497071	4134	KXW55		
			23 sri 3155	Ceylon Transport Board, Colombo, Ceylon	12/67
RTL706	497086	4050	KXW56		
			CA 30413	Golden Arrow Bus Service, Cape Town, South Africa 266	11/65
RTL707	497087	4111	KXW57		
				Wombwell Diesel Company (Dealer), Wombwell, Yorkshire	09/67
RTL708	497088	4082	KXW58		
				Passenger Vehicle Sales (London) Ltd (Dealer), Upminster, Essex	10/65
				S.Eynon & Sons, Trimsaran, Carmarthenshire	11/65
				Withdrawn by Executors of S.Eynon & Sons, Trimsaran	05/69
RTL709	500004	4072	KXW59		
			23 sri 3144	Ceylon Transport Board, Colombo, Ceylon	12/67
RTL710	500032	4054	KXW60		
				Pickersgill & Laverick (Dealer), Cudworth, Yorkshire	06/69
RTL711	500033	4278	KXW61		
			23 sri 2668	Ceylon Transport Board, Colombo, Ceylon	12/66
				Still in existence, but withdrawn	02/77
RTL712	500034	4010	KXW62		
				Bird's Commercial Motors (Dealer), Stratford-upon-Avon, Warwickshire	09/67
RTL713	500037	4070	KXW63		
			23 sri 2754	Ceylon Transport Board, Colombo, Ceylon	01/67
RTL714	500039	4087	KXW64		
				N.B. Blow, London WC2 as agent	09/65
				Louis Margo, t/a Margos Coaches of Streatham, London SW16 49	09/65
				Unknown dealer, London SE14	07/69
RTL715	500040	4088	KXW65		
				Leyland Motors Limited, (Dealer), London W1	09/65
			2753	Grand Bahama Port Authority, Freeport, Grand Bahama, Bahamas and used on sightseeing tours in L.T. Livery	09/65
RTL716	500041	4047	KXW66		
			CA 16531	City Tramways Co., Cape Town, South Africa 756	11/65
				Still in service	04/74

RTL717	500042	4276	KXW67		
			CA 59124	City Tramways Co., Cape Town, South Africa 757	11/65
				Still in service	04/74
RTL718	500043	4055	KXW68		
				Bird's Commercial Motors (Dealer), Stratford-upon-Avon, Warwickshire	08/67
RTL719	500052	4193	KXW69		
			23 sri 2759	Ceylon Transport Board, Colombo, Ceylon	01/67
RTL720	500055	4135	KXW70		
				Pickersgill & Laverick (Dealer), Cudworth, Yorkshire	06/69
RTL721	500056	3970	KXW71		
				Leyland Motors Limited (Dealer), London W1	05/66
				Exported to USA	—/66
RTL722	500057	4103	KXW72		
			CA 143 796	City Tramways Co., Cape Town, South Africa 758	10/66
				Still in service	04/74
RTL723	500058	4035	KXW73		
			23 sri 3071	Ceylon Transport Board, Colombo, Ceylon	10/67
RTL724	500059	4107	KXW74		
				Bird's Commercial Motors (Dealer), Stratford-upon-Avon, Warwickshire	09/67
RTL725	500060	4116	KXW75		
				West's Piling & Construction Company Limited, Colnbrook, Middlesex, being used at Bristol as a staff bus	06/66
				Noted on premises of Berresford, Cheddleton, Staffordshire in withdrawn condition	07/71
				Being converted to a breakdown lorry	08/74
				As a towing vehicle seen in the Sheffield area on trade plates 581RF	09/76
				Derelict at premises of Berresford	08/79
				Ripley, Carlton, Yorkshire for scrap	05/87
RTL726	500061	4059	KXW76		
			23 sri 3141	Ceylon Transport Board, Colombo, Ceylon	12/67
				Still in existence but withdrawn	02/77
RTL727	500062	4133	KXW77		
				W.North (Dealer), Sherburn-in-Elmet, Yorkshire	01/67
				Johnson, (Breakers), South Elmsall, Yorkshire	10/67
RTL728	500064	4030	KXW78		
			23 sri 2018	Ceylon Transport Board, Colombo, Ceylon	12/65
RTL729	500065	4123	KXW79		
				Scaffolding (GB) Limited, Mitcham, Surrey 6 as a staff bus	08/66
				H.J. Weston (Dealer), Mitcham for use as a store shed	03/71

RTL1049 is seen in Harlow New town on the 18th June 1966 when in the ownership of the Wrighton & Sons, furniture manufacturers. A practice in sporadic use with certain disposals was the painting through of previous London Transport identification and that, coupled with the loss of paint at roof level and an attempt to remove advertising makes the bus look very down at heel. (John Gascoine)

RTL730	500066	4096	KXW80		
			CA 147 385	Golden Arrow Bus Service, Cape Town, South Africa 303	11/66
				Scrapped	03/71
RTL731	500402	4008	KXW81		
				W.North (Dealer), Sherburn-in-Elmet, Yorkshire	02/67
				Johnson, (Breakers), South Elmsall, Yorkshire	09/67
RTL732	500404	4130	KXW82		
			23 sri 3029	Ceylon Transport Board, Colombo, Ceylon	08/67
RTL733	500405	4039	KXW83		
				F.Wilde, t/a Wimbledon Coaches, London SW19	05/66
				Withdrawn	by 09/70
RTL734	500407	4095	KXW84		
				Wombwell Diesel Company (Dealer), Wombwell, Yorkshire after mechanical units had been removed at Stonebridge Garage for Ceylon Transport Board	05/69
RTL735	500408	4131	KXW85		
			23 sri 2673	Ceylon Transport Board, Colombo, Ceylon	12/66
				Still in existence but withdrawn	02/77
RTL736	500409	4112	KXW86		
				W.North (Dealer), Sherburn-in-Elmet, Yorkshire	01/67
				Johnson, (Breakers), South Elmsall, Yorkshire	09/67
RTL737	500410	4066	KXW87		
				W.North (Dealer), Sherburn-in-Elmet, Yorkshire	10/65
				Broken up	03/66
RTL738	500411	4231	KXW88		
				Bird's Commercial Motors (Dealer), Stratford-upon-Avon, Warwickshire	09/67
RTL739	500412	4110	KXW89		
				Bird's Commercial Motors (Dealer), Stratford-upon-Avon, Warwickshire	08/67
RTL740	500413	4036	KXW90		
				Passenger Vehicle Sales (London) Ltd (Dealer), Upminster, Essex	10/65
				Garelochhead Coach Services, Garelochhead, Dumbartonshire 48	10/65
				Into service	01/66
				Withdrawn	07/68
				Ferry & Simpson, t/a P & M Coaches, Glasgow	07/68
				De-roofed in accident and withdrawn	by 12/68

Now carrying fleet number 1 with its new owners Harper Bros. of Heath Hayes, RTL26 has an air of wartime black-out white paint style with the new paint scheme it now carries. The bus, with Kingstanding showing in the much altered London route aperture boxes, carries a good load of passengers while viewed sometime in 1961 having just negotiated a roundabout which includes a direction sign to Lightfield. (Alan Mortimer)

The chassis of both vehicles in this view were built by Leyland while the lead bus as far as this book is concerned is the more interesting being RTL21. Both buses are on route to the coastal town of Ardrossan in 1958 and although no route numbers are carried the different routes being taken are clearly announced with the blind boxes. The bus operated for the A1 Service organisation for a very short time before moving over to Clyde Coast Services. (F. W. Ivey)

RTL741	500414	4118	KXW91		
				Bird's Commercial Motors (Dealer), Stratford-upon-Avon, Warwickshire	08/67
RTL742	400415	4120	KXW92		
			CA 147 375	Golden Arrow Bus Service, Cape Town, South Africa 293	10/66
RTL743	501085	4155	KXW93		
			23 sri 2987	Ceylon Transport Board, Colombo, Ceylon	09/67
				Still in existence but withdrawn	02/77
RTL744	501086	4056	KXW94		
			23 sri 3219	Ceylon Transport Board, Colombo, Ceylon	07/68
RTL745	501087	4092	KXW95		
			CA 147 373	Golden Arrow Bus Service, Cape Town, South Africa 291	10/66
RTL746	501088	4083	KXW96		
				F.Widle t/a Wimbledon Coaches, London SW19	09/65
				Withdrawn	01/70
RTL747	501090	4114	KXW97		
				Bird's Commercial Motors (Dealer), Stratford-upon-Avon, Warwickshire	08/67
RTL748	501093	4109	KXW98		
				W.M. Bird, Cholderton College, Cholderton, Salisbury, Wilts	09/66
RTL749	501094	4178	KXW99		
			23 sri 3129	Ceylon Transport Board, Colombo, Ceylon	11/67
RTL750	501095	4038	KXW100		
			CA 143 797	City Tramways Co., Cape Town, South Africa 759	11/66
				Still in service	04/74
RTL751	501097	4068	KYY721		
			23 sri 2746	Ceylon Transport Board, Colombo, Ceylon	01/67
RTL752	501098	4119	KYY722		
			23 sri 2988	Ceylon Transport Board, Colombo, Ceylon	09/67
RTL753	501099	4053	KYY723		
			23 sri 2993	Ceylon Transport Board, Colombo, Ceylon	08/67
RTL754	501100	4023	KYY724		
				W.North (Dealer), Sherburn-in-Elmet, Yorkshire	02/66
				Broken Up	03/66
RTL755	501101	4106	KYY725		
				Leyland Motors Limited (Dealer), London W1	11/66
				Cheshire Inn & Lodge, St. Louis, Missouri, USA	—/67
				Replaced and sold to unknown owners in St. Louis area	—/79
				Believed to be with G.Nicholas, Olympia Kebab House & Tavern, St. Louis, Missouri	by 11/94
RTL756	501102	4117	KYY726		
				W.North (Dealer), Sherburn-in-Elmet, Yorkshire	01/67
				Johnson, (Breakers), South Elmsall, Yorkshire	09/67
RTL757	501216	4146	KYY727		
			23 sri 3403	Ceylon Transport Board, Colombo, Ceylon	12/68

RTL758	501217	4315	KYY728		
				B.Walden t/a Walden's Coaches, Epping, Essex	09/66
				W.J.MacIntyre, t/a Golden Boy Coaches, Harlow, Essex	05/69
				Ben Johnson (Breakers), Cudworth, Barnsley, Yorkshire and scrapped	09/69
RTL759	501218	4115	KYY729		
			23 sri 3101	Ceylon Transport Board, Colombo, Ceylon	11/67
RTL760	501219	4197	KYY730		
				W.North (Dealer), Sherburn-in-Elmet, Yorkshire	01/67
				Johnson, (Breakers), South Elmsall, Yorkshire	10/67
RTL761	501220	4136	KYY731		
				Barton Transport Limited, Chilwell, Nottinghamshire. 1084	03/67
				Withdrawn	11/72
				Royal Army Veterinary Corps, (for dog training), Melton Mowbray, Leicestershire	02/73
				Appeared in "Blue Peter" programme (still in Barton Livery)	04/74
				Police Training College, Ashfordby, Leicestershire	by 07/86
RTL762	501221	4143	KYY732		
				Wombwell Diesel Company (Dealer), Wombwell, Yorkshire	11/67
RTL763	501222	4139	KYY733		
			23 sri 2762	Ceylon Transport Board, Colombo, Ceylon	01/67
				Still in existence but withdrawn	02/77
RTL764	501223	4100	KYY734		
			23 sri 3006	Ceylon Transport Board, Colombo, Ceylon	08/67
				Still in service	02/77
RTL765	501227	3979	KYY735		
				F.Wilde, t/a Wimbledon Coaches, London SW19	05/66
				Fisher & Ford (Dealer), Barnsley, Yorkshire, for scrap	03/69
RTL766	501228	4129	KYY736		
				W.North (Dealer), Sherburn-in-Elmet, Yorkshire	01/67
				Passenger Vehicle Sales (London) Ltd (Dealer), Upminster, Essex, as spares for RTL1036	01/67
				Linnard, (Breaker), London E17	04/67
RTL767	501229	4122	KYY737		
				Waldens Coaches Limited, Epping, Essex	05/67
				Passenger Vehicle Sales (London) Ltd (Dealer), Canvey Island, Essex	06/70
				Bexleyheath Transport Co.Ltd., Bexleyheath, Kent	06/70
				Withdrawn and being stripped for spares	03/73
				Jamieson (Dealer), Dunscroft	05/74
RTL768	501230	4113	KYY738		
				F.Ridler (Dealer), Whitton, Middlesex	07/65
				Seth Coaches, London NW5, used for spares only	08/65
				Dome fitted to RT759	—/65
RTL769	501231	4042	KYY739		
			23 sri 2750	Ceylon Transport Board, Colombo, Ceylon	01/67
RTL770	501232	4204	KYY740		
			23 sri 3164	Ceylon Transport Board, Colombo, Ceylon	12/67

RTL460 was first used by the Jersey Motor Transport Company Limited for a good number of years after its sale by the Executive. Eventually it was brought back to the mainland in 1974 only to be re-exported and put to use on a tourist service in much altered condition on Sentoza Island. A very informative bus stop number 3 is being passed on the other side of the road which points to some interesting locations. (L.W. Rowe)

RTL771	501233	4062	KYY741		
				W.North (Dealer), Sherburn-in-Elmet, Yorkshire	01/67
				Johnson, (Breakers), South Elmsall, Yorkshire	09/67
RTL772	501388	4151	KYY742		
				Wombwell Diesel Company (Dealer), Wombwell, Yorkshire	09/67
RTL773	501390	4052	KYY743		
				W.North (Dealer), Sherburn-in-Elmet, Yorkshire	01/67
				Johnson, (Breakers), South Elmsall, Yorkshire	09/67
RTL774	501394	4125	KYY744		
			23 sri 3085	Ceylon Transport Board, Colombo, Ceylon	10/67
				Still in existence but withdrawn	02/77
RTL775	501395	4147	KYY745		
				W.North (Dealer), Sherburn-in-Elmet, Yorkshire	01/67
				Unknown breaker	05/67
RTL776	501396	4185	KYY746		
				W.North (Dealer), Sherburn-in-Elmet, Yorkshire	02/67
				Johnson, (Breakers), South Elmsall, Yorkshire	09/67
RTL777	501398	4064	KYY747		
				Passenger Vehicle Sales (London) Ltd (Dealer), Upminster, Essex	03/67
				Berger Coaches, London N4	03/67
				Withdrawn	09/69
				R.Searle (Dealer), London E17 and scrapped	04/71
RTL778	501399	4210	KYY748		
			23 sri 3389	Ceylon Transport Board, Colombo, Ceylon	12/68
				Still in existence having been fitted with CTB single deck bodywork	02/77
				Withdrawn	01/79
RTL779	501496	4164	KYY749		
			23 sri 3115	Ceylon Transport Board, Colombo, Ceylon	11/67
RTL780	501498	4169	KYY750		
			23 sri 2098	Ceylon Transport Board, Colombo, Ceylon	01/66
RTL781	501499	4226	KYY751		
			23 sri 3100	Ceylon Transport Board, Colombo, Ceylon	11/67
				Still in existence but withdrawn	02/77
RTL782	501500	4150	KYY752		
			23 sri 2757	Ceylon Transport Board, Colombo, Ceylon	01/67
RTL783	501501	4191	KYY753		
				W.North (Dealer), Sherburn-in-Elmet, Yorkshire	01/67
				Johnson, (Breakers), South Elmsall, Yorkshire	10/67
RTL784	501502	4198	KYY754		
				F.Ridler (Dealer), Whitton, Middlesex	03/65
				N.Beldoz (Breaker), Hertford and broken up	07/65
RTL785	501503	4091	KYY755		
			23 sri 3125	Ceylon Transport Board, Colombo, Ceylon	11/67
RTL786	501504	4153	KYY756		
			CA 143 804	City Tramways Co., Cape Town, South Africa 765	12/66
				Still in service, renumbered 0765	02/76
RTL787	501505	4154	KYY757		
				Wombwell Diesel Company (Dealer), Wombwell, Yorkshire after mechanical units had been removed at Stonebridge Garage for Ceylon Transport Board	05/69
RTL788	501508	4200	KYY758		
			23 sri 3022	Ceylon Transport Board, Colombo, Ceylon	08/67
				Still in existence but withdrawn	02/77
RTL789	501509	4089	KYY759		
			23 sri 3183	Ceylon Transport Board, Colombo, Ceylon	04/68
				Still in existence but withdrawn	02/77
RTL790	501510	4090	KYY760		
				Wombwell Diesel Company (Dealer), Wombwell, Yorkshire	05/69
RTL791	501511	4145	KYY761		
			23 sri 3293	Ceylon Transport Board, Colombo, Ceylon	08/68
				Still in existence but withdrawn	02/77
RTL792	501512	4219	KYY762		
			CA 143 799	City Tramways Co., Cape Town, South Africa 761	11/66
				Still in service	04/74
RTL793	501513	4076	KYY763		
			23 sri 2755	Ceylon Transport Board, Colombo, Ceylon	01/67
RTL794	501514	4162	KYY764		
				W.North (Dealer), Sherburn-in-Elmet, Yorkshire	01/67
				Johnson, (Breakers), South Elmsall, Yorkshire	09/67
RTL795	501538	4085	KYY765		
			23 sri 3290	Ceylon Transport Board, Colombo, Ceylon	08/68
				Still in existence but withdrawn	02/77
RTL796	501540	4173	KYY766		
				Bird's Commercial Motors (Dealer), Stratford-upon-Avon, Warwickshire	08/67

RTL797	501541	4163	KYY767		
			23 sri 3163	Ceylon Transport Board, Colombo, Ceylon	12/67
RTL798	501543	4215	KYY768		
				Pickersgill & Laverick (Dealer), Cudworth, Yorkshire	06/69
RTL799	501544	4224	KYY769		
				Essoldo Circuits, London SW1 5 for members transport at Essoldo Bingo Club, Chippenham, Buckinghamshire	01/67
				J.Dreelan, t/a Langley Coaches, Slough, Buckinghamshire	08/68
				Lewis (Dealer), Maidenhead, Berkshire	c07/69
				Only chassis now remaining	07/70
RTL800	501546	4190	KYY770		
				Harper Bros., Heath Hayes, Cannock, Staffordshire 7	07/66
				Harper Bros., taken over by Midland Red and now operating on hire to Midland Red	—/74
				Midland Red 2207	09/74
				Withdrawn having never been operated by Midland Red	09/74
				Newman, Cannock, Staffordshire for preservation	04/75
				Linley, Bridge Cross Garage, Chase Terrace, Staffordshire for continued preservation	by 07/75
				Exported Japan	c —/78
				Macchen-Japan, Tokyo, Japan in LT red livery	by 03/93
RTL801	501547	4257	KYY771		
			23 sri 3004	Ceylon Transport Board, Colombo, Ceylon	08/67
RTL802	501549	4166	KYY772		
				Essoldo Circuits, London SW1, 1 used for members transport at Essoldo Bingo Club, Chippenham, Buckinghamshire	01/67
				J.Dreelan t/a Langley Coaches, Slough, Buckinghamshire	08/68
				Lewis (Dealer), Maidenhead, Berkshire	c03/69
				Broken up	by 04/69
RTL803	501550	4305	KYY773		
				John Walker & Sons Limited, London SW1	09/67
				Used in Belgium by Walkers Belgian agent promoting Johnnie Walker Whisky, roof rebuilt on hydraulics so that it could be lowered to 4 metres high	—/—
				London Bus Preservation Group, Cobham, Surrey	02/84
				E.Brakell (Dealer), Cheam, Surrey	06/84
				Fills Gancia, Canelli, Asti, Italy, sponsors of the Dangerous Sports Club 1985 ski extravaganza at St. Morritz	03/85
				Lord Rufus Isaacs, London of the dangerous sports club and stored on a farm near Kingham/Churchill, Oxfordshire	by 04/85
				PVS (Dealer), Carlton, Yorkshire for scrap	by 11/87

Staff bus RTL1283 is seen parked at Bexleyheath on the 2nd December 1967 while in the ownership of Collars 1940 Group Limited. It was to last nearly ten years before finally being disposed of but to who currently remains a mystery. (John G. S. Smith)

RTL804	501551	4196	KYY774		
				Wombwell Diesel Company (Dealer), Wombwell, Yorkshire	10/69
RTL805	501714	4195	KYY775		
			23 sri 3075	Ceylon Transport Board, Colombo, Ceylon	10/67
				Still in existence but withdrawn	02/77
RTL806	501715	4157	KYY776		
				W.North (Dealer), Sherburn-in-Elmet, Yorkshire	02/67
				Johnson, (Breakers), South Elmsall, Yorkshire	10/67
RTL807	501716	4189	KYY777		
				Leyland Motors Limited (Dealer), London WC1	12/66
				Grand Bahama Port Authority, Freeport, Bahamas 5 for sight seeing tours	01/67
			5222	To unknown dealer in Florida USA	c —/79
				Noted derelict on the Tamiami Trail, near Ochopee, Florida, USA, with for sale sign	—/83
RTL808	501717	4183	KYY778		
				Wombwell Diesel Company (Dealer), Wombwell, Yorkshire	09/67
RTL809	501718	4207	KYY779		
				Wombwell Diesel Company (Dealer), Wombwell, Yorkshire after mechanical units had been removed at Stonebridge Garage for Ceylon Transport Board	04/69
RTL810	501719	4170	KYY780		
				Barton Transport Limited, Chilwell, Nottinghamshires 1086	04/67
				Withdrawn	05/70
				East Midlands Transport Society, Plumtree, Nottinghamshire	08/70
				Broken up as means of raising funds from sale of scrap	08/70
RTL811	501720	4180	KYY781		
				West Kent College of Further Education for visit to the USSR in July and August	01/67
				Super Coaches, Upminster, Essex for spares	12/67
RTL812	501721	4222	KYY782		
				Goode, Durrant & Murray Limited, London EC1	11/66
				Marie Claire Boutique, Drummond Building, Catherine Street, West Montreal, Canada, built into entrance of premises.	by 05/71
				Still there	05/76
				Removed and not traced further	—/76
RTL813	501724	4105	KYY783		
			23 sri 3140	Ceylon Transport Board, Colombo, Ceylon	12/67
RTL814	501725	4206	KYY784		
				W.North (Dealer), Sherburn-in-Elmet, Yorkshire	01/67
				Johnson, (Breakers), South Elmsall, Yorkshire	09/67
RTL815	501726	4127	KYY785		
			23 sri 2749	Ceylon Transport Board, Colombo, Ceylon	01/67
RTL816	501727	4361	KYY786		
			23 sri 3379	Ceylon Transport Board, Colombo, Ceylon	12/68
				Still in existence but withdrawn	02/77
RTL817	501728	4156	KYY787		
			23 sri 3137	Ceylon Transport Board, Colombo, Ceylon	12/67
RTL818	501729	4233	KYY788		
			23 sri 3395	Ceylon Transport Board, Colombo, Ceylon	12/68
RTL819	501730	4211	KYY789		
			23 sri 3106	Ceylon Transport Board, Colombo, Ceylon	11/67
RTL820	501731	4178	KYY790		
				W.North (Dealer), Sherburn-in-Elmet, Yorkshire	01/67
				Johnson, (Breakers), South Elmsall, Yorkshire	10/67
RTL821	501908	4179	KYY791		
			23 sri 3239	Ceylon Transport Board, Colombo, Ceylon	07/68
RTL822	501909	4149	KYY792		
			CA 147 372	Golden Arrow Bus Service, Cape Town, South Africa 290	10/66
RTL823	501910	4161	KYY793		
				W.North (Dealer), Sherburn-in-Elmet, Yorkshire	01/67
				Johnson, (Breakers), South Elmsall, Yorkshire	09/67
RTL824	501911	4221	KYY794		
				Johnson, London SW16 as agent	04/66
				Louis Margo, t/a Margo's Coaches, Streatham, London, SW16	04/66
				Saunders (Dealer), London SE8	12/69
				Wombwell Diesel Company (Dealer), Wombwell, Yorkshire	12/69
RTL825	501912	4282	KYY795		
			23 sri 3134	Ceylon Transport Board, Colombo, Ceylon	12/67
				Still in existence having been fitted with CTB single deck bodywork	02/77
				Withdrawn	01/79
RTL826	501914	4159	KYY796		
			23 sri 3370	Ceylon Transport Board, Colombo, Ceylon	12/68
RTL827	501915	4270	KYY797		
				Don Everall (Commercial Vehicles), Wolverhampton	09/66
				Fellows-Stringer, Kidderminster, (Crane Manufacturers), Worcestershire as staff bus	09/66

RTL828	501916	4187	KYY798			
				23 sri 3159	Ceylon Transport Board, Colombo, Ceylon	12/67
RTL829	501917	4301	KYY799			
					Passenger Vehicle Sales (London) Ltd (Dealer), Upminster, Essex	10/66
					Executors of S.Ledgard, Armley, Yorkshire	10/66
					West Yorkshire Road Car Company, Harrogate, West Yorkshire upon take over of Ledgard business, not used	10/67
					W.North (Dealer), Sherburn-in-Elmet, Yorkshire	01/68
					A1 Service, (J.C.Stewart, Stevenston), Ardrossan, Ayrshire	02/68
					Withdrawn	—/70
					McKinnon, Kilmarnock	09/70
					Lawson (Dealer), Stevenston for scrap	09/70
RTL830	501921	4235	KYY800			
				23 sri 3292	Ceylon Transport Board, Colombo, Ceylon	08/68
					Still in existence but withdrawn	02/77
RTL831	501922	4186	KYY801			
					W.North (Dealer), Sherburn-in-Elmet, Yorkshire	02/67
					Johnson, (Breakers), South Elmsall, Yorkshire	09/67
RTL832	501923	4231	KYY802			
					Bird's Commercial Motors (Dealer), Stratford-upon-Avon, Warwickshire	09/67
RTL833	501926	4158	KYY803			
				23 sri 2989	Ceylon Transport Board, Colombo, Ceylon	09/67
					Still in existence but withdrawn	02/77
RTL834	502084	4250	KYY804			
					W.North (Dealer), Sherburn-in-Elmet, Yorkshire	01/67
					Johnson, (Breakers), South Elmsall, Yorkshire	09/67
RTL835	502085	4205	KYY805			
					Passenger Vehicle Sales (London) Ltd (Dealer), Upminster, Essex	01/67
				AWI 617	W.Kenneally, t/a Kenneally's Bus Service, Waterford, Eire	01/67
					Withdrawn	by 09/78
RTL836	502086	4379	KYY806			
					British Radio Corporation Limited, Chigwell, Essex	11/67
					Renamed Thorn Electrical Industries	—/—
					Withdrawn	03/72
RTL837	502087	4290	KYY807			
					Barton Transport Limited, Chilwell, Nottinghamshire 1085	03/67
					Withdrawn	03/72
					G.Lister (Dealer), Bolton	03/72
					Autospares (Dealer), Bingley	07/72
RTL838	502088	4381	KYY808			
				CA 143 798	City Tramways Co., Cape Town, South Africa 760	11/66
					Still in service	04/74
RTL839	502089	4220	KYY809			
				23 sri 3184	Ceylon Transport Board, Colombo, Ceylon	04/68
					Still in existence but withdrawn	02/77
RTL840	502090	4376	KYY810			
					Bird's Commercial Motors (Dealer), Stratford-upon-Avon, Warwickshire	09/67
RTL841	502091	4212	KYY811			
				CA 143 800	City Tramways Co., Cape Town, South Africa 762	11/66
					Repainted LT red to mark end of regular ex London bus operations	—/76
					Withdrawn	—/77
					David Rawden, Matjiesfontein, Karoo, South Africa, used for transport of tourists around Matjiesfontein to and from railway station and hotel	—/81
					Still owned	—/98
RTL842	502092	4292	KYY812			
					Passenger Vehicle Sales (London) Ltd (Dealer), Upminster, Essex	06/66
					McConnachie, Campletown, Argyllshire	06/66
					Craig, t/a West Coast Motors, Campbeltown, upon take over of McConnachie's business, not used	03/70
					Telefilms Transport (Dealer), Preston, Lands	05/70
RTL843	502093	4316	KYY813			
				23 sri 3280	Ceylon Transport Board, Colombo, Ceylon	08/68
RTL844	502094	4237	KYY814			
				23 sri 3148	Ceylon Transport Board, Colombo, Ceylon	12/67
RTL845	502096	4208	KYY815			
				CA 143 805	City Tramways Co., Cape Town, South Africa 766	12/66
					Still in service	02/76
RTL846	502099	4375	KYY816			
					Bird's Commercial Motors (Dealer), Stratford-upon-Avon, Warwickshire	09/67
RTL847	502100	3988	KYY817			
					H & C Transport, Garston, Hertfordshire	06/66
					Knightswood Coaches, Watford, Hertfordshire	05/68
					Broken up by showmen, Watford Heath, Hertfordshire	02/69

RTL1414 after a number of years in use as a passenger carrying bus with the Ceylon Transport Board was eventually transformed into this Police Command Post and mobile police station. It is seen here at Echelon Square, Columbo on the 2nd February 1978 looking ready for business complete with a confinement area situated at the front of the lower saloon. Operated and maintained by its original Ceylonese owners who have taken the precaution it would appear to state the correct engine oil required of the benefit of anyone unfamiliar. (Wijewardene Memorial Media Library & Documentation Centre)

RTL848	502101	4314	KYY818		
				Passenger Vehicle Sales (London) Ltd (Dealer), Upminster, Essex	09/66
				A.H.Kearsey, Cheltenham, Gloucestershire	10/66
				Marchant's Coaches, Cheltenham, Gloucestershire upon take over of Kearsey's business	—/68
				Withdrawn	04/74
				G.Lister (Dealers), Bolton	05/74
				Woods (Breakers), Doncaster	—/74
RTL849	502102	4257	KYY819		
			23 sri 3018	Ceylon Transport Board, Colombo, Ceylon	08/67
RTL850	502103	4216	KYY820		
			23 sri 3180	Ceylon Transport Board, Colombo, Ceylon	04/68
				Still in existence but withdrawn	02/77
RTL851	502190	4234	LLU841		
				Wombwell Diesel Company (Dealer), Wombwell, Yorkshire	09/67
RTL852	502192	4324	LLU842		
				Passenger Vehicle Sales (London) Ltd (Dealer), Upminster, Essex	08/66
				Executors of S.Ledgard, Armley, Yorkshire	08/66
				West Yorkshire Road Car Company, Harrogate, West Yorkshire upon takeover of Ledgard's business, not used	10/67
				Passenger Vehicle Sales (London) Ltd (Dealer), Canvey Island, Essex	01/68
				J.Keenan, Coalhall, Ayrshire	02/68
				Fitted with platform doors	03/68
				Licenced	04/68
				Withdrawn and derelict on premises	11/72
RTL853	502193	4297	LLU843		
			23 sri 3401	Ceylon Transport Board, Colombo, Ceylon	12/68
RTL854	502194	4244	LLU844		
				Bird's Commercial Motors (Dealer), Stratford-upon-Avon, Warwickshire	08/67
RTL855	502195	4260	LLU845		
			23 sri 3063	Ceylon Transport Board, Colombo, Ceylon	10/67
				Still in existence but withdrawn	02/77
RTL856	502196	4312	LLU846		
			23 sri 3286	Ceylon Transport Board, Colombo, Ceylon	08/68
				Still in existence but withdrawn	02/77
RTL857	502197	4303	LLU847		
				Wombwell Diesel Company (Dealer), Wombwell, Yorkshire	09/67
RTL858	502198	4302	LLU848		
			23 sri 3103	Ceylon Transport Board, Colombo, Ceylon	11/67
				Still in existence but withdrawn	02/77

In 1926 John Stevenson of Spath started operation in road transport having previously been in the dairy farming business. It was 1957 when the first ex-London Transport vehicles began to arrive in the fleet culminating with the large influx of DMS buses acquired over the period 1979 through to the late 80s. A 1964 acquisition was RTL1141, seen in their customary livery of yellow and black together with operator's name and rising sun. (Photobus)

RTL859	502201	4296	LLU849		
			23 sri 3003	Ceylon Transport Board, Colombo, Ceylon	08/67
RTL860	502202	4232	LLU850		
				W.North (Dealer), Sherburn-in-Elmet, Yorkshire	01/67
				Johnson, (Breakers), South Elmsall, Yorkshire	02/67
RTL861	502203	4299	LLU851		
				Bird's Commercial Motors (Dealer), Stratford-upon-Avon, Warwickshire	08/67
RTL862	402204	4264	LLU852		
				Wombwell Diesel Company (Dealer), Wombwell, Yorkshire	09/67
RTL863	502205	4261	LLU853		
				Passenger Vehicle Sales (London) Ltd (Dealer), Upminster, Essex	08/66
				Executors of S.Ledgard, Armley, Yorkshire	08/66
				West Yorkshire Road Car Co. Harrogate West Yorkshire, upon take over of Ledgard's business, not operated	10/67
				Passenger Vehicle Sales (London) Ltd (Dealer), Canvey Island, Essex	01/68
				W.North (Dealer), Sherburn-in-Elmet, Yorkshire	01/68
				J.Keenan, Coalhall	01/68
				Fitted with platform doors	02/68
				Licensed	04/68
				G.Lister (Dealer), Bolton	07/74
				Jamieson (Dealer), Dunscroft	by 10/74
RTL864	502206	4266	LLU854		
			23 sri 3294	Ceylon Transport Board, Colombo, Ceylon	08/68
RTL865	502209	4228	LLU855		
				Johnson, London SW16	08/66
				Louis Margo, t/a South London Coach Company, Streatham, London SW16	08/66
				Wombwell Diesel Company (Dealer), Wombwell, Yorkshire	08/70
RTL866	502212	4287	LLU856		
				Leyland Motors Limited (Dealer), London WC1	12/66
			5224	Grand Bahama Port Authority, Freeport, Bahamas for sightseeing tours in L.T. livery	01/67
RTL867	502398	4160	LLU857		
				B.S.Harris, London SW16, used for a holiday tour to Spain	08/66
				Passenger Vehicle Sales (London) Ltd (Dealer), Silver End, Essex	08/66
				Super Coaches, Upminster, Essex	11/66
				City Coach Lines, Upminster, Essex	02/69
				Romford Scrap & Salvage Company (Dealer), Collier Row, Essex	—/70
RTL868	502399	4325	LLU858		
			CA 147 382	Golden Arrow Bus Service, Cape Town, South Africa 300	12/66
RTL869	502400	4370	LLU859		
				Wombwell Diesel Company (Dealer), Wombwell, Yorkshire	09/67
RTL870	502401	4289	LLU860		
				W.North (Dealer), Sherburn-in-Elmet, Yorkshire	01/67
				Johnson, (Breakers), South Elmsall, Yorkshire	05/67
RTL871	502402	4174	LLU861		
			23 sri 3077	Ceylon Transport Board, Colombo, Ceylon	10/67
				Still in existence but withdrawn	02/77
RTL872	502403	4214	LLU862		
			23 sri 3383	Ceylon Transport Board, Colombo, Ceylon	12/68
				Still in existence but withdrawn	02/77
RTL873	502404	4400	LLU863		
			23 sri 3019	Ceylon Transport Board, Colombo, Ceylon	08/67
				Still in existence but withdrawn	02/77
RTL874	502405	4249	LLU864		
			23 sri 3023	Ceylon Transport Board, Colombo, Ceylon	08/67
RTL875	502407	4326	LLU865		
			23 sri 3025	Ceylon Transport Board, Colombo, Ceylon	08/67
RTL876	502410	4140	LLU866		
				Passenger Vehicle Sales (London) Ltd (Dealer), Upminster, Essex	10/65
				S.Eynon & Sons, Trimsaran, Carmarthenshire	11/65
				Withdrawn	09/67
				Arlington Motors (Dealer), Cardiff	09/67
				W.H.Way (Dealer), Cardiff Docks	11/67
				Scrapped	—/—
RTL877	502411	4172	LLU867		
				Leyland Motors Limited (Dealer), London WC1	12/66
				Grand Bahama Port Authority, Freeport, Bahamas 7 for sightseeing tours in L.T. livery	01/67
RTL878	502412	4022	LLU868		
				Wombwell Diesel Company (Dealer), Wombwell, Yorkshire	11/67
RTL879	502415	4188	LLU869		
			CA 147 383	Golden Arrow Bus Service, Cape Town, South Africa 301	12/66
				Withdrawn	between 11/70 – 04/71

RTL880	502578	4378	LLU870		
				W.North (Dealer), Sherburn-in-Elmet, Yorkshire	01/67
				Johnson, (Breakers), South Elmsall, Yorkshire	02/67
RTL881	502579	4332	LLU871		
			23 sri 3413	Ceylon Transport Board, Colombo, Ceylon	12/68
RTL882	502581	4176	LLU872		
				W.North (Dealer), Sherburn-in-Elmet, Yorkshire	01/67
				Johnson, (Breakers), South Elmsall, Yorkshire	09/67
RTL883	502582	4365	LLU873		
				Passenger Vehicle Sales (London) Ltd (Dealer), Upminster, Essex	08/66
				Executors of S.Ledgard, Armley, Yorkshire	08/66
				West Yorkshire Road Car Company, Harrogate, West Yorkshire, upon take over of Ledgard's business, not used	10/67
				W.North (Dealer), Sherburn-in-Elmet, Yorkshire	01/68
				Passenger Vehicle Sales (London) Ltd (Dealer), Upminster, Essex	03/68
				Clyde Coast Services (H.B.Frazer, Fairle), Saltcoats, Ayrshire	03/68
				Withdrawn and scrapped by Frazer for spares	05/70
RTL884	502583	4192	LLU874		
			CA 143 801	City Tramways Co., Cape Town, South Africa 763	11/66
				Still in service	04/74
RTL885	802584	4171	LLU875		
				Wombwell Diesel Company (Dealer), Wombwell, Yorkshire	09/67
RTL886	502586	4300	LLU876		
			CA 147 384	Golden Arrow Bus Service, Cape Town, South Africa 302	12/66
RTL887	502591	4353	LLU877		
				Wombwell Diesel Company (Dealer), Wombwell, Yorkshire	09/67
RTL888	502592	4286	LLU878		
				West's Piling & Construction Company Limited, Colnbrook (based at Altrincham, Lancs) as a staff bus	08/66
				Autospares (Dealer), Bingley, Yorkshire	02/70
				Broken up	by 03/70
RTL889	502593	4213	LLU879		
				Johnson, London SW16 as agent	08/66
				Louis Margo, Streatham, London SW16	08/66
				Saunders (Dealer), London SE8	09/70
RTL890	502594	4217	LLU880		
			23 sri 3194	Ceylon Transport Board, Colombo, Ceylon	04/68
RTL891	502595	4380	LLU881		
			23 sri 3121	Ceylon Transport Board, Colombo, Ceylon	11/67
				Still in existence but withdrawn	02/77
RTL892	502599	4271	LLU882		
				W.North (Dealer), Sherburn-in-Elmet, Yorkshire	01/67
				Johnson, (Breakers), South Elmsall, Yorkshire	03/67

Percy C,. Mounty Limited used RTL1412 as farm transport and for its next use it stands ready to transport Howfield picker. Currently preserved it is one of a small number of Leyland RTL and RTW buses which nowadays attend rally meetings. (John Gascoine)

RTL893	502600	4184	LLU883	Central Broadcasting Corporation, 4225 Franklin Road, Nashville, Tennessee, USA	10/66
				Sangro De Cristo Development Co., Sante Fe, New Mexico	by —/72
				British Promotions (Dealer), Norfolk, Virginia	07/72
				Red Dog Dan's Show Time Square / Pink Pussycat Topless Bar, Albequerque, New Mexico	—/72
				For sale	12/74
				London Bus & Cab Company, Canoga Park, California	by —/86
				Rent-It-Vehicle Rentals, Agoura Hills, California, probably never used	by —/90
				Still there, out of use	06/92
				Sold	—/92 to —/93
				Ranch Estates Remax Calabasas Realty, Calabasas, California	by 03/96
				Still owned	06/96
RTL894	502601	4288	LLU884		
			23 sri 3380	Ceylon Transport Board, Colombo, Ceylon	12/68
				Still in service	02/77
RTL895	502602	4199	LLU885		
			23 sri 3227	Ceylon Transport Board, Colombo, Ceylon	07/68
				Still in service	02/77
RTL896	502807	4209	LLU886		
			CA 143 806	City Tramways Co., Cape Town, South Africa 767	12/66
				Still in service	04/74
RTL897	502808	4245	LLU887		
				Wombwell Diesel Company (Dealer), Wombwell, Yorkshire	09/67
RTL898	502809	4077	LLU888		
			23 sri 2752	Ceylon Transport Board, Colombo, Ceylon	01/67
RTL899	502810	4293	LLU889		
				Wombwell Diesel Company (Dealer), Wombwell, Yorkshire	05/69
RTL900	502811	4202	LLU890		
				B.Waldens Coaches, Epping, Essex	08/66
				G.F.Ward, Epping, Essex	08/68
				Withdrawn	03/72
				Passenger Vehicle Sales (London) Ltd (Dealer), Silver End, Essex	05/72
				PVS Contract Fleet 65	05/72
				Queen Eleanor School, Waltham Cross	02/73
				E.Brakell (Dealer), Cheam, Surrey	01/77
				Continental Pioneer (in dealer capacity), Richmond, Surrey	09/77
				To unknown youth club, London SE as a static club house under a railway arch	—/77
RTL901	502812	4269	LLU891		
				Johnson, London SW16	08/66
				Louis Margo t/a South London Coach Co, Streatham, London SW16	08/66
				Margo t/a Bexleyheath Transport, Bexleyheath	09/70
				Withdrawn	09/71
				Jamieson (Dealer), Dunscroft, Yorkshire	05/74
RTL902	502813	4323	LLU892		
			23 sri 3251	Ceylon Transport Board, Colombo, Ceylon	07/68

RTL3, whose fleet number is still carried in its London Transport position, was converted to offside platform configuration in October 1958 as a demonstrator to prospective purchasers. It was eventually sold to the Mont Blanc Auto-Rental of Geneva and is shown parked looking like a mobile advertising hoarding near to the famous tunnel in Switzerland with many other road vehicles in evidence. At the base of the lighting column at the left of the picture a direction sign pointing the way to Lausanne is just visible. (John Gascoine collection)

RTL903	502814	4201	LLU893		
			23 sri 3076	Ceylon Transport Board, Colombo, Ceylon	10/67
				Still in existence but withdrawn	02/77
RTL904	502815	4280	LLU894		
			23 sri 3066	Ceylon Transport Board, Colombo, Ceylon	10/67
RTL905	502816	4345	LLU895		
			23 sri 3408	Ceylon Transport Board, Colombo, Ceylon	12/68
RTL906	502817	4223	LLU896		
			23 sri 3412	Ceylon Transport Board, Colombo, Ceylon	12/68
RTL907	502818	4354	LLU897		
				Pickersgill & Laverick (Dealer), Cudworth, Yorkshire	06/69
RTL908	502819	4344	LLU898		
				Wombwell Diesel Company (Dealer), Wombwell, Yorkshire	09/67
RTL909	502820	4307	LLU899		
			J 36677	Jersey Motor Transport Co. Ltd., St Helier, Jersey, Channel Islands 677	04/67
				Exported to France	02/73
				J.Buffard, Nantes, Loire Atlantique as an advertisement bus	02/73
			3756 QH 85	Unknown, Muséobus de la Vendee, painted green	by 07/81
				M.Dufresne, Monts, Indre-et-Loire, for 'Bric-a-Brac' museum at Azay le Rideau	11/84
				Still owned	—/96
RTL910	502821	4241	LLU900		
				Wombwell Diesel Company (Dealer), Wombwell, Yorkshire	11/69
RTL911	502822	4340	LLU901		
			23 sri 3080	Ceylon Transport Board, Colombo, Ceylon	10/67
RTL912	504002	4294	LLU902		
			23 sri 3024	Ceylon Transport Board, Colombo, Ceylon	08/67
RTL913	504003	4383	LLU903		
				W.North (Dealer), Sherburn-in-Elmet, Yorkshire	01/67
				Johnson, (Breakers), South Elmsall, Yorkshire	09/67
RTL914	504004	4230	LLU904		
				Wombwell Diesel Company (Dealer), Wombwell, Yorkshire	11/67
RTL915	504005	4124	LLU905		
			23 sri 3079	Ceylon Transport Board, Colombo, Ceylon	10/67
RTL916	504015	4277	LLU906		
				Passenger Vehicle Sales (London) Ltd (Dealer), Upminster, Essex	10/66
				A.A. Motor Services (R.Tumilty, Irvine), Ayrshire	10/66
				Withdrawn and dismantled by Tumilty	01/70

Initially disposed of in October 1966 it wasn't until March 1968 that RTL883 was acquitted by the Clyde Coast Services. On the 15th June 1959 the bus is seen in Ardrossan town waiting complete with rolled up shirt sleeved driver and standing next to a substantially built shelter provided for the travelling public. (A. R. Packer)

RTL				Event	Date
RTL917	504016	4313	LLU907		
				Passenger Vehicle Sales (London) Ltd (Dealer), Upminster, Essex	06/66
				McConnachie, Campeltown, Argyll	06/66
				Withdrawn	03/70
				Craig, Campbeltown, Argyll (never used)	03/70
				Telefilms Transport (Dealer), Preston, Lancs	05/70
RTL918	504019	4367	LLU908		
				Hills Patents Limited, Staines, Middlesex as a staff bus	11/67
				Wombwell Diesel Company (Dealer), Wombwell, Yorkshire for scrapping	by 05/69
RTL919	504020	4239	LLU909		
			23 sri 3064	Ceylon Transport Board, Colombo, Ceylon	10/67
RTL920	504021	4238	LLU910		
			23 sri 3073	Ceylon Transport Board, Colombo, Ceylon	10/67
				Still in service	02/77
RTL921	504022	4390	LLU911		
				Passenger Vehicle Sales (London) Ltd (Dealer), Canvey Island, Essex	05/67
				Leyland Motors Limited (Dealer), London W1	05/67
				"1700" Restaurant, Philadelphia, Pennsylvania, USA	05/67
RTL922	504023	4309	LLU912		
			23 sri 3074	Ceylon Transport Board, Colombo, Ceylon	10/67
				Still in existence but withdrawn	02/77
RTL923	504024	4268	LLU913		
				Centrax Limited, Newton Abbot, Devon for staff transport between Newton Abbott and Exeter, Devon, named "Lulu"	08/66
				Roof rebuilt after two low bridge accidents on delivery run, rebuild by Booker Motor Bodies, Newton Abbott before entering service	09/66
				Taghill (Breakers), Alphington, Exeter, Devon	01/69
RTL924	504025	4295	LLU914		
			23 sri 3061	Ceylon Transport Board, Colombo, Ceylon	10/67
RTL925	504166	4168	LLU915		
				Wombwell Diesel Company (Dealer), Wombwell, Yorkshire	11/69
RTL926	504167	4262	LLU916		
				Passenger Vehicle Sales (London) Ltd (Dealer), Upminster, Essex	06/66
				Super Coaches, t/a Upminster & Districty, Upminster, Essex 562 and fitted with doors	01/67
				City Coach Lines, Upminster, Essex	02/69
				Science Research Council, Rutherford Laboratory, Chilton, Didcot, Berks for internal transport	02/70
				Unknown owner, Reading, Berkshire, together with RTL958, for spares	—/74
RTL927	504168	4310	LLU917		
				Wombwell Diesel Company (Dealer), Wombwell, Yorkshire	10/69
RTL928	504169	4247	LLU918		
				J.Keenan, Coalhall, Ayrshire	06/69
				Derelict on site	11/72
RTL929	504170	4291	LLU919		
			23 sri 3083	Ceylon Transport Board, Colombo, Ceylon	10/67
				Still in existence but withdrawn	02/77
RTL930	504171	4317	LLU920		
				W.North (Dealer), Sherburn-in-Elmet, Yorkshire	01/67
				Unknown breaker	06/67
RTL931	504172	4364	LLU921		
				Wombwell Diesel Company (Dealer), Wombwell, Yorkshire after mechanical units had been removed at Stonebridge Garage for Ceylon Transport Board	05/69
RTL932	504173	4243	LLU922		
			23 sri 3377	Ceylon Transport Board, Colombo, Ceylon	12/68
				Still in service	02/77
RTL933	504174	4242	LLU923		
				Wombwell Diesel Company (Dealer), Wombwell, Yorkshire	05/69
RTL934	504176	4311	LLU924		
			23 sri 3366	Ceylon Transport Board, Colombo, Ceylon	12/68
RTL935	504177	4275	LLU925		
				Wombwell Diesel Company (Dealer), Wombwell, Yorkshire after mechanical units had been removed at Stonebridge Garage for Ceylon Transport Board	04/69
RTL936	504178	4356	LLU926		
			23 sri 3149	Ceylon Transport Board, Colombo, Ceylon	12/67
RTL937	504179	4389	LLU927		
			23 sri 3369	Ceylon Transport Board, Colombo, Ceylon	12/68
				Still in service	02/77
RTL938	504181	4327	LLU 928		
			23 sri 2997	Ceylon Transport Board, Colombo, Ceylon	08/67
RTL939	504182	4375	LLU929		
			23 sri 3400	Ceylon Transport Board, Colombo, Ceylon	12/68
				Still in service	

RTL940	504183	4203	LLU930	Passenger Vehicle Sales (London) Ltd (Dealer), Upminster, Essex	02/67
				P.Irvine t/a Golden Eagle, Salsburgh	02/67
				Still in service	01/72
				Tiger Coaches (Dealer), Salsburgh	by 04/72
RTL941	504184	4246	LLU931		
			23 sri 3289	Ceylon Transport Board, Colombo, Ceylon	08/68
RTL942	504185	4254	LLU932		
				Mobile Oil Company Limited, London SW and used as internal transport at Coryton Refinery, Essex	02/67
				H.S.Motors (Breaker), Basildon for scrap	—/72
RTL943	504186	4251	LLU933		
			23 sri 3368	Ceylon Transport Board, Colombo, Ceylon	12/68
				Still in service	02/77
RTL944	504187	4225	LLU934		
			23 sri 3191	Ceylon Transport Board, Colombo, Ceylon	04/68
				Still in existence but withdrawn	02/77
RTL945	504188	4132	LLU935		
				W.North (Dealer), Sherburn-in-Elmet, Yorkshire	01/67
				Johnson, (Breakers), South Elmsall, Yorkshire	10/67
RTL946	504339	4333	LLU936		
			23 sri 3020	Ceylon Transport Board, Colombo, Ceylon	08/67
				Still in existence but withdrawn	02/77
RTL947	504340	4284	LLU937		
			23 sri 3248	Ceylon Transport Board, Colombo, Ceylon	07/68
				Still in existence but withdrawn	02/77
RTL948	504341	4360	LLU938		
			23 sri 3245	Ceylon Transport Board, Colombo, Ceylon	07/68
				Still in existence having been fitted with CTB single deck bodywork, now withdrawn	02/77
				Sold	01/80
RTL949	504344	4318	LLU939		
				Passenger Vehicle Sales (London) Ltd (Dealer), Upminster, Essex	07/66
				J.Keenan, Coalhall, Ayrshire	08/66
				Withdrawn and used for spares	08/69
RTL950	504345	4256	LLU940		
			23 sri 3250	Ceylon Transport Board, Colombo, Ceylon	07/68
				Still in existence but withdrawn	07/78

Quite obviously what might have been had London Transport decided that some RTL's should have been placed in service as Green Line vehicles like their counterparts the RT. The date is unknown but a Volkswagen Beetle, drop-head keeps RTL1323 company while posing for the camera.

RTL951	504346	3969	LUC326		
			23 sri 2048	Ceylon Transport Board, Colombo, Ceylon	12/65
RTL952	504347	4329	LUC327		
			23 sri 3249	Ceylon Transport Board, Colombo, Ceylon	07/68
RTL953	504348	4182	LUC328		
				W.North (Dealer), Sherburn-in-Elmet, Yorkshire	01/67
				Johnson, (Breakers), South Elmsall, Yorkshire	07/67
RTL954	504350	4218	LUC329		
				Passenger Vehicle Sales (London) Ltd (Dealer), Upminster, Essex	02/67
				P.Irvine t/a Golden Eagle, Salsburgh	02/67
				Still in service	01/72
				Tiger Coaches (Dealer), Salsburgh	by 04/72
RTL955	504351	4387	LUC330		
			23 sri 3409	Ceylon Transport Board, Colombo, Ceylon	12/68
				Still in service	02/77
RTL956	504354	4279	LUC331		
				Wombwell Diesel Company (Dealer), Wombwell, Yorkshire	11/67
RTL957	504355	4259	LUC332		
			23 sri 3102	Ceylon Transport Board, Colombo, Ceylon	11/67
				Still in service	02/77
RTL958	504356	4330	LUC333		
				W.North (Dealer), Sherburn-in-Elmet, Yorkshire	08/66
				Body to Johnson (Breakers), South Elmsall	02/67
		4078		Rebodied by W.North with the body from RTL676	03/67
				Passenger Vehicle Sales (London) Ltd (Dealer), Upminster, Essex	06/67
				Super Coaches, Upminster, Essex	06/67
				City Coach Lines, Upminster, Essex	02/69
				Passenger Vehicle Sales (London) Ltd (Dealer), Upminster, Essex	02/70
				Science Research Council, Rutherford Laboratory, Chilton for internal transport	02/70
				Unknown owner, Reading, Berkshire, together with RTL926, for use as a mobile caravan	—/74
				Parked in a field nerar Pau Pyrenees, Atlantiques, France painted orange/yellow/cream and dark roof	by 04/88
				Still there	—/93
RTL959	504347	4349	LUC334		
			23 sri 3287	Ceylon Transport Board, Colombo, Ceylon	08/68
				Still in existence but withdrawn	02/77
RTL960	504358	4334	LUC335		
			J 36678	Jersey Motor Transport Co. Ltd., St Helier, Jersey, Channel Islands 678	04/67
				Exported to France	02/73
				J.Buffard, Nantes, Loire-Atlantique as advertisement bus painted red	02/73
				Office Enfance Jeunesse, Saint-Sebastien-Sur-Loire, Loire Atlantique for spares for their RT	03/88
				Body dismantled	—/—
				Chassis to D.Chabaud, Lavoux, Vienne	by 05/93
				Still owned	05/98
RTL961	504366	4167	LUC336		
				W.North (Dealer), Sherburn-in-Elmet, Yorkshire	01/67
				Johnson, (Breakers), South Elmsall, Yorkshire	09/67
RTL962	504367	4384	LUC337		
			23 sri 3367	Ceylon Transport Board, Colombo, Ceylon	12/68
RTL963	504368	4255	LUC338		
			23 sri 3082	Ceylon Transport Board, Colombo, Ceylon	10/67
RTL964	504572	4328	LUC339		
				J. Keenan, Coalhall, Ayrshire	06/69
				Still in service	11/72
				Remains burnt	by 11/73
RTL965	504573	4322	LUC340		
			23 sri 3197	Ceylon Transport Board, Colombo, Ceylon	04/68
RTL966	504574	4336	LUC341		
			23 sri 3002	Ceylon Transport Board, Colombo, Ceylon	08/67
				Still in existence but withdrawn	02/77
RTL967	504575	4367	LUC342		
			23 sri 3088	Ceylon Transport Board, Colombo, Ceylon	10/67
				Still in service	02/77
RTL968	504576	4335	LUC343		
				Wombwell Diesel Company (Dealer), Wombwell, Yorkshire after mechanical units had	
				been removed at Stonebridge Garage for Ceylon Transport Board	04/69
RTL969	504577	4227	LUC344		
				Wombwell Diesel Company (Dealer), Wombwell, Yorkshire	10/69
RTL970	504578	4002	LUC345		
				Barton Transport Limited, Chilwell, Nottinghamshire 1031	12/65
				Withdrawn	03/72
				Unidentified dealer for scrap	04/72

RTL358, which appeared in an episode of "Some Mothers Do 'Ave 'Em" on BBC 1 later in its career, is one of a number of buses whose history is documented in the pages of this book which have appeared in film or on TV. In its earlier years with Red Rover it is seen departing Kingsway Square at Aylesbury with London Transport owned RT4189 in use in route 301 soon to depart for Watford Junction. (Roy Marshall Collection)

RTL971	504579	4308	LUC346		
				Stringer t/a Prince of Wales Coaches, Ampthill, Bedfordshire	06/67
				L.W.Vass (Dealer), Ampthill, Bedfordshire	10/70
				Morris (Dealer), Rounds, near Rushden, Bedfordshire for intended local public house transport, but not taken up	05/71
				E.Brakell, T.Robertson, T.Hornby, Cheam, Surrey for preservation	06/71
				Singapore Port Authority, Singapore as agent	06/75
			PB 40 J	Sentoza Development Corporation 23 and used on tourist services on Sentoza Island	06/75
				Placed on the sea bed off the Island's lagoon for use as fish breeding grounds	by 12/80
RTL972	504580	4274	LUC347		
				Pickersgill & Laverick (Dealer), Cudworth, Yorkshire	05/69
RTL973	504581	4265	LUC348		
			23 sri 3114	Ceylon Transport Board, Colombo, Ceylon	11/67
				Still in service	02/77
RTL974	504583	4273	LUC349		
			23 sri 3108	Ceylon Transport Board, Colombo, Ceylon	11/67
				Withdrawn and scrapped by CTB	by 04/81
RTL975	504584	4253	LUC350		
				Passenger Vehicle Sales (London) Ltd (Dealer), Upminster, Essex	07/66
				J.Keenan, Coalhall, Ayrshire	08/66
				Withdrawn	—/72
				Being Cannibalised	11/73
RTL976	504586	4272	LUC351		
				W.North (Dealer), Sherburn-in-Elmet, Yorkshire	01/67
				Johnson, (Breakers), South Elmsall, Yorkshire	09/67
RTL977	504723	4258	LUC352		
			23 sri 3363	Ceylon Transport Board, Colombo, Ceylon	12/68
RTL978	504724	4175	LUC353		
			23 sri 3139	Ceylon Transport Board, Colombo, Ceylon	12/67
				Still in existence but withdrawn	02/77
				Stripped chassis derelict by side of road at Homagana	01/82
RTL979	504725	4304	LUC354		
			CA 147 376	Golden Arrow Bus Service, Cape Town, South Africa 294	10/66
				Still in service	04/74
RTL980	504726	4152	LUC355		
				R. Armstrong Bus Limited, Moordale Motor Services, Newcastle-on-Tyne	10/66
				Withdrawn	07/72
RTL981	504727	4181	LUC356		
				J.Keenan, Coalhall, Ayrshire	07/67
				Still in service	11/72
				Being Cannibalised	11/73

RTL982	504728	4177	LUC357		
			23 sri 2984	Ceylon Transport Board, Colombo, Ceylon	09/67
RTL983	504729	4306	LUC358		
				Clyde Coast Services (Fraser, Fairlie), Ayrshire	10/66
				Withdrawn and reported scrapped	by 01/70
RTL984	504730	4320	LUC359		
			23 sri 3295	Ceylon Transport Board, Colombo, Ceylon	08/68
RTL985	504731	4374	LUC360		
			23 sri 3406	Ceylon Transport Board, Colombo, Ceylon	12/68
				Still in existence but withdrawn	02/77
RTL986	504732	4357	LUC361		
				Wombwell Diesel Company (Dealer), Wombwell, Yorkshire after mechanical units had	
				been removed at Stonebridge Garage for Ceylon Transport Board	04/69
RTL987	504733	4248	LUC362		
			23 sri 3373	Ceylon Transport Board, Colombo, Ceylon	12/68
				Still in existence but withdrawn	02/77
RTL988	504734	4369	LUC363		
			J 36679	Jersey Motor Transport Co. Ltd., St Helier, Jersey, Channel Islands 679	04/67
				Out of use and in store	—/74
			PGK 202P	E.Brakell, T.Robertson, T.Hornsby, Cheam, Surrey for preservation	11/74
				On hire to Brown & Root (UK) Limited, London SW19 from E.Brakell	12/77
				Returned from hire and used for promotional hire	06/79
			RTK 930	Star Groundwork, Chadwell St,. Mary, Essex converted to open-top	c09/88
				J.Mould, Burghfield, Reading, Berkshire as a hospitality vehicle	08/90
				Still owned	06/97
RTL989	504735	4240	LUC364		
				Mobil Oil Company Limited, London SW1 and used as internal transport at	
				Coryton Refinery, Essex	02/67
				H.S. Motors (Breaker), Basildon, for scrap	—/72
				Still there, derelict	—/78
RTL990	504736	4327	LUC365		
			23 sri 3391	Ceylon Transport Board, Colombo, Ceylon	12/68
				Still in existence but withdrawn	02/77
RTL991	504737	4338	LUC366		
			23 sri 2990	Ceylon Transport Board, Colombo, Ceylon	09/67
				Still in existence but withdrawn	02/77
RTL992	504740	4281	LUC367		
				W.North (Dealer), Sherburn-in-Elmet, Yorkshire	01/67
				Johnson, (Breakers), South Elmsall, Yorkshire	03/67
RTL993	504742	4263	LUC368		
			23 sri 3421	Ceylon Transport Board, Colombo, Ceylon	12/68
				Still in existence but withdrawn	02/77
RTL994	504836	4386	LUC369		
			23 sri 2986	Ceylon Transport Board, Colombo, Ceylon	09/67
RTL995	504838	4388	LUC370		
				Wombwell Diesel Company (Dealer), Wombwell, Yorkshire	09/67
RTL996	504846	4342	LUC371		
			23 sri 3196	Ceylon Transport Board, Colombo, Ceylon	04/68
				Still in existence but withdrawn	02/77
RTL997	504849	4352	LUC372		
			23 sri 3372	Ceylon Transport Board, Colombo, Ceylon	12/68
				Still in service	02/77
RTL998	505510	4252	LUC373		
				Passenger Vehicle Sales (London) Ltd (Dealer), Upminster, Essex	05/67
				J.Dengate & Son, Rye, Sussex	05/67
				Fitted with platform doors	—/6-
				Withdrawn	12/70
				Passenger Vehicle Sales (London) Ltd (Dealer), Canvey Island, Essex	12/70
				PVS Contracts fleet 57	by 02/71
				Withdrawn	01/73
				J.Read, Frog Island Drag Racing Team, Brightwell-cum-Sotwell, Oxfordshire with staircase and	
				rear platform area rebuilt with roller shutter at rear, access to top deck via a ladder	11/73
				Dumped at Santa Pod, Northamptonshire	08/83
				M.Bollens, Rushden, Northamptonshire and used for spares	11/83
				G.Lister (Dealer), Bolton	03/85
				Blackett (Dealer), Butterknowle, Durham for scrap	04/88
RTL999	505518	4319	LUC374		
			23 sri 3028	Ceylon Transport Board, Colombo, Ceylon	08/67
RTL1000	505520	4194	LUC375		
				W.North (Dealer), Sherburn-in-Elmet, Yorkshire	10/65
				Broken up	03/66

RTL1001	501924	3708	KYY644		
				Bird's Commercial Motors (Dealer), Stratford-upon-Avon, Warwickshire	12/69
RTL1002	501920	3795	KYY645		
			23 sri 3222	Ceylon Transport Board, Colombo, Ceylon	07/68
RTL1003	501918	5784	KYY646		
			23 sri 3221	Ceylon Transport Board, Colombo, Ceylon	07/68
RTL1004	502098	3784	KYY647		
				Public Safety Officer, London Borough of Lambeth, London SW2 as an exhibition unit	06/67
				Noted in white/dark blue livery as mobile safety unit	03/73
				Unknown Colchester dealer	—/78
				D.Burton, London NW6 and Slator, Royston, Hertfordshire for preservation	04/79
				Abbots Langley Transport Circle, Abbots Langley, Hertfordshire for continued preservation	03/80
				J.Young, Nottingham for continued preservation	by 11/87
				Guernseybus, St. Peter Port, Guernsey 19	10/94
			995	Converted to front entrance with central staircase, seating 29 up, 23 down entering service	12/95
			47312	Reregistered	—/97
RTL1005	502097	4371	KYY648		
			23 sri 3127	Ceylon Transport Board, Colombo, Ceylon	11/67
RTL1006	502095	3574	KYY649		
				Bird's Commercial Motors (Dealer), Stratford-upon-Avon, Warwickshire	12/69
RTL1007	501919	3540	KYY705		
			23 sri 3266	Ceylon Transport Board, Colombo, Ceylon	07/68
RTL1008	502207	3594	KYY706		
			22 sri 1601	Ceylon Transport Board, Colombo, Ceylon	04/58
RTL1009	502199	3909	KYY707		
			23 sri 3178	Ceylon Transport Board, Colombo, Ceylon	04/68
				Still in existence but withdrawn	02/77
RTL1010	502208	9220	KYY708		
			23 sri 3232	Ceylon Transport Board, Colombo, Ceylon	07/68
				Still in existence but withdrawn	02/77
RTL1011	502191	9218	KYY709		
			23 sri 3181	Ceylon Transport Board, Colombo, Ceylon	04/68
				Still in existence having been fitted with CTB single deck bodywork	02/77
				Withdrawn	01/79
			27 sri 1982	Sold and rebuilt as a private lorry	—/—
RTL1012	502200	5491	KYY710		
			23 sri 1601	Ceylon Transport Board, Colombo, Ceylon	04/65
RTL1013	502408	3666	KYY711		
				Wombwell Diesel Company (Dealer), Wombwell, Yorkshire	12/69
RTL1014	502210	9145	KYY712		
				Passenger Vehicle Sales (London) Ltd (Dealer), Upminster, Essex	09/67
				Leyland Motors Ltd (Dealer) London W1	09/67
			E 815591	University Transport System, University of California, Davis, California, USA,	09/67
				Still current	—/97

RTL1050 acts as a tow vehicle for broken down RTL1023 when seen on the 21st December 1968 at Hanworth. Someone has reasoned that roughly the total length of this road hazard is 70 feet and with other information added very cleverly using the grime and dust as a means of warning following road users of this hazard. Both vehicles were owned by the School Holidays branch of Continental Pioneer, Richmond at the time of this most unusual occurrence. (John G.S. Smith)

Operating in red livery RTL1515 is seen on the tourist island of Sentoza now with alien registration PB35 A and fleet number 22. Nowadays its remains sitting on the sea bed providing a very unusually habitat for commercial bred and reared fish for discerning far Eastern palates. (L. W. Rowe)

RTL1015	502211	3779	KYY713		
			23 sri 3135	Ceylon Transport Board, Colombo, Ceylon	12/67
RTL1016	502406	9146	KYY714		
				Bird's Commercial Motors (Dealer), Stratford-upon-Avon, Warwickshire	08/67
				Partially dismantled	01/68
RTL1017	502409	3906	KYY715		
			22 sri 7931	Ceylon Transport Board, Colombo, Ceylon	01/61
				Still in existence but withdrawn	02/77
RTL1018	502417	3498	LLU772		
				Pickersgill & Laverick (Dealer), Cudworth, Yorkshire	02/70
RTL1019	502414	9149	LLU773		
			23 sri 3371	Ceylon Transport Board, Colombo, Ceylon	12/68
RTL1020	502413	6790	LLU774		
			SA 55 32	Gradeka Saobracaine Preduzece, Sarajevo, Yugoslavia, 22	05/64
RTL1021	502416	3914	LLU775		
			23 sri 3110	Ceylon Transport Board, Colombo, Ceylon	11/67
RTL1022	502588	3852	LLU776		
			23 sri 3145	Ceylon Transport Board, Colombo, Ceylon	12/67
				Still in existence but withdrawn	02/77
RTL1023	502580	9217	LLU777		
				Continental Pioneer School Holidays Limited, Richmond, Surrey 5	02/68
				Withdrawn	04/70
				Broken up at Pioneers yard by contractor	by 11/70
RTL1024	502598	3858	LLU778		
				Wombwell Diesel Company (Dealer), Wombwell, Yorkshire after mechanical units had	
				been removed at Stonebridge Garage for Ceylon Transport Board	04/69
RTL1025	502597	3851	LLU779		
			23 sri 1575	Ceylon Transport Board, Colombo, Ceylon	04/65
RTL1026	502798	5975	LLU780		
				R.Richard, Margny Les Compiegne, Oise, France	12/68
RTL1027	502799	9225	LLU781		
			23 sri 3158	Ceylon Transport Board, Colombo, Ceylon	12/67
RTL1028	502596	3714	LLU782		
				Ceylon Transport Board, Colombo, Ceylon – bus severley damaged during loading at docks.	12/67
				Sale to CTB cancelled and salvage passed to Crown Agents Shipping Dept, London EC3	
				Registration number 23 sri 3157 had been allocated for operation in Ceylon.	
				Wombwell Diesel Company (Dealer), Wombwell, Yorkshire	04/69
RTL1029	502803	3709	LLU783		
			22 sri 7925	Ceylon Transport Board, Colombo, Ceylon	01/61
RTL1030	502800	3793	LLU784		
			23 sri 3150	Ceylon Transport Board, Colombo, Ceylon	12/67
RTL1031	502801	3787	LLU785		
			23 sri 3117	Ceylon Transport Board, Colombo, Ceylon	11/67
				Still in existence but withdrawn	02/77
RTL1032	502587	3794	LLU786		
				Pickersgill & Laverick (Dealer), Cudworth, Yorkshire	06/69

RTL1033	502598	3898	LLU787		
				J.Keenan, Coalhall, Ayrshire	07/67
				Lister (Dealer), Bolton	07/74
				Unknown dealer, Carlton and scrapped	07/74
RTL1034	502590	3783	LLU788		
			23 sri 3190	Ceylon Transport Board, Colombo, Ceylon	04/68
RTL1035	502585	5663	LLU789		
			23 sri 3192	Ceylon Transport Board, Colombo, Ceylon	04/68
				Still in existence but withdrawn	02/77
RTL1036	502805	3778	LLU790		
				Passenger Vehicle Sales (London) Ltd (Dealer), Upminster, Essex	01/67
				H.O. Hambridge, t/a Hambridge Coaches, Kidlington, Oxon	02/67
				Withdrawn	12/70
				Still on premises of Hambridge, disused and again	10/73
RTL1037	502806	6154	LLU791		
			E 535 397	Long Beach Public Transport Corporation, Long Beach, California, USA 5 used on services to and from the liner "Queen Mary" at Long Beach	07/68
				Static exhibit alongside stern of the liner 'Queen Mary', Long Beach, California	c05/79
				Larry Greer, Orange County, California	11/82
RTL1038	502802	3901	LLU792		
			23 sri 1316	Ceylon Transport Board, Colombo, Ceylon	11/64
RTL1039	502804	3895	LLU793		
			SA 54 26	Gradeka Saobracaine Preduzece, Sarajevo, Yugoslavia 50	07/64
RTL1040	504009	6063	LLU819		
			23 sri 3161	Ceylon Transport Board, Colombo, Ceylon	12/67
RTL1041	504008	5968	LLU820		
				Pickersgill & Laverick (Dealer), Cudworth, Yorkshire, after mechanical units had been removed at Stonebridge Garage for Ceylon Transport Board	06/69
RTL1042	504014	3788	LLU821		
			22 sri 7936	Ceylon Transport Board, Colombo, Ceylon	01/61
RTL1043	504011	9219	LLU822		
				Pickersgill & Laverick (Dealer), Cudworth, Yorkshire	06/69
RTL1044	504012	6785	LLU823		
			SA 55 31	Gradeka Saobracaine Preduzece, Sarajevo, Yugoslavia 21	05/64
RTL1045	504006	5723	LLU824		
			23 sri 3193	Ceylon Transport Board, Colombo, Ceylon	04/68
				Still in existence but withdrawn	02/77
				Sold	01/80
			27 sri 457	Rebuilt as a private lorry	by 04/81

RTL1348 stands at the familiar bus station in St. Helier, Jersey before departure to Gorey on route 1. The livery worn is green and cream and this particular use of the lighter colour enhanced the appearance considerably from its previous nearly all over red colour scheme. (John Gascoine)

RTL1046	504010	3861	LLU825		
			23 sri 3376	Ceylon Transport Board, Colombo, Ceylon	12/68
				Still in service	02/77
				Sold	by 04/81
			27 sri 7400	Rebuilt as a private lorry	by 04/81
RTL1047	504007	3860	LLU826		
			23 sri 3136	Ceylon Transport Board, Colombo, Ceylon	12/67
RTL1048	504013	3790	LLU827		
			23 sri 3274	Ceylon Transport Board, Colombo, Ceylon	08/68
RTL1049	504017	5493	LLU828		
				Wrighton & Son (Furniture Manufacturers), Broxbourne Aerodrome, Waltham Abbey, Nazeing, Hertfordshire as a staff bus	05/64
				Salisbury Hall Garages (Dealer), London E4	06/67
				Johnson (Breaker), London E9	by 01/68
RTL1050	504001	3946	LLU829		
				B.Lewis, St. Margaret's Hertfordshire	03/64
				Used by Richmond Liberal party for GLC election campaign	04/64
				Noted outside Westminster Abbey decorated with flags of all nations and labelled "An Authentic London Bus" for unknown use	10/64
				Continental Pioneer Holidays, Richmond, Surrey 1	06/66
				Withdrawn	05/72
				E.Brakell, T.Robertson, T.Hornby, Cheam, Surrey for preservation	05/72
				Noted now in open-top condition	10/75
				E.Brakell (Dealer), Cheam, Surrey	—/75
				D.Hardcastle, Wallington, Surrey for preservation	by 01/81
				D.Hardcastle using the title Rally Racing Limited	01/81
				D.Hardcastle moved to Silverstone, Northamptonshire	07/82
				On view at Wickstead Park, Kettering, Northamptonshire	07/82
				D.Thrower, Manchester later of Stockton Heath, Warrington for preservation	01/87
				Replacement roof and upper deck windows fitted	—/91
RTL1051	504018	3711	LLU830		
				Passenger Vehicle Sales (London) Ltd (Dealer), Upminster, Essex	08/67
				Used on a shuttle service to and from the British Fair at the Canadian National Exhibition Grounds during a British week in Toronto, Ontario, Canada	10/67
				British Promotions, Boston, Massachusetts, USA	10/67
				Hired by McGinn Bus Company, Sears City, Leominster, USA	by 06/68
				De-roofed and converted to open-top	by 06/68
				Robert Stebbins, -?-, Florida	c—/72
RTL1052	504175	5403	LUC23		
				Bird's Commercial Motors (Dealer), Stratford-upon-Avon, Warwickshire	05/63
				T.W.Beach Limited (Canners), Evesham, Worcestershire	by 05/63
				Withdrawn	01/66
				F.C.Cowley (Dealer), Dunchurch, Warwickshire	01/66
RTL1053	504180	5451	LUC24		
			23 sri 1569	Ceylon Transport Board, Colombo, Ceylon	04/65
RTL1054	504190	5754	LUC25		
				Passenger Vehicle Sales (London) Ltd (Dealer), Canvey Island, Essex	12/67
				Barton Transport, Chilwell, Nottinghamshire. 1108	12/67
				Withdrawn, after accident	04/68
				E. Keeble (Dealer), Sutton-in-Ashfield for scrap	04/68
RTL1055	504189	5441	LUC26		
				Gradeka Saobracaine Preduzece, Sarajevo, Yugoslavia	05/64
RTL1056	504342	3910	LUC27		
				Gradeka Saobracaine Preduzece, Sarajevo, Yugoslavia	05/64
RTL1057	504343	3905	LUC28		
			23 sri 1608	Ceylon Transport Board, Colombo, Ceylon	04/65
RTL1058	504353	6723	LUC41		
			23 sri 1257	Ceylon Transport Board, Colombo, Ceylon	09/64
RTL1059	504352	9221	LUC42		
			23 sri 3296	Ceylon Transport Board, Colombo, Ceylon	08/68
RTL1060	504349	5460	LUC43		
			SA 55 24	Gradeka Saobracaine Preduzece, Sarajevo, Yugoslavia 14	05/64
RTL1061	504359	6285	LUC68		
			23 sri 3198	Ceylon Transport Board, Colombo, Ceylon	04/68
				Now fitted with CTB single deck bodywork	by 04/81
RTL1062	504568	5488	LUC69		
			23 sri 1568	Ceylon Transport Board, Colombo, Ceylon	04/65
RTL1063	504571	5461	LUC70		
			23 sri 1587	Ceylon Transport Board, Colombo, Ceylon	04/65
RTL1064	504570	3883	LUC71		
				Bird's Commercial Motors (Dealer), Stratford-upon-Avon, Warwickshire	08/63
				Griffin Motors, t/a G & G Coaches, Leamington Spa, Warwickshire	08/64

RTL1065	504569	5443	LUC72		
				Bird's Commercial Motors (Dealer), Stratford-upon-Avon, Warwickshire	08/63
				Dunoon Motor Service, Dunoon	by 06/64
				Withdrawn upon acquisition of business by Cowal Motor Services, Dunoon	12/64
				A & C McLennan, Spittalfield, Perthshire	02/65
				Entered service	11/65
				Withdrawn	—/72
				Henderson (fruit farmer), Carnoustie, Angus and used by berry pickers	07/72
			AGS 72B	Forfar Potato Company (Seed Growers), Suttleside, Forfar, Angus	by 10/83
				Urquart, Forfar and partly scrapped	11/94
				D.Thrower, M.Hurst, M.Lloyd and B.Simmonds for preservation	04/95
				Body scrapped	c 08/96
			LUC250	Chassis still owned and reregistered	11/97
RTL1066	504363	3917	LUC73		
			23 sri 1606	Ceylon Transport Board, Colombo, Ceylon	04/65
				Still in existence but withdrawn	02/77
RTL1067	504362	5722	LUC74		
				Parker Laundry Group, Bromley, Kent	09/64
				Forest Gate Laundry, London E15 as a staff bus	—/—
				Renamed Industrial Linens Services Limited,. London E15	09/72
				Pickersgill & Laverick (Dealer), Cudworth, Yorkshire	10/73
RTL1068	504361	3913	LUC75		
			22 sri 7928	Ceylon Transport Board, Colombo, Ceylon	01/61
RTL1069	504364	5552	LUC76		
			CA 119 184	Golden Arrow Bus Service, Cape Town, South Africa 151	11/63
RTL1070	504360	5543	LUC77		
			23 sri 1603	Ceylon Transport Board, Colombo, Ceylon	04/65
				Still in existence but withdrawn	02/77
RTL1071	504567	5756	LUC78		
			CA 119 185	Golden Arrow Bus Service, Cape Town, South Africa 152	11/63
RTL1072	504365	3949	LUC79		
			23 sri 1620	Ceylon Transport Board, Colombo, Ceylon	04/65
				Still in existence but withdrawn	02/77
RTL1073	504741	5763	LUC250		
			23 sri 3111	Ceylon Transport Board, Colombo, Ceylon	11/67
RTL1074	504831	5445	LUC251		
				Bird's Commercial Motors (Dealer), Stratford-upon-Avon, Warwickshire	04/64
				Scrapped	by c04/65
RTL1075	504834	5406	LUC252		
			23 sri 1500	Ceylon Transport Board, Colombo, Ceylon	02/65
RTL1076	504832	5577	LUC253		
				The Agent General, Canadian Atlantic Province, London WC2 as agent	06/64
			PV 020	C.Murphy t/a Abegweit Sightseeing Tours, Charlottetown, Prince Edward Island, Canada,	07/64
			PVA 081	Reregistered	—/—
				Still in service	05/98
RTL1077	504835	5489	LUC254		
				Gradeka Saobracaine Preduzece, Sarajevo, Yugoslavia	06/64
RTL1078	504585	5601	LUC255		
				Bird's Commercial Motors (Dealer), Stratford-upon-Avon, Warwickshire	04/64
				Scrapped	c4/65
RTL1079	504830	5603	LUC256		
			23 sri 1256	Ceylon Transport Board, Colombo, Ceylon	09/64
RTL1080	504582	5598	LUC257		
			23 sri 1565	Ceylon Transport Board, Colombo, Ceylon	04/65
RTL1081	504833	5761	LUC258		
			23 sri 3116	Ceylon Transport Board, Colombo, Ceylon	11/67
RTL1082	504840	5497	LUC259		
			CA 119 186	Golden Arrow Bus Service, Cape Town, South Africa 153	11/63
RTL1083	504837	3785	LUC260		
			23 sri 3195	Ceylon Transport Board, Colombo, Ceylon	04/68
RTL1084	504845	5764	LUC261		
			CA 57255	Golden Arrow Bus Service, Cape Town, South Africa 139	08/63
				Withdrawn after accident and dismantled	02/70
RTL1085	504843	5682	LUC262		
			23 sri 3112	Ceylon Transport Board, Colombo, Ceylon	11/67
RTL1086	504739	5670	LUC263		
				Gradeka Saobracaine Preduzece, Sarajevo, Yugoslavia	05/64
RTL1087	504844	5545	LUC264		
			23 sri 1598	Ceylon Transport Board, Colombo, Ceylon	04/65
RTL1088	504738	6282	LUC265		
			23 sri 3300	Ceylon Transport Board, Colombo, Ceylon	08/68

One could be forgiven for thinking RTL554 has just been delivered to London Transport from the bodybuilders Metro-Cammell, but in reality is a fine example of a preserved 7RT7. After having spent a number of years as a staff bus with an engineering organisation it then moved into the preservation movement eventually to emerge after many hours of work to bring it to its almost new condition. (John Fozard)

RTL1089	504848	5550	LUC282		
			23 sri 1305	Ceylon Transport Board, Colombo, Ceylon	11/64
RTL1090	505508	3919	LUC283		
			23 sri 1110	Ceylon Transport Board, Colombo, Ceylon	05/64
RTL1091	505511	5444	LUC284		
			23 sri 1313	Ceylon Transport Board, Colombo, Ceylon	11/64
RTL1092	505507	3791	LUC285		
			23 sri 3281	Ceylon Transport Board, Colombo, Ceylon	08/68
RTL1093	504841	5558	LUC286		
			23 sri 1576	Ceylon Transport Board, Colombo, Ceylon	04/65
RTL1094	504839	5731	LUC287		
			23 sri 2985	Ceylon Transport Board, Colombo, Ceylon	09/67
				Still in service having been fitted with CTB single deck bodywork	02/77
				Withdrawn	01/79
RTL1095	505522	3918	LUC305		
				Bird's Commercial Motors (Dealer), Stratford-upon-Avon, Warwickshire	10/63
				A1 Service, (A.Hunter, Dreghorn), Ardrossan, Ayrshire 16, to replace RTL1	02/64
				Still in service	12/70
RTL1096	505519	5580	LUC306		
				Biss Bros. Bishop's Stortford, Hertfordshire	03/64
				Little (Dealer), Totham	04/71
RTL1097	505516	5610	LUC307		
			CA 57254	Golden Arrow Bus Service, Cape Town, South Africa 138	09/63
				Withdrawn between	11/70 – 03/71
				Scrapped	02/71 – 03/71
RTL1098	505521	5446	LUC308		
			23 sri 1355	Ceylon Transport Board, Colombo, Ceylon	11/64
RTL1099	505512	5575	LUC309		
			CA 57249	Cape Electric Tramways, Cape Town, South Africa 137	09/63
				Withdrawn and scrapped	11/70
RTL1100	505509	3950	LUC310		
			23 sri 1254	Ceylon Transport Board, Colombo, Ceylon	09/64
RTL1101	505506	5490	LUC311		
			SA 55 21	Gradeka Saobracaine Preduzece, Sarajevo, Yugoslavia, 46	08/64
RTL1102	505513	5557	LUC312		
				Gradeka Saobracaine Preduzece, Sarajevo, Yugoslavia	07/64
RTL1103	505505	3900	LUC313		
			SA 55 25	Gradeka Saobracaine Preduzece, Sarajevo, Yugoslavia 15	07/64
RTL1104	505517	5755	LUC314		
			23 sri 1618	Ceylon Transport Board, Colombo, Ceylon	04/65
RTL1105	504842	6286	LUC315		
				The Agent General, Canadian Atlantic Provinces, London WC2	04/67
			PVA 080	C.Murphy t/a Abegweit Sightseeing Tours, Charlottetown, Prince Edward Island, Canada	04/67
				Still in service	05/98
RTL1106	505515	5738	LUC316		
			23 sri 1605	Ceylon Transport Board, Colombo, Ceylon	04/65
			26 sri 266	Sold and rebuilt as a private lorry	—/—
RTL1107	505523	6294	LUC317		
			23 sri 3394	Ceylon Transport Board, Colombo, Ceylon	12/68
				Still in existence but withdrawn	02/77
				Sold	06/78
			27 sri 6779	Rebuilt as a private lorry	—/81
RTL1108	505514	5678	LUC318		
				A1 Service, (Brown, Dreghorn), Ardrossan, Ayrshire, acquired minus roof, for spares only	11/63
				Still being used for spares	10/64
RTL1109	505524	5735	LUC319		
			23 sri 1611	Ceylon Transport Board, Colombo, Ceylon	04/65
RTL1110	510084	3856	LYF34		
			SA 54 16	Gradeka Saobracaine Preduzece, Sarajevo, Yugoslavia 42	06/64
RTL1111	504847	5549	LYF35		
				Bird's Commercial Motors (Dealer), Stratford-upon-Avon, Warwickshire	08/63
				S.Eynon & Sons, Trimsaran, Carmarthenshire	12/63
				Withdrawn	08/71
				P.Sykes, Barnsley, Yorkshire, for scrap	08/71
RTL1112	510147	5423	LYF36		
			SA 55 64	Gradeka Saobracaine Preduzece, Sarajevo, Yugoslavia 29	06/64
RTL1113	510083	5714	LYF37		
			23 sri 1599	Ceylon Transport Board, Colombo, Ceylon	04/65
RTL1114	510151	5600	LYF38		
				Bird's Commercial Motors (Dealer), Stratford-upon-Avon, Warwickshire	08/63
				S.Eynon & Sons., Trimsaran, Carmarthenshire	10/63
				Withdrawn	08/71
				P.Sykes, Barnsley, Yorkshire, for scrap	08/71

RTL1115	510144	5710	LYF39		
				King Korn Stamp Company, Finchley, London N12 as a publicity and gift bus	05/64
				Sperry & Hutchinson, (Pink Stamps) Limited, as a gift centre on take-over of King Korn	11/64
				G.A.Gill, Harefield, Middlesex as mobile supermarket	12/66
				A.C.Bowles Transport Company Limited, Cowley, Middlesex, believed for use as a film dining bus, but at 12/67 was still unconverted	02/67
				J. Anderson (Transport) Limited, Cowley, Buckinghamshire	c 01/71
				Withdrawn	03/73
RTL1116	510148	5664	LYF40		
				Bird's Commercial Motors (Dealer), Stratford-upon-Avon, Warwickshire	08/63
				S.Eynon & Sons., Trimsaran, Carmarthenshire	10/63
				Withdrawn	08/71
				P.Sykes, Barnsley, Yorkshire, for scrap	08/71
RTL1117	510146	5659	LYF41		
				Bird's Commercial Motors (Dealer), Stratford-upon-Avon, Warwickshire	04/64
				Partially scrapped	04/65
RTL1118	510145	5495	LYF42		
			23 sri 1356	Ceylon Transport Board, Colombo, Ceylon	11/64
RTL1119	510150	5548	LYF43		
				Bird's Commercial Motors (Dealer), Stratford-upon-Avon, Warwickshire	10/63
				Hutfield Coaches, Warwick	02/64
				Withdrawn	04/65
				T.H.Griffin t/a G & G Coaches, Leamington Spa, Warwickshire upon take over of Hutfield's business	04/65
RTL1120	510188	5766	LYF44		
			CA 57315	Golden Arrow Bus Service, Cape Town, South Africa 145	09/63
				Withdrawn	by 09/70
				Scrapped	09/70
RTL1121	510149	5785	LYF45		
				A1 Service, (Brown, Dreghorn), Ardrossan, Ayrshire	07/67
				Still in service	01/72
				Out of service	11/73
RTL1122	510187	5713	LYF46		
				Gradeka Saobracaine Preduzece, Sarajevo, Yugoslavia	05/64
RTL1123	510274	5679	LYF47		
			23 sri 1574	Ceylon Transport Board, Colombo, Ceylon	04/65
				Still in service	12/81

Now in operation with its fourth owner, Riverway Coaches, RTL1241 negotiates the Mill roundabout within Harlow new town on the 5th June 1973. Unfortunately nothing is recorded after its withdrawal in January 1974 and although it probably went for scrap any information would be welcome.
(John G.S. Smith)

RTL No.			Reg.	Operator / Notes	Date
RTL1124	510191	3624	LYF48		
				Wombwell Diesel Company (Dealer), Wombwell, Yorkshire	05/69
RTL1125	510273	5680	LYF49		
			23 sri 1567	Ceylon Transport Board, Colombo, Ceylon	04/65
				Still in existence but withdrawn	02/77
RTL1126	510189	3547	LYF50		
			23 sri 3203	Ceylon Transport Board, Colombo, Ceylon	04/68
				Still in existence but withdrawn	02/77
RTL1127	510192	3538	LYF51		
			23 sri 3282	Ceylon Transport Board, Colombo, Ceylon	08/68
				Still in existence but withdrawn	02/77
RTL1128	510190	5672	LYF52		
			CA 125 292	City Tramways Co., Cape Town, South Africa 485	04/64
				Still in service and renumbered 0485	04/74
RTL1129	510278	5660	LYF53		
				A & C McLennan, Spittalfield, Perthshire	06/63
				Not yet in service, rear doors fitted but after overhaul, engine removed	08/64
				Withdrawn	—/72
				Porter (Fruit farmer), Balhungie Farm, Broughty Ferry, Monifieth as workers rest hut	07/72
				Still owned	06/73
RTL1130	510277	5608	LYF54		
			SA 55 37	Gradeka Saobracaine Preduzece, Sarajevo, Yugoslavia 27	05/64
RTL1131	510294	5405	LYF55		
				J.Keenan, Coalhall, Ayrshire	07/67
				Still in service	11/72
				Being Cannibalised	11/73
RTL1132	510295	5576	LYF56		
			23 sri 1578	Ceylon Transport Board, Colombo, Ceylon	04/65
				Still in service	02/77
RTL1133	510275	5654	LYF57		
				A & C McLennan, Spittalfield, Perthshire	06/63
				Withdrawn	11/65
				Davidson (Farmer), Dundee, as workers bus	06/72
				Unknown breaker, Carlton	06/78
RTL1134	510293	5605	LYF58		
			23 sri 1604	Ceylon Transport Board, Colombo, Ceylon	04/65
RTL1135	510291	5762	LYF59		
			23 sri 1307	Ceylon Transport Board, Colombo, Ceylon	11/64
RTL1136	510290	5607	LYF60		
				A & C McLennan, Spittalfield, Perthshire and fitted with platform doors	06/63
				Withdrawn and sold for scrap	—/72
				Noted at Metheun Castle	11/73 and 06/74
				Gone	by 11/74

This posed view of RTL2 taken on the 21st September 1963 with Transport enthusiasts enjoying conversation and refreshments clearly shows the very high standards for which OK Motor Services were renowned. The paint scheme would prove an accountant's nightmare in these days of cost cutting but nevertheless superbly suits this style of bodywork.

Stonier & Sons of Goldenhill, Stoke-on-Trent owned RTL34 between July 1958 until disposed of to Tiger Coaches of Salsburgh in November 1967. It is employed on service to a newly developing housing estate and is seen in company with a Bedford TJ model truck and a Singer Super 10 car manufactured sometime between 1937 and 1949. With only the removal of the London Transport inscribed plate from the radiator and painted over route number aperture box together with abolition of advertising material, the bus is still basically as disposed by the Executive.

RTL1137	510423	5492	LYF61		
			23 sri 1616	Ceylon Transport Board, Colombo, Ceylon	04/65
				Still in existence but withdrawn	02/77
RTL1138	510276	5674	LYF62		
			23 sri 1308	Ceylon Transport Board, Colombo, Ceylon	11/64
RTL1139	510281	3770	LYF63		
			23 sri 3242	Ceylon Transport Board, Colombo, Ceylon	07/68
RTL1140	510279	5555	LYF64		
			23 sri 3126	Ceylon Transport Board, Colombo, Ceylon	11/67
				Still in existence as a staff bus with enlcosed rear platform (no doors fitted)	02/77
				Still in use	04/81
RTL1141	510280	5671	LYF65		
				Bird's Commercial Motors (Dealer), Stratford-upon-Avon, Warwickshire	10/63
				J.Stevenson, Spath, Uttoxeter, Staffordshire 17	10/63
				Fitted with platform doors	10/64
				Renumbered 14	01/72
				Withdrawn	06/75
				Being used for spares to keep RTL270 in road worthy condition	10/75
				Bloor (Dealer), Spath for scrap	03/76
RTL1142	510292	5749	LYF66		
			SA 55 23	Gradeka Saobracaine Preduzece, Sarajevo, Yugoslavia, 47	08/64
RTL1143	510422	5675	LYF67		
				Gradeka Saobracaine Preduzece, Sarajevo, Yugoslavia	05/64
RTL1144	510282	5551	LYF68		
			23 sri 1612	Ceylon Transport Board, Colombo, Ceylon	04/65
RTL1145	510427	5747	LYF69		
				Wombwell Diesel Company (Dealer), Wombwell, Yorkshire	04/69
RTL1146	510428	5721	LYF70		
			23 sri 3235	Ceylon Transport Board, Colombo, Ceylon	07/68
RTL1147	510426	5709	LYF71		
			23 sri 1566	Ceylon Transport Board, Colombo, Ceylon	04/65
				Still in existence but withdrawn	02/77
RTL1148	510425	5732	LYF89		
				A & C McLennan, Spittalfield, Perthshire	06/63
				Withdrawn	—/7–
				S & N Motors (Dealer), Glasgow	08/72
RTL1149	510424	5665	LYF90		
			23 sri 3268	Ceylon Transport Board, Colombo, Ceylon	07/68
				Still in existence but withdrawn	02/77

RTL1150	510430	5546	LYF91		
				Gradeka Saobracaine Preduzece, Sarajevo, Yugoslavia	05/64
RTL1151	510429	5606	LYF92		
			23 sri 1497	Ceylon Transport Board, Colombo, Ceylon	02/65
RTL1152	510519	5775	LYF93		
				Passenger Vehicle Sales (London) Ltd (Dealer), Upminster, Essex	08/67
				Leyland Motors Limited (Dealer), London W1	—/67
				Exported to unknown Toronto owner, Canada	—/67
RTL1153	510524	5741	LYF94		
			CA 134 465	Golden Arrow Bus Service, Capetown, South Africa 225	12/64
				Withdrawn	between 11/70 – 04/71
RTL1154	510520	5702	LYF95		
			23 sri 1499	Ceylon Transport Board, Colombo, Ceylon	02/65
RTL1155	510522	5407	LYF96		
			23 sri 1588	Ceylon Transport Board, Colombo, Ceylon	04/65
RTL1156	510521	5744	LYF97		
			23 sri 3393	Ceylon Transport Board, Colombo, Ceylon	12/68
				Still in existence but withdrawn	02/77
RTL1157	510593	5669	LYF98		
			23 sri 3132	Ceylon Transport Board, Colombo, Ceylon	12/67
RTL1158	510527	5553	LYF99		
			23 sri 3147	Ceylon Transport Board, Colombo, Ceylon	12/67
				Still in existence but withdrawn	02/77
RTL1159	510523	5753	LYF100		
			23 sri 1317	Ceylon Transport Board, Colombo, Ceylon	11/64
				Still in existence but withdrawn	02/77
RTL1160	510525	5602	LYF101		
			23 sri 1410	Ceylon Transport Board, Colombo, Ceylon	12/64
RTL1161	510431	9215	LYF102		
				Wombwell Diesel Company (Dealer), Wombwell, Yorkshire	11/69
RTL1162	510600	5554	LYF103		
			23 sri 1584	Ceylon Transport Board, Colombo, Ceylon	04/65
RTL1163	510599	5760	LYF104		
				A.R.Harling, t/a Harlings Coaches, London SE1 for spares	07/63
				Acquired for the engine which was then fitted to RTL1256, then used as a store shed	09/63
				C.Maycock, Barnet, Hertfordshire for preservation, after fitting of further engine	11/69
				Essex Transport Group (G.Burgess and others)	by 05/75
				E.Brakell (Dealer), Cheam, Surrey	04/84
				R.Ford, London N1 for continued preservation	by —/85
				Bracknell Omnibus Sales, (Dealer) Ceham, Surrey	—/90
				P.Cousins & Hobbs, Torquay, Devon for continued preservation	05/91
				Still owned	08/97
RTL1164	510595	5718	LYF105		
			23 sri 3128	Ceylon Transport Board, Colombo, Ceylon	11/67
				Still in existence as a trainer	02/77
				Sold	12/79
RTL1165	510596	3849	LYF106		
				F.Ridler (Dealer), Whitton, Middlesex	07/65
				N.Beldoz (Breaker), Hertford and broken up	07/65
RTL1166	510594	5442	LYF107		
			23 sri 1619	Ceylon Transport Board, Colombo, Ceylon	04/65
RTL1167	510526	5734	LYF108		
			CA 57298	Golden Arrow Bus Service, Cape Town, South Africa 144	09/63
				Withdrawn	between 11/70 – 02/71
				Scrapped	02/71
RTL1168	510669	5737	LYF109		
			E 535398	Long Beach Public Transport Corporation, Long Beach, California, USA 6	07/68
				Taken our of service	by —/78
				Static display alongside stern of the liner 'Queen Mary'. Long Beach, California	c05/79
				Larry Greer, Orange County, California	11/82
RTL1169	510668	5599	LYF110		
				Bird's Commercial Motors (Dealer), Stratford-upon-Avon, Warwickshire	04/64
				Scrapped	c04/65
RTL1170	510597	5609	LYF111		
			23 sri 3070	Ceylon Transport Board, Colombo, Ceylon	10/67
RTL1171	510675	5725	LYF112		
				C.F.Ward, t/a Wards Coaches, Epping, Essex	10/67
				Passenger Vehicle Sales (London) Ltd (Dealer), Silver End, Essex	10/70
				PVS (Contracts Fleet) 58 on contract hire to Lesney Products	02/71
				Ensign Bus Company, Hornchurch, Essex 58 on contract hire to Lesney Products	06/73
				Hartwood Finance (Dealer), Barnsley, Yorkshire	09/73
RTL1172	510670	5578	LYF113		
			23 sri 3107	Ceylon Transport Board, Colombo, Ceylon	11/67

RTL18 is seen in the vicinity of the Bishop Auckland terminus on the 5th August 1958 just six months after entering service with Anderson Bros. who traded as Blue Belle. An attractive livery which includes lining out has been applied to the bus which in October 1959 together with Anderson's other RTL moved into the fleet of the OK Motor Services when the latter operator was acquired. (A. R. Parker)

RTL1173	510672	5579	LYF114		
			23 sri 1312	Ceylon Transport Board, Colombo, Ceylon	11/64
				Still in existence but withdrawn	02/77
				Sold	12/78
RTL1174	510673	5662	LYF115		
				Bird's Commercial Motors (Dealer), Stratford-upon-Avon, Warwickshire	10/63
				Dunoon Motor Services, Dunoon, Ayrshire	by 06/64
				Withdrawn upon acquisition of business by Cowal Motor Services, Dunoon, Ayrshire	12/64
				A & C McLennon, Spittalfield, Perthshire	02/65
				Entered Service	08/65
				Still in service	12/74
				East London Traction Society	by 06/77
				Ray Reid, London N16 for preservation	—/79
				RT1784 Preservation Group, Bishops Stortford, Hertfordshire for preservation	10/85
				R.Brown t/a London Bus Export Company, (Dealer), Chepstow	by 12/87
				D.E. Bartolini, Buchloe, Germany converted to open top	02/88
RTL1175	510528	5656	LYF116		
			23 sri 1413	Ceylon Transport Board, Colombo, Ceylon	12/64
RTL1176	510671	5657	LYF117		
				British Travel & Holidays Association, London SW1	09/63
				Shipped to Canada and used on a promotional tour visiting more than 20 towns and cities from Montreal to Vancouver. Lower deck converted to mobile information office, upper deck retained seating, so that rides could be given	02/64
				London Omnibus Tours Limited, Victoria, Vancouver Island, British Columbia, Canada	—/65
				British Columbia Hydro and Power Authority t/a Royal Blue Line Motor Tours, Victoria Vancouver Island, British Columbia, Canada 658	01/73
			4523 JE	London Transport Limited, Victoria, Vancouver Island, British Columbia 208	09/79
				Operated under the Victoria Tours Ltd name, Vancouver Island, British Columbia 208	—/82
				Grayline of Victoria Ltd, Victoria, Vancouver Island, British Columbia	c 09/83
			2779 DF	Rainbow Blackfish Tours Company, Ketchikan, Alaska as tour bus	04/95
				Still in use	09/97
RTL1177	510602	5724	LYF118		
				Bird's Commercial Motors (Dealer), Stratford-upon-Avon, Warwickshire	10/63
				A1 Service, (T & E Docherty, Irvine), Ardrossan, Ayrshire	02/64
				One piece front window screen and non opening upper deck windows fitted	09/64
				Sold within group to Reid, Saltcoats, Ayrshire	05/66
				Reid sold out to T.Docherty, Irvine and vehicle repurchased by Dorcherty	12/66
				Withdrawn	by 03/70
				Clyde Coast Services (McGregor, Saltcoats), Saltcoats, Ayrshire	07/70
				Into service	08/70
				Withdrawn	by 06/72
				Tiger Coaches (Dealer), Salsburgh	06/72
RTL1178	510601	9141	LYF119		
			23 sri 3165	Ceylon Transport Board, Colombo, Ceylon	12/67

RTL1179	510677	5494	LYF120		
			23 sri 1607	Ceylon Transport Board, Colombo, Ceylon	04/65
RTL1180	510715	3855	LYF121		
			23 sri 3390	Ceylon Transport Board, Colombo, Ceylon	12/68
RTL1181	510720	5667	LYF122		
			23 sri 1503	Ceylon Transport Board, Colombo, Ceylon	02/65
RTL1182	510674	5487	LYF123		
			CA 57290	Golden Arrow Bus Service, Cape Town, South Africa 143	09/73
				Withdrawn after accident in 02/64 and dismantled	05/69
RTL1183	510719	3871	LYF124		
				British Twin Discs Limited, Strood, Kent	11/67
RTL1184	510676	5728	LYF125		
				Gradeka Saobracaine Preduzece, Sarajevo, Yugoslavia	05/64
RTL1185	510820	3782	LYF126		
				Wombwell Diesel Company (Dealer), Wombwell, Yorkshire after mechanical units had been removed at Stonebridge Garage for Ceylon Transport Board	04/69
RTL1186	510598	5668	LYF127		
			23 sri 3067	Ceylon Transport Board, Colombo, Ceylon	10/67
RTL1187	510716	5547	LYF128		
			23 sri 1570	Ceylon Transport Board, Colombo, Ceylon	04/65
RTL1188	510718	5677	LYF129		
			23 sri 1318	Ceylon Transport Board, Colombo, Ceylon	11/64
RTL1189	510717	6293	LYF130		
			23 sri 3146	Ceylon Transport Board, Colombo, Ceylon	12/67
				Still in existence but withdrawn	02/77
RTL1190	510722	5708	LYF131		
			23 sri 3272	Ceylon Transport Board, Colombo, Ceylon	08/68
				Still in existence but withdrawn	02/77
RTL1191	510721	5496	LYF132		
			CA 57281	Golden Arrow Bus Service, Cape Town, South Africa 142	09/63
RTL1192	510724	5485	LYF133		
				J.Keenan, Coalhall, Ayrshire	07/67
				Withdrawn	06/74
				Unknown Barnsley dealer	—/74
RTL1193	510821	5767	LYF134		
			23 sri 3247	Ceylon Transport Board, Colombo, Ceylon	07/68
				Still in existence but withdrawn	02/77
RTL1194	510723	5774	LYF135		
				Passenger Vehicle Sales (London) Ltd (Dealer), Upminster, Essex	09/67
				Leyland Motors Ltd (Dealer) London W1	09/67
			E 815590	University Transport System, University of California, Davis, California, USA	09/67
				Bob Jeffrey (Ram Reality), Sacramento, California, USA	09/77
				Stored in open, near Ranches, Cordova, north-east of Sacramento, semi derelict	04/88
				Still there	01/95
RTL1195	510842	5782	LYF136		
			23 sri 3119	Ceylon Transport Board, Colombo, Ceylon	11/67
RTL1196	510844	5486	LYF137		
			23 sri 1255	Ceylon Transport Board, Colombo, Ceylon	09/64
RTL1197	510847	5544	LYF138		
				Gradeka Saobracaine Preduzece, Sarajevo, Yugoslavia	06/64
RTL1198	510841	9139	LYF139		
			23 sri 3204	Ceylon Transport Board, Colombo, Ceylon	04/68
				Still in existence having been fitted with CTB single deck bodywork, now withdrawn	02/77
				Sold	01/79
RTL1199	510845	5736	LYR140		
			23 sri 1577	Ceylon Transport Board, Colombo, Ceylon	04/65
RTL1200	510850	5773	LYR141		
			23 sri 3243	Ceylon Transport Board, Colombo, Ceylon	07/68
				Still in existence but withdrawn	02/77
RTL1201	510846	6283	LYR142		
			23 sri 3399	Ceylon Transport Board, Colombo, Ceylon	12/68
				Still in existence but withdrawn	02/77
RTL1202	510849	5733	LYR143		
			23 sri 3407	Ceylon Transport Board, Colombo, Ceylon	12/68
RTL1203	510848	5686	LYR144		
			23 sri 1583	Ceylon Transport Board, Colombo, Ceylon	04/65
				Still in existence but withdrawn	02/77
RTL1204	510843	5727	LYR145		
			23 sri 3151	Ceylon Transport Board, Colombo, Ceylon	12/67
				Still in existence but withdrawn	02/77
RTL1205	510924	5712	LYF146		
			23 sri 1600	Ceylon Transport Board, Colombo, Ceylon	04/65
				Still in existence but withdrawn	02/77

RTL1206	510923	5783	LYF147		
			23 sri 3297	Ceylon Transport Board, Colombo, Ceylon	08/68
RTL1207	510919	5655	LYF148		
				Gradeka Saobracaine Preduzece, Sarajevo, Yugoslavia	05/64
RTL1208	510920	5757	LYF149		
			CA 57267	Golden Arrow Bus Service, Cape Town, South Africa 141	09/63
RTL1209	510925	5556	LYF150		
				Bird's Commercial Motors (Dealer), Stratford-upon-Avon, Warwickshire	07/62
				S.Eynon & Sons, Trimsaran, Carmarthenshire	08/62
				Withdrawn	05/68
				Arlington Motors (Dealer), Cardiff	05/68
				W.H.Way (Breakers), Cardiff East Docks, Cardiff	06/68
				Scrapped	—/77
RTL1210	510927	5676	LYF151		
			CA 57264	Golden Arrow Bus Service, Cape Town, South Africa 140	09/63
RTL1211	511047	5653	LYF152		
			23 sri 1602	Ceylon Transport Board, Colombo, Ceylon	04/65
RTL1212	510922	5743	LYF153		
			23 sri 1415	Ceylon Transport Board, Colombo, Ceylon	12/64
RTL1213	510926	5689	LYF154		
			23 sri 1416	Ceylon Transport Board, Colombo, Ceylon	12/64
				Still in existence but withdrawn	02/77
RTL1214	511050	5707	LYF155		
			CA 57329	Golden Arrow Bus Service, Cape Town, South Africa 146	09/63
				Withdrawn	by 11/70
				Scrapped	11/70
RTL1215	510921	5684	LYF156		
				Pickersgill & Laverick (Dealer), Cudworth, Yorkshire	05/69
RTL1216	511048	5764	LYF157		
			23 sri 3214	Ceylon Transport Board, Colombo, Ceylon	05/68
RTL1217	511049	5658	LYF158		
				Edward Bowman & Son, London EC1 as mobile showroom	05/63
				Multihire Sound Amplification, Syston, Leicestershire still as showroom	09/71
RTL1218	511052	3665	LYF159		
				Wombwell Diesel Company (Dealer), Wombwell, Yorkshire	11/69
RTL1219	510928	5739	LYF160		
			23 sri 3298	Ceylon Transport Board, Colombo, Ceylon	08/68
				Still in existence but withdrawn	02/77

Gradeka Saobracaine Preduzece abbreviated to GSP is carried centrally on the lower deck panelling by RTL1110, when photographed in Llidza, Yugoslavia on the 28th June, 1965. The rebuilt loading platform and staircase area is interesting in that the old offside route number stencil bracketery from its London Transport years has been retained, but not used. Can anyone state where these conversions were carried out? (John G.S. Smith)

F. Wilde trading as Wimbledon Coaches of London SW19 operated RTL659 for a number of years and it is seen less any route blinds or advertising almost as if it has just emerged from a repaint. It does carry legal ownership information aft of the front wheel which thankfully allows it otherwise anonymity to be uncovered. (Kevin Lane)

RTL1220	511054	5717	LYF161		
			23 sri 3405	Ceylon Transport Board, Colombo, Ceylon	12/68
RTL1221	511051	5673	LYF162		
			23 sri 3138	Ceylon Transport Board, Colombo, Ceylon	12/67
RTL1222	511053	5781	LYF163		
				Burnt out at Walworth Garage 01/53	
				Withdrawn	01/53
				Cut up at Chiswick works	04/53
RTL1223	511055	5726	LYF164		
			23 sri 3241	Ceylon Transport Board, Colombo, Ceylon	07/68
RTL1224	511057	5771	LYF165		
				Passenger Vehicle Sales (London) Ltd (Dealer), Canvey Island, Essex	12/67
				Barton Transport, Chilwell, Nottinghamshire 1090	12/67
				Withdrawn	10/70
				Unidentified dealer for scrap	01/71
RTL1225	511058	5688	LYF166		
			23 sri 3123	Ceylon Transport Board, Colombo, Ceylon	11/67
				Still in existence but withdrawn	02/77
RTL1226	511056	5683	LYF167		
			23 sri 3081	Ceylon Transport Board, Colombo, Ceylon	10/67
RTL1227	514777	5687	LYR759		
			23 sri 3283	Ceylon Transport Board, Colombo, Ceylon	08/68
				Still in existence but withdrawn	02/77
RTL1228	514732	5769	LYR760		
			23 sri 3133	Ceylon Transport Board, Colombo, Ceylon	12/67
				Still in existence as a trainer	02/77
RTL1229	514731	5730	LYR761		
			23 sri 3143	Ceylon Transport Board, Colombo, Ceylon	12/67
RTL1230	514695	5768	LYR762		
			23 sri 3118	Ceylon Transport Board, Colombo, Ceylon	11/67
				Still in existence but withdrawn	02/77
RTL1231	514773	5740	LYR763		
				Atlantic National Advertising Agency, Hampton, Virginia, USA	08/68
				City of Hampton Commerce Dept, City Hall, Hampton, Virginia and used by Hampton City Transit on sightseeing tours	—/—
				Busch Gardens, Williamsburgh, Virginia, USA, for use on park and ride shuttle service	by 12/76
				Unknown owner, Greensboro, North Carolina, USA	by 01/91

RTL1232	514775	5742	LYR764		
				Pickersgill & Laverick (Dealer), Cudworth, Yorkshire	04/71
RTL1233	512921	5681	LYR765		
			23 sri 3217	Ceylon Transport Board, Colombo, Ceylon	05/68
				Still in service	02/77
RTL1234	514774	5666	LYR766		
			23 sri 3202	Ceylon Transport Board, Colombo, Ceylon	04/68
RTL1235	514722	5759	LYR767		
				Wombwell Diesel Company (Dealer), Wombwell, Yorkshire	05/69
RTL1236	512920	5711	LYR768		
			23 sri 3200	Ceylon Transport Board, Colombo, Ceylon	04/68
RTL1237	512697	5779	LYR769		
				Wombwell Diesel Company (Dealer), Wombwell, Yorkshire	05/69
RTL1238	512916	5611	LYR770		
				Passenger Vehicle Sales (London) Ltd (Dealer), Canvey Island, Essex	12/67
				Barton Transport, Chilwell, Nottinghamshire, 1107	12/67
				Withdrawn	10/70
				Unidentified dealer, for scrap	01/71
RTL1239	512919	5604	LYR771		
			23 sri 3213	Ceylon Transport Board, Colombo, Ceylon	05/68
				Still in existence but withdrawn	02/77
RTL1240	512917	5776	LYR772		
			23 sri 3152	Ceylon Transport Board, Colombo, Ceylon	12/67
RTL1241	512918	5729	LYR773		
				B.Walden's Coaches, Epping, Essex	02/68
				G.Ward, t/a Ward's Coaches, Epping, Essex	04/70
				Riverway Coaches, Harlow, Essex	01/72
				Withdrawn	01/74
RTL1242	512698	5715	LYR774		
				Pickersgill & Laverick (Dealer), Cudworth, Yorkshire	02/70
RTL1243	514932	3912	LYR775		
			23 sri 3267	Ceylon Transport Board, Colombo, Ceylon	07/68
				Still in existence but withdrawn	02/77
RTL1244	512701	5406	LYR776		
			23 sri 3271	Ceylon Transport Board, Colombo, Ceylon	08/68
RTL1245	514694	6321	LYR777		
				B.Walden's Coaches, Epping, Essex	03/64
				G.Ward, t/a Ward's Coaches, Epping, Essex	06/66
				Withdrawn	12/69
				Luton Commercial Motors (Dealer), Dunstable, Bedfordshire	12/69
				Weaton Commercial (Dealer), London SW1	12/69
				R.E.Doyle (Breaker), London NW1 for scrap	12/69

R.C. Doughty & Sons of Kings Lynn favoured a rather plain livery for RTL6 which they had acquired in March 1958 but at least it does change the appearance of the Park Royal built body from its London operation. With a route blind announcing Islington as the destination confusion could creep in, as the bus is seen in Kings Lynn.

RTL1246	512699	4978	LYR778		
			23 sri 1960	Ceylon Transport Board, Colombo, Ceylon	10/65
				Still in existence but withdrawn	02/77
RTL1247	512700	5751	LYR779		
				Pickersgill & Laverick (Dealer), Cudworth, Yorkshire	06/69
RTL1248	514930	5233	LYR780		
				Pickersgill & Laverick (Dealer), Cudworth, Yorkshire	05/69
RTL1249	514931	5208	LYR781		
			23 sri 1613	Ceylon Transport Board, Colombo, Ceylon	04/65
RTL1250	514929	2164	LYR782		
			CA 28541	Golden Arrow Bus Service, Cape Town, South Africa 205	09/64
RTL1251	514928	3899	LYR873		
			23 sri 3237	Ceylon Transport Board, Colombo, Ceylon	07/68
				Still in service	02/77
RTL1252	514926	4941	LYR784		
			23 sri 2046	Ceylon Transport Board, Colombo, Ceylon	12/65
RTL1253	514927	5292	LYR785		
				Pickersgill & Laverick (Dealer), Cudworth, Yorkshire	05/69
RTL1254	514934	3638	LYR786		
				Bird's Commercial Motors (Dealer), Stratford-upon-Avon, Warwickshire	01/70
RTL1255	514933	3422	LYR787		
				J.A.Elliott Limited (Plant and Crane Hire), Bishops Stortford, Hertfordshire, as staff bus	09/65
				Fitted with platform doors	10/65
				Sold for scrap	—/—
RTL1256	514925	6299	LYR788		
				A.R. Harling t/a Harlings Coaches, London SE1, without roof following an accident with LTE, at the same time body of RT1067 in damaged condition purchased and its roof fitted to this bus and used for nurses transports between Westminster and St. Georges hospitals and nurses hostels	09/62
				Phillips t/a Enterprise Safety Coaches, Chatteris, Cambridgeshire	11/69
				E.Brakell (Dealer), Cheam, Surrey	12/75
				On hire to Brown & Root (UK) Limited, London SW19 as staff bus	12/77
				Returned from hire	01/79
				J.C.Riddiough, Bingley, West Yorkshire for preservation	05/84
				Still owned	08/96
RTL1257	514923	6333	LYR789		
			23 sri 3285	Ceylon Transport Board, Colombo, Ceylon	08/68
RTL1258	512915	6309	LYR790		
			SA 55 33	Gradeka Saobracaine Preduzece, Sarajevo, Yugoslavia, 23	
RTL1259	514776	5265	LYR791		
				Pickersgill & Laverick (Dealer), Cudworth, Yorkshire	02/70
				Hartwood Finance (Dealer), Barnsley and scrapped	03/70
RTL1260	514937	5227	LYR792		
			CA 134 702	City Tramways Co., Cape Town, South Africa 731	05/65
				Still in service and renumbered 0731	04/74
RTL1261	514938	3908	LYR793		
			23 sri 3131	Ceylon Transport Board, Colombo, Ceylon	11/67
RTL1262	514935	6427	LYR794		
			SA 55 34	Gradeka Saobracaine Preduzece, Sarajevo, Yugoslavia, 24	05/64
RTL1263	514936	4947	LYR795		
				Passenger Vehicle Sales (London) Ltd (Dealer), Upminster, Essex	02/67
				P.Irvine, t/a Golden Eagle, Salsburgh, Lanarkshire	02/67
				Johnson, Glasgow	08/67
				Withdrawn after accident	03/70
RTL1264	515026	6306	LYR796		
			CA 125 282	City Tramways Co., Cape Town, South Africa 478	02/64
				Still in service	04/74
				Sold and used as a chicken coup still in CT livery	—/—
				David Munton, Cape Town for intended body restoration and eventual fitting to chassis of RT222	—/91
				Elwierda Tours, Stellenbosch, upon take over of Mr. Munton's business, unrenovated	—/96
RTL1265	515027	6311	LYR797		
				Roydonian Coaches, Roydon, Essex	09/63
				Out of use	06/66
				Re-instated	07/67
				Withdrawn and scrapped by Roydonian Coaches	by 10/70
RTL1266	514940	6298	LYR798		
			CA 125 276	City Tramways Co., Cape Town, South Africa 475	03/64
				Still in service renumbered 0475	03/74
RTL1267	514924	6320	LYR799		
			23 sri 3225	Ceylon Transport Board, Colombo, Ceylon	07/68
RTL1268	514942	6304	LYR800		
			SA 55 36	Gradeka Saobracaine Preduzece, Sarajevo, Yugoslavia, 26	05/64
RTL1269	515025	6300	LYR801		
				Wombwell Diesel Company (Dealer), Wombwell, Yorkshire	01/70

Silver Star of Porton Down used an unusually livery of silver in keeping with their fleet name and RTL305 looks splendid as it shines in the sunshine within Salisbury City Centre. The London radiator badge has been replaced by a 'Silver Star' example which all adds up to the high standards aimed for by the proprietors. Once considered for preservation, the bus was unfortunately gutted by fire and one is only left with photograph memories.

RTL27 shows off the rather attractive livery of A & C McLennan of Spittalfield. Other changes include a door having been added to the platform boarding area and the removal of the London Transport running duty plate holders. (A. B. Cross)

RTL1270	514939	6331	LYR802		
			23 sri 3258	Ceylon Transport Board, Colombo, Ceylon	07/68
RTL1271	515034	6357	LYR803		
			23 sri 3410	Ceylon Transport Board, Colombo, Ceylon	12/68
				Still in existence but withdrawn	02/77
RTL1272	515033	6332	LYR804		
			23 sri 3411	Ceylon Transport Board, Colombo, Ceylon	12/68
				Still in existence but withdrawn	02/77
RTL1273	514941	6317	LYR805		
			CA 125 283	City Tramways Co., Cape Town, South Africa 479	03/64
				Still in service	04/74
RTL1274	515028	6336	LYR806		
				Bird's Commercial Motors (Dealer), Stratford-upon-Avon, Warwickshire	08/67
RTL1275	515030	6310	LYR807		
			SA 55 36	Gradeka Saobracaine Preduzece, Sarajevo, Yugoslavia 26	05/64
RTL1276	515031	6345	LYR808		
				Passenger Vehicle Sales (London) Ltd (Dealer), Ilford, Essex	09/63
				S.Eynon & Sons, Trimsara, Carmarthenshire	10/63
				Withdrawn	08/71
				P.Sykes, (Dealer), Barnsley, Yorkshire for scrap	08/71
RTL1277	515158	6318	LYR809		
			SA 54 17	Gradeka Saobracaine Preduzece, Sarajevo, Yugoslavia, 43	07/64
RTL1278	515032	6316	LYR810		
				Gradeka Saobracaine Preduzece, Sarajevo, Yugoslavia	06/64
RTL1279	515029	6363	LYR811		
				Ford & Walton, London E15 (Contractors) as staff bus	03/64
				Out of use	by 05/66
				Gone	by 10/66
RTL1280	515084	6319	LYR812		
			23 sri 3374	Ceylon Transport Board, Colombo, Ceylon	12/68
RTL1281	515157	6216	LYR813		
				Empress Cleaning Service (Ilford) Limited, Barkingside, Essex	12/67
				Noted at South Weald Garage, Brentwood with roof ripped off by accident	12/68
RTL1282	515036	6375	LYR814		
			23 sri 3277	Ceylon Transport Board, Colombo, Ceylon	08/68
				Still in use now fitted with a Leyland 0680 Power Plus engine and used for private hire contracts	04/81
RTL1283	515087	6358	LYR815		
				Collars 1940 Group Limited, Dartford, Kent as staff bus	10/67
				Sold	03/77
RTL1284	515088	5778	LYR816		
			23 sri 3384	Ceylon Transport Board, Colombo, Ceylon	12/68
				Still in use now fitted with a Leyland 0680 Power Plus engine, numbered RL31	12/81
RTL1285	515089	6313	LYR817		
				Gradeka Saobracaine Preduzece, Sarajevo, Yugoslavia	05/64
RTL1286	515056	6328	LYR818		
			23 sri 3253	Ceylon Transport Board, Colombo, Ceylon	07/68
				Still in existence but withdrawn	02/77
				Sold	12/77
				Rebuilt as a private lorry, not reregistered	by 04/81
RTL1287	515082	6308	LYR819		
			23 sri 3418	Ceylon Transport Board, Colombo, Ceylon	12/68
RTL1288	515083	6242	LYR820		
			23 sri 3415	Ceylon Transport Board, Colombo, Ceylon	12/68
				Still in existence but withdrawn	02/77
RTL1289	515156	6340	LYR821		
				Pickersgill & Laverick (Dealer), Cudworth, Yorkshire	02/70
RTL1290	515159	6302	LYR822		
			SA 54 18	Gradeka Saobracaine Preduzece, Sarajevo, Yugoslavia, 45	02/64
RTL1291	515085	5748	LYR823		
			23 sri 3156	Ceylon Transport Board, Colombo, Ceylon	12/67
RTL1292	515054	5780	LYR824		
				Passenger Vehicle Sales (London) Ltd (Dealer), Kelvedon, Essex	12/67
				Barton Transport, Chilwell, Nottinghamshire 1109	12/67
				Withdrawn	01/72
				G.Lister (Dealer), Bolton, Lancashire	01/72
				Barraclough (Dealer), Barnsley, Yorkshire	02/72
RTL1293	515035	5772	LYR825		
			23 sri 3199	Ceylon Transport Board, Colombo, Ceylon	04/68
RTL1294	515055	2402	LYR828		
			23 sri 3269	Ceylon Transport Board, Colombo, Ceylon	07/68
RTL1295	515270	6292	LYR829		
				Wombwell Diesel Company (Dealer), Wombwell, Yorkshire	05/69

RTL1296	515086	6330	LYR830		
			23 sri 3201	Ceylon Transport Board, Colombo, Ceylon	04/68
				Still in existence but withdrawn	02/77
RTL1297	515057	6307	LYR831		
			CA 125285	City Tramways Co., Cape Town, South Africa 481	03/64
				Withdrawn	by 11/70
				Scrapped	11/70
RTL1298	515160	6335	LYR832		
				Hays International Services (London) Limited, Waltham Abbey, Essex as staff bus	02/68
				G.Ward t/a Ward's Coaches, Epping, Essex	by 07/69
				On loan to Alder Valley	09/74
				Returned from loan	12/74
				Withdrawn	06/75
				M.Biddell, Woodford, Essex for preservation	—/—
				Advertised as for sale	10/77
				E.Brakell (Dealer), Cheam, Surrey	01/78
				Hanover Street Productions, EMI, Borehamwood and used in the film, 'Hanover Street', masquerading as RT35, FXT210 and seen severely damaged in a Second World War bombing scene	c02/78
RTL1299	515272	4949	LYR833		
				Pickersgill & Laverick (Dealer), Cudworth, Yorkshire	05/69
RTL1300	515354	6315	LYR834		
			23 sri 1111	Ceylon Transport Board, Colombo, Ceylon	05/64
RTL1301	515275	3443	LYR835		
				Pickersgill & Laverick (Dealer), Cudworth, Yorkshire	05/69
RTL1302	515353	6314	LYR936		
			23 sri 3264	Ceylon Transport Board, Colombo, Ceylon	07/68
RTL1303	515274	6334	LYR937		
			23 sri 3416	Ceylon Transport Board, Colombo, Ceylon	12/68
RTL1304	515271	7160	LYR938		
			23 sri 3236	Ceylon Transport Board, Colombo, Ceylon	07/68
RTL1305	515355	5716	LYR939		
			23 sri 3234	Ceylon Transport Board, Colombo, Ceylon	07/68
RTL1306	515356	6225	LYR940		
				McDonald, Saussey & Partners (Shipping Agents), London W1	09/67
				Exported to USA	—/67
				Radio Station W-SHO, New Orleans, Louisiana, USA	by 12/70
				Discovery Bay, Pass Christian, Mississippi	c—/73
RTL1307	515357	7706	LYR935		
			23 sri 1310	Ceylon Transport Board, Colombo, Ceylon	11/64
RTL1308	515161	3629	LYR956		
				Pickersgill & Laverick (Dealer), Cudworth, Yorkshire	02/70
RTL1309	515273	3554	LYR957		
				Bird's Commercial Motors (Dealer), Stratford-upon-Avon, Warwickshire	12/69
RTL1310	515361	4462	LYR958		
			CA 80967	City Tramways Co., Cape Town, South Africa 718	12/64
				Still in service	04/74
RTL1311	515360	7311	LYR959		
				Passenger Vehicle Sales (London) Ltd (Dealer), Upminster, Essex	09/63
				S.Eynon & Sons, Trimsaran, Carmarthenshire	10/63
				Withdrawn	08/71
				P.Sykes, Barnsley, Yorkshire, for scrap	08/71
RTL1312	515358	2260	LYR960		
				Pickersgill & Laverick (Dealer), Cudworth, Yorkshire	05/69
RTL1313	515359	5182	LYR961		
				Pickersgill & Laverick (Dealer), Cudworth, Yorkshire	05/69
RTL1314	520925	4499	MLL676		
			23 sri 1498	Ceylon Transport Board, Colombo, Ceylon	02/65
RTL1315	520926	6303	MLL677		
				Passenger Vehicle Sales (London) Ltd (Dealer), Upminster, Essex	09/67
				Used on a shuttle service to and from the British Fair at the Canadian National Exhibition Grounds during a British week in Toronto, Ontario, Canada	10/67
			BA 4802	Double Deck Tours Ltd, Niagara Falls, Ontario, Canada, subsequently carried various licence plates while owned by DDT	10/67
				Chip Bar situated at Niagara Falls	c—/93
			DD FRY	R.Mitchinson, Kincardine, Ontario, parked at Sutton Park Mall, Kincardie as Double Deck Fries Chip Bar	by 05/95
				Still owned	09/95
RTL1316	520923	4419	MLL678		
			23 sri 1524	Ceylon Transport Board, Colombo, Ceylon	02/65
RTL1317	520924	5168	MLL679		
				Pickersgill & Laverick (Dealer), Cudworth, Yorkshire	05/69

RTL1318	520928	6367	MLL680		
				Pickersgill & Laverick (Dealer), Cudworth, Yorkshire	05/69
RTL1319	520927	7220	MLL681		
			23 sri 3244	Ceylon Transport Board, Colombo, Ceylon	07/68
RTL1320	520921	6312	MLL682		
			23 sri 3417	Ceylon Transport Board, Colombo, Ceylon	12/68
				Still in existence but withdrawn	02/77
RTL1321	520922	3444	MLL683		
				Pickersgill & Laverick (Dealer), Cudworth, Yorkshire	05/69
RTL1322	521295	4529	MLL684		
			CA 119 169	City Tramways Co., Cape Town, South Africa 468	02/64
RTL1323	521293	4402	MLL685		
				Williams Furniture Supermarkets, NW6	08/64
				Shaw & Kilburn (Dealer), London W5	—/66
				A & D Allmey, Pinner, Middlesex, for preservation	08/66
				Repainted into green line livery	—/—
				D.Allmey, Eastcote for continued preservation	07/78
				Still owned	01/98
RTL1324	521294	6343	MLL686		
			23 sri 1311	Ceylon Transport Board, Colombo, Ceylon	11/64
RTL1325	521296	6388	MLL687		
			CA 11011	Golden Arrow Bus Service, Cape Town, South Africa 204	08/64
RTL1326	521454	4545	MLL697		
				Continental Pioneer, Richmond, Surrey	05/68
				Being used for spares	11/68
				Broken up	11/69
RTL1327	521297	4751	MLL698		
			SA 52 62	Gradeka Saobracaine Preduzece, Sarajevo, Yugoslavia, 35	06/64
RTL1328	521298	2102	MLL699		
				Pickersgill & Laverick (Dealer), Cudworth, Yorkshire	05/69
RTL1329	521299	6360	MLL700		
				Passenger Vehicle Sales (London) Ltd (Dealer), Ilford, Essex	09/64
				Taylor-Woodrow Limited (Contractors), London W5 as staff bus	09/64
				Used as immobile canteen at Gloucester Road, N17 site and later Lisson Grove, NW	08/70
RTL1330	521300	5236	MLL701		
				Pickersgill & Laverick (Dealer), Cudworth, Yorkshire	05/69
RTL1331	521453	3577	MLL702		
				Pickersgill & Laverick (Dealer), Cudworth, Yorkshire	02/70
RTL1332	521455	6337	MLL703		
				Wombwell Diesel Company (Dealer), Wombwell, Yorkshire	10/69
RTL1333	521460	6344	MXX32		
			23 sri 3378	Ceylon Transport Board, Colombo, Ceylon	12/68
RTL1334	521458	6381	MXX33		
			CA 80822	City Tramways Co., Cape Town, South Africa 705	08/64
				Withdrawn after accident	09/69
				Used for spares	10/69
RTL1335	521457	6288	MXX34		
				Passenger Vehicle Sales (London) Ltd (Dealer), Canvey Island, Essex	12/67
				Barton Transport, Chilwell, Nottinghamshire, 1110	12/67
				Withdrawn	11/70
				W.J.Lowndes, Draycott Metals, (Dealer), Spondon, Derbyshire	11/70
RTL1336	521456	9143	MXX35		
			23 sri 3189	Ceylon Transport Board, Colombo, Ceylon	04/68
RTL1337	521459	3555	OLD813		
				Bird's Commercial Motors (Dealer), Stratford-upon-Avon, Warwickshire	12/69
RTL1338	521646	3435	MXX61		
				Wombwell Diesel Company (Dealer), Wombwell, Yorkshire after mechanical units had been removed at Stonebridge Garage for Ceylon Transport Board	12/69
RTL1339	521640	4521	MXX62		
			23 sri 1112	Ceylon Transport Board, Colombo, Ceylon	05/64
RTL1340	521641	5357	MXX63		
				Bird's Commercial Motors (Dealer), Stratford-upon-Avon, Warwickshire	12/69
RTL1341	521903	3947	MXX64		
			23 sri 3210	Ceylon Transport Board, Colombo, Ceylon	04/68
				Still in existence but withdrawn	02/77
RTL1342	521645	3581	MXX65		
				Pickersgill & Laverick (Dealer), Cudworth, Yorkshire	02/70
RTL1343	521643	6326	MXX66		
				Bird's Commercial Motors (Dealer), Stratford-upon-Avon, Warwickshire	05/69
RTL1344	521639	9168	MXX67		
			23 sri 3257	Ceylon Transport Board, Colombo, Ceylon	07/68

RTL1345	521642	9144	MXX68		
			23 sri 3087	Ceylon Transport Board, Colombo, Ceylon	10/67
RTL1346	521644	6353	MXX69		
			CA 80843	City Tramways Co., Cape Town, South Africa 706	08/64
				Still in service	04/74
RTL1347	521908	5017	MXX70		
			SA 55 67	Gradeka Saobracaine Preduzece, Sarajevo, Yugoslavia, 38	05/64
RTL1348	522155	3605	MXX71		
			J 8629	Jersey Motor Transport Co. Ltd., St Helier, Jersey, Channel Islands 11	03/59
				Out of use and in store	—/74
				E.Brakell (Dealer), Cheam, Surrey	11/74
			MXX71	Previous registration obtained	—/75
				After use as a towing vehicle returned to LT livery	10/79
				D.Ladd, Iver, Buckinghamshire for preservation	08/84
				Still owned	06/91
RTL1349	522409	2215	MXX72		
				Bird's Commercial Motors (Dealer), Stratford-upon-Avon, Warwickshire	12/58
				Stonier & Sons, Goldenhill, Stoke-on-Trent, Staffordshire 10	12/58
				S.Hughes (Dealer), Gomershall, Yorkshire	04/68
				Hornsby, Ashby, Lincolnshire	06/68
				Withdrawn	02/74
				Wombwell Diesel Company (Dealer), Wombwell, Yorkshire	09/74
RTL1350	522151	6382	MXX73		
			23 sri 1358	Ceylon Transport Board, Colombo, Ceylon	11/64
				Rebuilt as a CTB service lorry	by 02/77
				Still extant	—/81
RTL1351	522514	6354	MXX74		
			CA 80816	City Tramways Co., Cape Town, South Africa 702	08/64
				Still in service	04/74
RTL1352	522416	4519	MXX75		
			23 sri 1060	Ceylon Transport Board, Colombo, Ceylon	04/64
				Still in existence but withdrawn	02/77
RTL1353	522410	6380	MXX76		
			CA 28521	Golden Arrow Bus Service, Cape Town, South Africa 203	08/64
				Withdrawn	by 11/70
RTL1354	521905	4446	MXX77		
			23 sri 1319	Ceylon Transport Board, Colombo, Ceylon	11/64

RTL269 belonging to Walter Mills Tours Limited of Gornal Woods is seen at that time of day when the sun casts long shadows when you least need them. But the picture is included as this was the only RTL which found further service with this operator. Very little work appears to have been carried out on the exterior except for the removal of advertising material. (Alan Mortimer)

RTL1355	521907	4542	MXX78		
				Passenger Vehicle Sales (London) Ltd (Dealer), Upminster, Essex	03/67
				Barton Transport Limited, Chilwell, Nottinghamshire 1088	04/67
				Withdrawn	07/71
				Unidentified Dealer for scrap	08/71
RTL1356	521906	4620	MXX79		
			CA 119 170	City Tramways Co., Cape Town, South Africa 469	02/64
				Still in service	04/74
RTL1357	522148	4587	MXX80		
			23 sri 1109	Ceylon Transport Board, Colombo, Ceylon	05/64
RTL1358	522152	6348	MXX81		
			23 sri 1306	Ceylon Transport Board, Colombo, Ceylon	11/64
RTL1359	522612	4459	MXX82		
			22 sri 3239	Ceylon Transport Board, Colombo, Ceylon	03/59
RTL1360	522149	2422	MXX83		
			23 sri 3396	Ceylon Transport Board, Colombo, Ceylon	12/68
RTL1361	521904	6351	MXX84		
			CA 9002	Golden Arrow Bus Service, Cape Town, South Africa 202	08/64
				Withdrawn and scrapped	04/70
RTL1362	521910	2399	MXX85		
				Camplins European Catering Company, London SW9 as a dining unit	01/69
				Withdrawn	09/75
RTL1363	522150	5253	MXX86		
				Pickersgill & Laverick (Dealer), Cudworth, Yorkshire	05/69
RTL1364	522419	4527	MXX87		
				Cobham Hire Services, t/a Caroline Coaches, Great Yarmouth, Norfolk	06/64
				Sold to local Gypsies for breaking at Fleggburgh, Norfolk.	—/71
				Still in existence in scrap yard at Fleggburgh, Norfolk	—73
				Remains scrapped	—/88
RTL1365	522689	4465	MXX88		
			23 sri 1309	Ceylon Transport Board, Colombo, Ceylon	11/64
RTL1366	522411	4652	MXX89		
			23 sri 3224	Ceylon Transport Board, Colombo, Ceylon	07/68
				Still in existence but withdrawn	02/77
RTL1367	522512	5092	MXX90		
			23 sri 1108	Ceylon Transport Board, Colombo, Ceylon	05/64
RTL1368	522408	2041	MXX91		
			23 sri 3259	Ceylon Transport Board, Colombo, Ceylon	07/68
RTL1369	522687	2238	MXX92		
			22 sri 3284	Ceylon Transport Board, Colombo, Ceylon	03/59
RTL1370	522611	4526	MXX93		
			CA 125 284	City Tramways Co., Cape Town, South Africa 480	03/64
RTL1371	522412	4548	MXX94		
				Wombwell Diesel Company (Dealer), Wombwell, Yorkshire	10/69
RTL1372	522153	4557	MXX95		
			23 sri 1061	Ceylon Transport Board, Colombo, Ceylon	04/64
RTL1373	522154	4444	MXX96		
			23 sri 1409	Ceylon Transport Board, Colombo, Ceylon	12/64
RTL1374	522616	4455	MXX97		
			23 sri 1502	Ceylon Transport Board, Colombo, Ceylon	02/65
RTL1375	522691	4564	MXX98		
			23 sri 1062	Ceylon Transport Board, Colombo, Ceylon	04/64
RTL1376	522615	4608	MXX99		
				Wombwell Diesel Company (Dealer), Wombwell, Yorkshire	10/69
RTL1377	521909	4401	MXX100		
			22 sri 3282	Ceylon Transport Board, Colombo, Ceylon	03/59
RTL1378	522511	4449	MXX101		
			23 sri 1357	Ceylon Transport Board, Colombo, Ceylon	11/64
RTL1379	522413	3499	MXX102		
				Pickersgill & Laverick (Dealer), Cudworth, Yorkshire	05/69
RTL1380	522414	4578	MXX103		
			23 sri 1129	Ceylon Transport Board, Colombo, Ceylon	05/64
RTL1381	522415	4579	MXX104		
			CA 119 168	City Tramways Co., Cape Town, South Africa 470	02/64
				Still in service	02/76
RTL1382	522417	4561	MXX105		
			CA 130 870	Golden Arrow Bus Service, Cape Town, South Africa 219	01/65
RTL1383	522515	2058	MXX106		
				Pickersgill & Laverick (Dealer), Cudworth, Yorkshire	05/69
RTL1384	522418	4565	MXX107		
			SA 55 70	Gradeka Saobracaine Preduzece, Sarajevo, Yugoslavia 40	05/64
RTL1385	522510	4662	MXX108		
			23 sri 1130	Ceylon Transport Board, Colombo, Ceylon	05/64

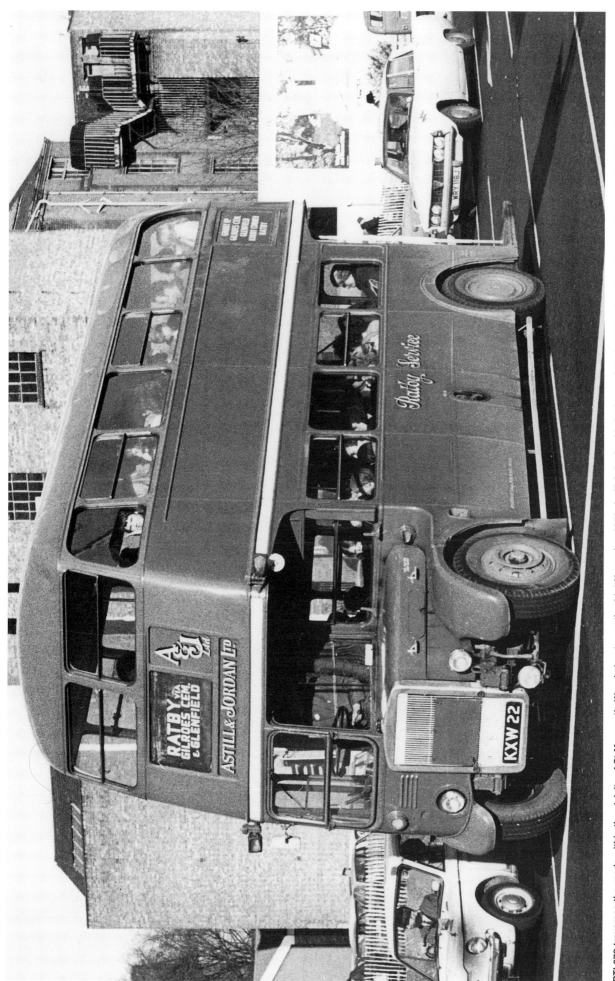

RTL672 traverses the roads within the vicinity of St Margaret's Way, Leicester on the 21st November 1970. Astill & Jordan Limited owned the bus from October 1965 through to the summer of 1972, their premises being situated at Ratby. Competition for road space is shared with a Hillman Imp on the left and Rover 2000, P6 model soon to pull up behind the Imp. (John G. S. Smith)

RTL1386	522613	4678	MXX109		
			CA 134 682	City Tramways Co., Cape Town, South Africa 727	02/65
				Golden Arrow Bus Service, Cape Town, South Africa 236	03/65
RTL1387	522693	7135	MXX110		
				Wombwell Diesel Company (Dealer), Wombwell, Yorkshire after mechanical units	
				had been removed at Stonebridge Garage for Ceylon Transport Board	04/69
RTL1388	522739	5010	MXX111		
				Faron Limited (Overseas Removals), London EC3	04/68
				H.Salt, San Francisco, California, USA, used for free transport to and from a fish and chip shop	04/68
				Tom Porter (Dealer), Burnsville, Minnesota, converted to open-top	by 02/81
			03.658	Lord Fletcher's Restaurant, Minnetonka, Minnesota in use as a refreshment stand	by 02/81
				Still owned	09/82
RTL1389	522688	4457	MXX112		
			CA 81063	City Tramways Co., Cape Town, South Africa 726	01/65
				Golden Arrow Bus Service, Capetown, South Africa. 233	03/65
RTL1390	522690	6341	MXX113		
			23 sri 3226	Ceylon Transport Board, Colombo, Ceylon	07/68
RTL1391	522513	5087	MXX114		
				Bosch Limited, Watford, Hertfordshire, used as a mobile cinema and exhibition unit	11/68
				First licensed	03/69
				Withdrawn	11/70
				Market Pulse (NPSV), Cobham, Surrey	07/71
				Withdrawn	03/72
				Vehicle abandoned at Oxhey, Hertfordshire and subsequently removed for scrap	02/74
RTL1392	522614	4601	MXX115		
				Pickersgill & Laverick (Dealer), Cudworth, Yorkshire	05/69
RTL1393	522692	5006	MXX116		
			SA 55 61	Gradeka Saobracaine Preduzece, Sarajevo, Yugoslavia, 33	06/64
RTL1394	522796	4530	MXX117		
			CA 119 172	City Tramways Co., Cape Town, South Africa 471	02/64
				Still in service, open top condition	04/74
				Transferred to Springbok Atlas Tours, Capetown, South Africa painted red for sightseeing tours	
				renumbered 0471	c06/75
				Still in service renumbered SA001	11/77
				David Rawden, Matjiesfontein, Karoo, South Africa for preservation and use by hotel guests	—/83
				Still owned	07/92
				David Munton, Cape Town, South Africa for preservation	11/92
			CA 5037	Fully restored to PSV status completed	12/94
				Elwierda Tours, Stellenbosch upon take over of Mr. Munton's business	—/96

This photograph of RTL641 was taken from the top deck of another vehicle travelling in the opposite direction while passing through Irvine. The non opening front windows of the upper deck and driver's cab together with the triangular shaped destination aperture were fitted while the bus was owned by members of the A1 Service. Throughout the book it will be noticed how the different members have applied the blue, white and maroon livery.
(John G. S. Smith)

RTL1395	522741	4413	MXX118		
			CA 80819	City Tramways Co., Cape Town, South Africa 703	09/64
				Still in service	04/74
RTL1396	522799	2136	MXX119		
			CA 35085	Golden Arrow Bus Service, Cape Town, South Africa 206	10/64
				Withdrawn	by 11/70
				Scrapped	12/70
RTL1397	522743	4574	MXX120		
			CA 59132	City Tramways Co., Cape Town, South Africa 701	08/64
RTL1398	522745	4765	MXX121		
				Wombwell Diesel Company (Dealer), Wombwell, Yorkshire	11/69
RTL1399	522794	4681	MXX122		
				Wombwell Diesel Company (Dealer), Wombwell, Yorkshire after mechanical units had been removed at Stonebridge Garage for Ceylon Transport Board	05/69
RTL1400	522740	4610	MXX123		
				Wombwell Diesel Company (Dealer), Wombwell, Yorkshire after mechanical units had been removed at Stonebridge Garage for Ceylon Transport Board	04/69
RTL1401	522793	5052	MXX124		
				Pickersgill & Laverick (Dealer), Cudworth, Yorkshire	05/69
RTL1402	522742	4535	MXX125		
				Wombwell Diesel Company (Dealer), Wombwell, Yorkshire after mechanical units had been removed at Stonebridge Garage for Ceylon Transport Board	04/69
RTL1403	522820	2218	MXX126		
				Bird's Commercial Motors (Dealer), Stratford-upon-Avon, Warwickshire	03/59
				J.Laurie t/a Chieftain, Burnbank, Hamilton, Lanarkshire 45	04/59
				Central SMT Motherwell, Lanarkshire HL202 upon take over of Laurie's business	10/61
				E.Corocan (Dealer), Motherwell, Lanarkshire and scrapped	09/66
RTL1404	522797	4422	MXX127		
			23 sri 1501	Ceylon Transport Board, Colombo, Ceylon	02/65
RTL1405	522824	4569	MXX128		
			J 34656	Jersey Motor Transport Co. Ltd., St Helier, Jersey, Channel Islands 656	04/65
				Withdrawn	02/71
				Amos (Dealer), Ludlow, Shropshire	02/71
				National Car Parks, St. Pancras, London being converted to an office and painted blue and cream	by 03/71
				Removed from Phoenix Road National Car Park premises	by 05/72
				S.Twell (Dealer), Ingham, Lincolnshire, still with Jersey registration and partially converted to mobile caravan, but never used and scrapped	05/72
RTL1406	522822	2417	MXX129		
				Wombwell Diesel Company (Dealer), Wombwell, Yorkshire after mechanical units had been removed at Stonebridge Garage for Ceylon Transport Board	05/69
RTL1407	522826	5064	MXX130		
			23 sri 3273	Ceylon Transport Board, Colombo, Ceylon	08/68
				Still in existence but withdrawn	02/77
RTL1408	522821	5114	MXX215		
				Pickersgill & Laverick (Dealer), Cudworth, Yorkshire	05/69
RTL1409	522744	4619	MXX216		
			23 sri 1880	Ceylon Transport Board, Colombo, Ceylon	09/65
RTL1410	522795	5185	MXX217		
				Wombwell Diesel Company (Dealer), Wombwell, Yorkshire	06/69
RTL1411	522825	4515	MXX218		
			J 34657	Jersey Motor Transport Co. Ltd., St Helier, Jersey, Channel Islands 657	03/65
				Withdrawn	02/71
				Amos (Dealer), Ludlow, Shropshire	02/71
			VUK 374J	Harry's Coaches Limited, Cheltenham, Gloucestershire	09/71
				G.Lister (Dealer), Bolton	c03/72
				Merseyside Coachways Limited, Garston, Liverpool	06/73
				Licenced but never used	07/73
				G.Lister (Dealer), Bolton	07/73
				T.Walton, Sutton-on-Trent, Nottinghamshire for conversion to mobile workshop for racing team,. but work never carried out	01/74
				Unknown breaker, Carlton, Yorkshire	—/74
RTL1412	522892	4543	MXX219		
				Passenger Vehicle Sales (London) Ltd (Dealer), Upminster, Essex	05/69
				Autoyachts Ltd (Dealer), Gillingham, Kent	05/69
				Percey C. Mount Limited, (Farmer), Chartham. Kent	06/69
				Scott & Knowles (Farmer), Chatham, Kent	—/70
				Still there	04/78
				Gone	10/78
				Parked at Kingsnorth Trailers, Kingsnorth, Ashford, Kent	12/81
				Still there	12/84
				M. Biddell, Woodford Bridge, Essex, for preservation	by 01/87
				Still owned	04/98

RTL			Reg	History	Date
RTL1413	522800	4461	MXX220		
			22 sri 3283	Ceylon Transport Board, Colombo, Ceylon	03/59
RTL1414	522891	4700	NLE501		
			23 sri 3397	Ceylon Transport Board, Colombo, Ceylon	12/68
				Still in service	02/77
				Mobile Police Post, Colombo, painted blue and operated by Ceylon Transport Board on behalf of the authorities	by 12/81
RTL1415	522798	5050	NLE502		
			23 sri 3270	Ceylon Transport Board, Colombo, Ceylon	07/68
				Still in existence but withdrawn	02/77
RTL1416	522890	4650	NLE503		
			23 sri 3233	Ceylon Transport Board, Colombo, Ceylon	07/68
				Still in existence but withdrawn	02/77
RTL1417	522827	4518	NLE504		
			23 sri 1411	Ceylon Transport Board, Colombo, Ceylon	12/64
RTL1418	522823	4810	NLE505		
				Pickersgill & Laverick (Dealer), Cudworth, Yorkshire	05/69
RTL1419	522895	4577	NLE506		
			CA 125 277	City Tramways Co., Cape Town, South Africa 476	03/64
				Still in service	02/76
RTL1420	522893	5057	NLE507		
				Wombwell Diesel Company (Dealer), Wombwell, Yorkshire	05/69
RTL1421	522896	4666	NLE508		
			23 sri 1586	Ceylon Transport Board, Colombo, Ceylon	04/65
RTL1422	522894	2051	NLE509		
				Wombwell Diesel Company (Dealer), Wombwell, Yorkshire	05/69
RTL1423	524952	4656	NLE510		
				Pickersgill & Laverick (Dealer), Cudworth, Yorkshire	02/70
RTL1424	524953	5110	NLE511		
				Pickersgill & Laverick (Dealer), Cudworth, Yorkshire	06/69
RTL1425	524965	4847	NLE512		
				Wombwell Diesel Company (Dealer), Wombwell, Yorkshire	05/69
RTL1426	524996	4822	NLE513		
				Pickersgill & Laverick (Dealer), Cudworth, Yorkshire	05/69
RTL1427	524964	2086	NLE701		
				Passenger Vehicle Sales (London) Ltd (Dealer), Canvey Island, Essex	05/69
				Howard (Contractor) Gillingham, Kent	05/69
				Autoyachts Ltd. (Dealer), Gillingham, Kent	05/69
				H.B. Low (Fruit Grower), Barons Place, Mereworth, Kent	04/70
				Autoyachts Ltd. (Dealer), Gillingham, Kent	by 04/70
				1784 Preservation Group, Smith, et al, Purley for preservation	11/77
				Group renamed RTL1427 Preservation Group	—/—
				Group renamed Purley Transport Preservation Group	—/91
RTL1428	524998	5034	NLE702		
				Wombwell Diesel Company (Dealer), Wombwell, Yorkshire	11/69
RTL1429	530002	2411	NLE703		
				Pickersgill & Laverick (Dealer), Cudworth, Yorkshire	06/69
RTL1430	524997	5194	NLE704		
				Wombwell Diesel Company (Dealer), Wombwell, Yorkshire	11/69
RTL1431	530005	4463	NLE705		
				Bird's Commercial Motors (Dealer), Stratford-upon-Avon, Warwickshire	04/59
				J.Laurie t/a Chieftain, Burnbank, Hamilton, Lanarkshire 46	04/59
				Central SMT Motherwell, Lanarkshire HL203 upon take over of Laurie's business	10/61
				E.Corocan (Dealer), Motherwell, Lanarkshire and scrapped	09/66
RTL1432	530006	2395	NLE706		
				Wombwell Diesel Company (Dealer), Wombwell, Yorkshire	01/70
RTL1433	530003	4763	NLE707		
				Pickersgill & Laverick (Dealer), Cudworth, Yorkshire, after mechanical units had been removed at Stonebridge Garage for Ceylon Transport Board	06/69
RTL1434	530008	4418	NLE708		
			22 sri 3286	Ceylon Transport Board, Colombo, Ceylon	03/59
				In use as a rest room at Colombo bus station	by 04/81
RTL1435	530007	4771	NLE709		
				Mr Hawkins, London, SW2 and exported to Holland	04/68
				Lips Autotron Museum (Motor Museum), Drunen, Holland	06/68
				Still on display	06/90
				Europaclub disco, Bladel, Holland	by 08/95
				F.Kuyers, Biezenmortel, near Udenhout, Holland	c 03/96
				Still owned	06/96
RTL1436	530158	4604	NLE710		
				A.Magistretti, London SW1, for conversion to caravan for overseas holiday	05/68
RTL1437	530157	4883	NLE711		
				Pickersgill & Laverick (Dealer), Cudworth, Yorkshire	05/69

In August 1986 an unidentifiable RTL, now converted to a private lorry complete with a different fuel tank, is pictured in Colombo. Large numbers of these substantially built public service buses and coaches were put to further use after withdrawal but the task of identifying them was almost impossible, especially when they were reregistered but the wheel drums of this example give clue to its origins. (Alan Mortimer)

This rear ¾ view of RTL1515, together with other pictures clearly show that, except for the rebuilding carried out to the saloon side windows and panel area beneath, nothing else was altered. Revised brake light clusters, direction indicators together with uniform notices in the platform area and main front and rear blind boxes were applied to the vehicles. The pale green and blue lining out was added to the entire fleet of Sentosa Development Corporation RTLs and RTs. (Alan Mortimer)

The last resting place of RTL1364 was among the greenery within a scrap dealer's premises hidden away in a field at Fleggburgh, Norfolk. Some years after this picture was taken the site was cleared and one must assume the bus finally met its end. (John A.S. Hambley)

RTL1568 looks very impressive in its newer guise as a lorry, the conversion having been undertaken by the Ceylon Transport Board who also still own the vehicle. It was photographed in April 1981 at the company's Rathmalana premises the driver having very kindly placed the vehicle in position for the benefit of the photographer. In the background stand some newer-single deck buses but this half cab low slung fuel tank Leyland must surely be the depot's pride and joy. (Bruce Harris)

Wanneroo Lion Park near Perth, Western Australia is an unlikely setting to come across RTL547, owed by the Transport museum. It was used as a tour bus to roam the park as part of fund raising activities for the museum, this picture having been taken in January 1976. Having paused to allow passengers to feed the small group of donkeys in the area where less ferocious animals roam, no doubt the animals welcoming the sight of the big red bus as did Londoners in earlier years. (Alan Mortimer)

RTL1123, now with rebuilt opening window apertures to both decks, is seen running empty at Galle Face in January 1982. Further small alterations have been made to the external bodywork since the bus arrived in Ceylon and include the deletion of the life rail but not all the attaching brackets. An extra piece of metalwork has been added to the nearside corner of the lower deck front bulkhead in addition to an offside fog light and non-opening driver's windscreen. (Bruce Harris)

This amazing view with centre stage occupied by RTL281 was recorded for the historian of future years having been taken in January 1982. The location is Mount Lavinia, Sri Lanka with the local populace going about their everyday business which includes a bullock cart and driver making slow passage along the wide thoroughfare. Note how additional ventilation has been provided with a rebuilt window arrangement to the upper deck but the driver has to sweat it out even more so with the one piece front windscreen that now replaces the former opening unit. (Bruce Harris)

Viewed in Colombo during January 1982 and seen negotiating their Hyde Park Corner at speed is RTW365, having been a resident of Ceylon since December 1966. Following closely behind is one of the hundreds of Ashok Leyland Comets which mainly replaced the London vehicles much to the dismay of the enthusiasts who had visited the island in the previous two decades for the London flavour. (Bruce Harris)

This view of RTL579 with operator's fleet number 657 and local registration 732.802 mirrors the alterations to RTL506 but with the addition of a flashing direction indicator afixed to the driver's cab. It is parked within the grounds of the B.C. Hydro Hotel waiting for further use in June 1975. (Alan Mortimer)

A nearside view of well laden RTW365 clearly shows its use on service 138 and all the additional embellishments which now adorn the bus. All the photographs used in this book of the RTL and RTW classes in use in Ceylon (or Sri Lanka as it was from 1972) have one thing in common, which is the incredibly traffic free conditions on the wide thoroughfares. It is January 1982 and the private car is still in the minority in the High Street of Nugcgoda. (Bruce Harris)

With the removal panels to the air tank and battery carrier now permanently discarded RTL1219 still operates in service and is seen on route 166 to Pettah in October 1972 as it leaves central Colombo. The old colonial structure is known as Bogala Building looks somewhat out of place with the modern tower block which has been built alongside. The road side sign about to be passed by the bus looks intriguing, are there really headless pedestrians walking about? And how about the shop titled Elephant House, it doesn't really look large enough to house such an animal of those proportions. (Alan Mortimer)

A perfect example of the ingenuity before the 'use and throw away' era in which we now live had arrived. RTL448 is almost completely unrecognisable as a front entrance single deck bus except for the registration and unmistakable Leyland and London Transport pedigree of the front portion. Now owned by Elk Arc it is seen in service on the outskirts of Colombo in April 1981 with another British built product, in this case a 'Mini', seen travelling in the opposite direction and about to overtake a coach. (Bruce Harris)

Although this picture was taken in Colombo, Ceylon, in British fashion two buses come along at the same time, in this instance on service 138 to Pettah. The lead bus RTL1345 has now gained the classic CTB lean, caused by heavy loads of passengers occupying the staircase and rear platform for long periods of time. RTL1003 following manages to sit upright at the present time and appears in overall better condition. No exterior alterations except for the removal of the lower panel to the engine compartment and loss of the lifeguard have been made to either vehicle although they now operate in completely different climatic conditions. (Alan Mortimer)

The Sri Lankan vehicle scrap yard follows much the same as British lines but judging by this picture does overspill at times on to adjoining land. The remains of an RTL has its bones picked by the locals for useful parts or is it a piece of memorabilia that they are after? This sorry state of at least the chassis, now sitting on two brake drums at the front, was photographed in what was its last resting place in April 1981. (Bruce Harris)

Another view of RTL547 but this time complete with a lion sitting on the engine bonnet, not something which can be seen everyday. As a safety feature wire mesh is affixed to the drivers cab window and at the rear of the bus a swinging cage enclosed the platform area effectively keeping the passengers in and the animals out. An Australian correspondent has written to say that the bus is not in operation nowadays, residing within the depot at Whiteman Park, Perth. (Alan Mortimer)

RTL1438	530004	2061	NLE712		
				Pickersgill & Laverick (Dealer), Cudworth, Yorkshire	05/69
RTL1439	530010	4433	NLE713		
			22 sri 3285	Ceylon Transport Board, Colombo, Ceylon	03/59
RTL1440	530156	5099	NLE714		
				Pickersgill & Laverick (Dealer), Cudworth, Yorkshire, after mechanical units had been removed at Stonebridge Garage for Ceylon Transport Board	06/69
RTL1441	530204	4701	NLE715		
			23 sri 3246	Ceylon Transport Board, Colombo, Ceylon	07/68
				Still in existence but withdrawn	02/77
RTL1442	530206	5096	NLE716		
				Wombwell Diesel Company (Dealer), Wombwell, Yorkshire	05/69
RTL1443	530009	4775	NLE717		
				Wombwell Diesel Company (Dealer), Wombwell, Yorkshire	05/69
RTL1444	530207	4426	NLE718		
				Bird's Commercial Motors (Dealer), Stratford-upon-Avon, Warwickshire	03/59
				A.Hornsby (Primrose Coaches), Scunthorpe, Lincolnshire	03/59
				Withdrawn	05/70
				T.P.E. (Dealer) and scrapped	05/70
RTL1445	530215	5165	NLE719		
				Pickersgill & Laverick (Dealer), Cudworth, Yorkshire, after mechanical units had been removed at Stonebridge Garage for Ceylon Transport Board	06/69
RTL1446	530216	4779	NLE720		
				Pickersgill & Laverick (Dealer), Cudworth, Yorkshire	05/69
RTL1447	530208	5164	NLE721		
				Pickersgill & Laverick (Dealer), Cudworth, Yorkshire, after mechanical units had been removed at Stonebridge Garage for Ceylon Transport Board	06/69
RTL1448	530159	4554	NLE722		
				Gradeka Saobracaine Preduzece, Sarajevo, Yugoslavia	05/64
RTL1449	530205	4458	NLE723		
			23 sri 1496	Ceylon Transport Board, Colombo, Ceylon	02/65
RTL1450	530219	4447	NLE724		
				Bird's Commercial Motors (Dealer), Stratford-upon-Avon, Warwickshire	08/59
				J.Lloyd & Sons Limited, Nuneaton, Warwickshire	10/59
				Withdrawn after accident	06/65
				Scrapped	07/65
RTL1451	530217	4634	NLE725		
			CB 27024	Port Elizabeth Transport, South Africa 384	01/65
				Withdrawn	between 11/70 – 04/71
RTL1452	530209	4582	NLE726		
			23 sri 1523	Ceylon Transport Board, Colombo, Ceylon	02/65
RTL1453	530229	5084	NLE727		
				Passenger Vehicle Sales (London) Ltd (Dealer), Upminster, Essex	05/69
				On hire to Don Partridge and the Buskers (Pop Group)	05/69
				Broke down while on tour with mechanical failure at Leeds	05/69
				Martin & Sons (Dealer), Weaverham	05/69
				Pickersgill & Laverick (Dealer), Cudworth, for scrap	05/69
RTL1454	530234	4730	NLE728		
			CB 27022	Port Elizabeth Transport, South Africa 383	01/65
				Withdrawn and scrapped	02/70
RTL1455	530218	4456	NLE729		
			23 sri 1414	Ceylon Transport Board, Colombo, Ceylon	12/64
RTL1456	530230	2099	NLE730		
				Pickersgill & Laverick (Dealer), Cudworth, Yorkshire	05/69
RTL1457	530235	5156	NLE731		
				Wombwell Diesel Company (Dealer), Wombwell, Yorkshire	11/69
RTL1458	530231	5083	NLE732		
				Wombwell Diesel Company (Dealer), Wombwell, Yorkshire	05/69
RTL1459	530220	8343	NLE733		
				Wombwell Diesel Company (Dealer), Wombwell, Yorkshire	04/69
RTL1460	530236	5066	NLE734		
				Wombwell Diesel Company (Dealer), Wombwell, Yorkshire	05/69
RTL1461	530233	4552	NLE735		
			23 sri 1585	Ceylon Transport Board, Colombo, Ceylon	04/65
RTL1462	530238	2430	NLE736		
			23 sri 3254	Ceylon Transport Board, Colombo, Ceylon	07/68
RTL1463	530232	5157	NLE737		
				A.Harling,t/a Harlings Coaches, Waterloo, London, SE1	11/64
				Not used	
				Unknown breakers, Barnsley, Yorkshire	by 05/69

With two Morris Minors following RTL43 is seen in the lower picture with its original rear platform and in the upper view in its rebuilt form to front entrance layout. The driver's windscreen together with the upstairs front windows have been replaced by one piece examples while other detail changes have been made which all add up to make this a unique vehicle. Thankfully the bus is currently preserved and one day will be the highlight of many a rally.
(F. W. Ivey and K. Lane)

RTL1464	530237	4431	NLE738		
				Bird's Commercial Motors (Dealer), Stratford-upon-Avon, Warwickshire	03/59
				J.Laurie t/a Chieftain, Burnbank, Hamilton, Lanarkshire 47	04/59
				Central SMT Motherwell, Lanarkshire HL204 upon take over of Laurie's business	10/61
				E.Corocan (Dealer), Motherwell, Lanarkshire, and scrapped	09/66
RTL1465	530241	5193	NLE739		
				Bird's Commercial Motors (Dealer), Stratford-upon-Avon, Warwickshire	04/69
RTL1466	530239	4403	NLE751		
			22 sri 3287	Ceylon Transport Board, Colombo, Ceylon	03/59
RTL1467	530242	3507	NLE752		
			23 sri 3402	Ceylon Transport Board, Colombo, Ceylon	12/68
RTL1468	530240	4450	NLE753		
			CA 134 467	Golden Arrow Bus Service, Capetown, South Africa 227	12/64
				Overturned, withdrawn and dismantled	05/65
RTL1469	532672	4572	NXP955		
			23 sri 1522	Ceylon Transport Board, Colombo, Ceylon	02/65
RTL1470	532617	4808	NXP956		
				Walsall Corporation Transport, Walsall, Staffordshire 202	08/59
				Withdrawn	02/68
				Unknown Dealer, Barnsley, Yorkshire	05/68
RTL1471	532693	4780	NXP957		
				Wombwell Diesel Company (Dealer), Wombwell, Yorkshire	05/69
RTL1472	532680	4747	NXP958		
			22 SRI 3251	Ceylon Transport Board, Colombo, Ceylon	03/59
RTL1473	532732	4977	NXP959		
			23 SRI 2042	Ceylon Transport Board, Colombo, Ceylon	12/65
RTL1474	532679	5326	NXP960		
			23 SRI 2019	Ceylon Transport Board, Colombo, Ceylon	12/65
RTL1475	532731	2118	OLD571		
				Pickersgill & Laverick (Dealer), Cudworth, Yorkshire	05/69
RTL1476	540004	3506	OLD572		
			23 SRI 2020	Ceylon Transport Board, Colombo, Ceylon	12/65
				Still in existence, unlicenced	02/77
			27 SRI 8486	Sold as a private lorry	07/80
RTL1477	540002	5277	OLD573		
			CA 134 701	City Tramways Co., Cape Town, South Africa 730	05/65
				Converted to front entrance retaining rear staircase	by 04/74
				Still in service	02/76

A further RTL eventually to enter the preservation movement is RTL48, which first saw service with F. Lockey & Sons of West Auckland after its years spent with London Transport. It is seen here with very clear and readable route details having just passed some decidedly strong purpose built passenger shelters and still to journey past the well stocked window display of a local stationery and newsagent on the corner of Chester Street, Bishop Auckland. Of special interest is the cigarette machine attached to the wall, a type of vending machine now only seen inside secure premises.
(Alan Mortimer)

At the Ardrossan terminus RTL135 displays the triangular shaped blind box with which quite a number of ex-London vehicles were equipped over the years. This particular bus was the property of McKinnon, Kilmarnock, part of the A1 Service of bus operators and was in use from January 1959 although its eventual withdrawal and fate has not come to be documented yet. (K. Lane)

RTL1478	540003	5325	OLD574		
			CA 140 509	City Tramways Co., Cape Town, South Africa 737	06/65
				Withdrawn	by 11/70
				Scrapped	11/70
RTL1479	540005	4856	OLD575		
				Barton Transport Limited , Chilwell, Nottinghamshire 1036	01/66
				Withdrawn	08/71
				Unidentified owner	09/71
RTL1480	532733	4796	OLD576		
			23 SRI 1573	Ceylon Transport Board, Colombo, Ceylon	04/65
RTL1481	540006	5220	OLD590		
			23 SRI 1579	Ceylon Transport Board, Colombo, Ceylon	04/65
RTL1482	540009	4807	OLD591		
				Barton Transport Limited, Chilwell, Nottinghamshire 1032	12/65
				Withdrawn	08/71
				Fisher & Ford (Dealer), Royston, Barnsley	08/71
RTL1483	532743	4865	OLD592		
				Barton Transport Limited, Chilwell, Nottinghamshire 1037	01/66
				Withdrawn	08/71
				Fisher & Ford (Dealer), Calton	09/71
RTL1484	540010	4954	OLD593		
			CA 58705	City Tramways Co., Cape Town, South Africa 753	09/65
				Still in service renumbered 0753	04/74
RTL1485	540012	3496	OLD594		
				Passenger Vehicle Sales (London) Ltd (Dealer), Upminster, Essex	06/66
				Barton Transport Limited, Chilwell, Nottinghamshire 1047	06/66
				Withdrawn	02/68
				W.J. Lowndes Draycott Metals, (Dealer), Spondon, Derbyshire for scrap	02/68
RTL1486	540008	3504	OLD595		
				Passenger Vehicle Sales (London) Ltd (Dealer), Upminster, Essex	01/66
				Barton Transport Limited, Chilwell, Nottinghamshire 1042	01/66
				Withdrawn	09/68
				W.J. Lowndes Draycott Metals, (Dealer), Spondon, Derbyshire for scrap	09/68
RTL1487	540011	3503	OLD596		
				Walsall Corporation Transport, Walsall, Staffordshire 203	08/59
				West Midlands PTE (Northern Division) 203L	10/69
				Withdrawn	06/71
				Wombwell Diesel Company (Dealer), Wombwell, Yorkshire	11/71

RTL1488	540013	3425	OLD597

Passenger Vehicle Sales (London) Ltd (Dealer), Upminster, Essex	06/66
Barton Transport Limited, Chilwell, Nottinghamshire 1048	06/66
Withdrawn	03/71
B.S.Russell, Sutton Coldfield, Warwickshire	04/71
Withdrawn	10/71

RTL1489	540014	4892	OLD598

Passenger Vehicle Sales (London) Ltd (Dealer), Upminster, Essex	01/66
Barton Transports Limited, Chilwell, Nottinghamshire 1044	01/66
Withdrawn	02/68
W.J. Lowndes Draycott Metals, (Dealer), Spondon, Derbyshire for scrap	02/68

RTL1490	540007	3513	OLD599
		22 sri 1600	Ceylon Transport Board, Colombo, Ceylon 04/58
RTL1491	540017	4835	OLD600
		23 sri 2021	Ceylon Transport Board, Colombo, Ceylon 12/65
RTL1492	540016	4973	OLD601

Walsall Corporation Transport, Walsall, Staffordshire 204	08/59
West Midlands PTE, (Northern Division) 204L	10/69
Withdrawn	09/71
Wombwell Diesel Company (Dealer), Wombwell, Yorkshire	12/71

RTL1493	540271	3427	OLD602

Passenger Vehicle Sales (London) Ltd (Dealer), Upminster, Essex	04/66
Barton Transport Limited, Chilwell, Nottinghamshire 1044	04/66
Withdrawn	02/68
W.J.Lowndes Draycott Metals, (Dealer), Spondon, Derbyshire, for scrap	02/68

RTL1494	540015	4970	OLD603

Walsall Corporation Transport, Walsall, Staffordshire 205	08/59
Withdrawn	02/68
Unknown Dealer, Barnsley, Yorkshire	02/68

RTL1495	540272	3468	OLD604
		23 sri 2001	Ceylon Transport Board, Colombo, Ceylon 11/65
RTL1496	540293	5274	OLD605
		23 sri 1904	Ceylon Transport Board, Colombo, Ceylon 09/65
RTL1497	540281	3421	OLD606
		22 sri 1604	Ceylon Transport Board, Colombo, Ceylon 04/58
RTL1498	540322	5331	OLD607
		23 sri 1905	Ceylon Transport Board, Colombo, Ceylon 09/65
RTL1499	540436	3663	OLD608

Pickersgill & Laverick (Dealer), Cudworth, Yorkshire	02/70

RTL1500	540321	5309	OLD609
		23 sri 1882	Ceylon Transport Board, Colombo, Ceylon 09/65

RTL1050 is seen in Braintree, Essex on the 28th June 1969 some considerable distance from its usual haunts of Richmond, Surrey where it was used on route 235 which had been surrendered by London Transport in 1966. Very informative route information is carried making excellent use of all the areas as originally intended, but of somewhat confusing value to the people of Braintree. (John G.S. Smith)

RTL1501	540292	4938	OLD610			
			CA 140 514	City Tramways Co., Cape Town, South Africa 742		07/65
				Converted to front entrance retaining rear staircase		by 04/74
				Still in service		02/76
RTL1502	540282	3607	OLD611			
				Wombwell Diesel Company (Dealer), Wombwell, Yorkshire		11/69
RTL1503	540457	5327	OLD612			
			CA´140 515	City Tramways Co., Cape Town, South Africa 743		08/65
RTL1504	540466	4983	OLD613			
			23 sri 2022	Ceylon Transport Board, Colombo, Ceylon		12/65
RTL1505	540456	3601	OLD614			
			J 8633	Jersey Motor Transport Co. Ltd., St Helier, Jersey, Channel Islands 14		03/59
				Withdrawn and in store		—/74
				E.Brakell, (Omnibus Sales), London		11/74
				Singapore Port Authority, Singapore as agent		06/75
			PB 41 G	Sentoza Development Corporation 25 and used on Tourist services on Sentoza Island		06/75
				Withdrawn and placed on the sea bed off the Islands lagoon for use as fish breeding grounds		12/80
RTL1506	540437	3911	OLD615			
			23 sri 3188	Ceylon Transport Board, Colombo, Ceylon		04/68
RTL1507	540630	3725	OLD616			
				Bird's Commercial Motors (Dealer), Stratford-upon-Avon, Warwickshire		12/69
				Unknown owner		—/70
				Saunders, Redditch, Worcestershire, as a caravan		by 11/71
				Bird's Commercial Motors (Dealer), Stratford-upon-Avon, Warwickshire		10/74
RTL1508	540639	4942	OLD617			
			23 sri 2060	Ceylon Transport Board, Colombo, Ceylon		01/66
RTL1509	540519	5942	OLD618			
				Passenger Vehicle Sales (London) Ltd (Dealer), Silver End, Essex		04/69
				Allan Pond Limited t/a Pond's Coaches, Roydon Hamlet, Essex		04/69
				W.J.McIntyre t/a Golden Boy Coaches, Roydon Hamlet, Essex		by 05/70
				Withdrawn		09/71
				Passenger Vehicle Sales (London) Ltd (Dealer), Silver End,. Essex		09/71
				P.Sykes (Dealer), Worsborough Dale, Yorkshire for scrap		09/71
RTL1510	540663	3527	OLD619			
			22 sri 1592	Ceylon Transport Board, Colombo, Ceylon		04/58
RTL1511	540670	5752	OLD620			
				J.Cooper, London N16 used as "Birds Paradise" a mobile boutique 1		05/67
				Orange & blue livery on west of England tour		
				Withdrawn		—/75
RTL1512	540664	5972	OLD621			
				Wombwell Diesel Company (Dealer), Wombwell, Yorkshire		01/70
RTL1513	540687	5961	OLD622			
				Wombwell Diesel Company (Dealer), Wombwell, Yorkshire		10/69
RTL1514	540671	3678	OLD623			
				Bird's Commercial Motors (Dealer), Stratford-upon-Avon, Warwickshire		01/70
RTL1515	540695	3525	OLD624			
			J 8683	Jersey Motor Transport Co. Ltd., St Helier, Jersey, Channel Islands 17		03/59
				Withdrawn		09/71
				E.Brakell, T.Robertson, T.Hornby, Cheam, Surrey for preservation		10/72
				E.H.Brakell, (Omnibus Sales), London		—/—
				Singapore Port Authority, Singapore as agent		06/75
			PB 35A	Sentoza Development Corporation 22 and used on a Tourist services on Sentoza Island		06/75
				Still in service		03/79
				Placed on the sea bed off the Island's lagoon for use as fish breeding grounds		12/80
RTL1516	540688	4889	OLD625			
			CA 140 510	City Tramways Co., Cape Town, South Africa 738		07/65
				Still in service		04/74
RTL1517	540696	3501	OLD626			
			23 sri 2160	Ceylon Transport Board, Colombo, Ceylon		03/66
RTL1518	540708	3552	OLD627			
				Bird's Commercial Motors (Dealer), Stratford-upon-Avon, Warwickshire		05/69
				Carlton Bingo, Leicester, Leics		by 09/69
RTL1519	540725	4920	OLD628			
				Pickersgill & Laverick (Dealer), Cudworth, Yorkshire		02/70
RTL1520	540716	3446	OLD629			
			23 sri 2002	Ceylon Transport Board, Colombo, Ceylon		11/65
RTL1521	540726	5285	OLD630			
			23 sri 1890	Ceylon Transport Board, Colombo, Ceylon		09/65
RTL1522	540735	5287	OLD631			
			23 sri 1898	Ceylon Transport Board, Colombo, Ceylon		09/65
RTL1523	540734	3502	OLD632			
			23 sri 2100	Ceylon Transport Board, Colombo, Ceylon		01/66

RTL523 carrying fleet number 2 is seen at the bus station situated on the sea front at St. Helier, Jersey waiting to depart on route number 1 which will take visitors near to Mount Orgueil Castle. Note the inscription above the lower deck saloon windows which reads 'Five day Rover Ticket 22/6d. Choose your days, any five from seven', complete freedom of the Island for as little as £1.12½p. (John Gascoine)

RTL1524	540745	5300	OLD633		
			23 sri 2023	Ceylon Transport Board, Colombo, Ceylon	12/65
RTL1525	540746	5979	OLD634		
				Wombwell Diesel Company (Dealer), Wombwell, Yorkshire	06/69
RTL1526	540753	3700	OLD635		
				Wombwell Diesel Company (Dealer), Wombwell, Yorkshire after mechanical units had been removed at Stonebridge Garage for Ceylon Transport Board	01/70
RTL1527	540754	3526	OLD636		
			22 sri 1612	Ceylon Transport Board, Colombo, Ceylon	04/58
RTL1528	540769	3673	OLD637		
				Wombwell Diesel Company (Dealer), Wombwell, Yorkshire	05/69
RTL1529	540770	3632	OLD638		
				Wombwell Diesel Company (Dealer), Wombwell, Yorkshire	11/69
RTL1530	540762	5286	OLD639		
			23 sri 1957	Ceylon Transport Board, Colombo, Ceylon	10/65
			24 sri 8216	Rebuilt as a CTB service lorry	—/—
				Noted being scrapped	04/81
RTL1531	540761	3703	OLD640		
				Wombwell Diesel Company (Dealer), Wombwell, Yorkshire	12/69
RTL1532	540777	3615	OLD641		
			23 sri 2172	Ceylon Transport Board, Colombo, Ceylon	03/66
RTL1533	540778	5250	OLD642		
			23 sri 1952	Ceylon Transport Board, Colombo, Ceylon	10/65
RTL1534	540788	3564	OLD643		
				Pickersgill & Laverick (Dealer), Cudworth, Yorkshire	02/70
				P.Sykes (Breaker), Barnsley, Yorkshire and partly scrapped	05/70
RTL1535	540791	4900	OLD644		
			23 sri 1885	Ceylon Transport Board, Colombo, Ceylon	09/65
RTL1536	540789	5345	OLD645		
				Wombwell Diesel Company (Dealer), Wombwell, Yorkshire	12/69
RTL1537	540792	5336	OLD646		
				Barton Transport Limited, Chilwell, Nottinghamshire 1033	12/65
				Withdrawn	10/70
				Unidentified dealer for scrap	01/71
RTL1538	540799	3500	OLD647		
			22 sri 1591	Ceylon Transport Board, Colombo, Ceylon	04/58
RTL1539	540814	3515	OLD648		
				Barton Transport Limited, Chilwell, Nottinghamshire. 1034	12/65
				Withdrawn after low bridge accident	06/67
				W.E.Andrews for use by Boy Scouts , engineless at premises bedside a canal in Nottingham	11/67
				Located at rear of Derry & Son, Nottingham as a storeshed, still used by the same scout troop	by 06/69
				Still there with water tank fitted to roof.	07/70
RTL1540	540815	3497	OLD649		
				Passenger Vehicle Sales (London) Ltd (Dealer), Upminster, Essex	10/65
				A1 Service, (T.Hunter, Kilmarnock), Ardrossan, Ayrshire	10/65
				Still owned and being used for spares	01/68
				Frews, (Breakers), Kilmarnock	c09/69
RTL1541	540807	5339	OLD650		
			23 sri 1907	Ceylon Transport Board, Colombo, Ceylon	09/65
RTL1542	540800	5344	OLD651		
			23 sri 2082	Ceylon Transport Board, Colombo, Ceylon	01/66
RTL1543	540862	3660	OLD652		
			23 sri 2043	Ceylon Transport Board, Colombo, Ceylon	12/65
RTL1544	540821	5971	OLD653		
				Wombwell Diesel Company (Dealer), Wombwell, Yorkshire	11/69
RTL1545	540883	5324	OLD654		
				Wombwell Diesel Company (Dealer), Wombwell, Yorkshire	05/69
RTL1546	540876	5408	OLD655		
			23 sri 1617	Ceylon Transport Board, Colombo, Ceylon	04/65
				Still in existence but withdrawn	02/77
RTL1547	540827	3572	OLD656		
				Wombwell Diesel Company (Dealer), Wombwell, Yorkshire after mechanical units had been removed at Stonebridge Garage for Ceylon Transport Board	04/69
RTL1548	540835	3662	OLD657		
				Wombwell Diesel Company (Dealer), Wombwell, Yorkshire	11/69
RTL1549	540836	3616	OLD658		
				M.R.Bruneau, La Praine, Six Fours-Les-Plages, France	05/69
				Seen at the Grand Prix de France motor race at the Paul Ricard Circuit, Le Castellet as a mobile dinining room "Bibo's Restaurant"	—/72
RTL1550	540882	4888	OLD659		
			23 sri 1968	Ceylon Transport Board, Colombo, Ceylon	10/65

RTL1551	540875	9156	OLD660		
				Wombwell Diesel Company (Dealer), Wombwell, Yorkshire after mechanical units	
				had been removed at Stonebridge Garage for Ceylon Transport Board	04/69
RTL1552	540848	3576	OLD661		
				Wombwell Diesel Company (Dealer), Wombwell, Yorkshire	11/69
RTL1553	540897	3417	OLD662		
			CA 10866	City Tramways Co., Cape Town, South Africa 747	08/65
				Still in service	04/74
RTL1554	540891	5363	OLD663		
				Wombwell Diesel Company (Dealer), Wombwell, Yorkshire	11/69
RTL1555	540907	3549	OLD664		
				Passenger Vehicle Sales (London) Ltd (Dealer), Silver End, Essex	04/69
				Alan Pond Limited t/a Pond's Coaches Limited, Roydon Hamlet, Essex	04/69
				W.J.McIntrye t/a Golden Boy Coaches, Roydon Hamlet, Essex	by 05/70
				Passenger Vehicle Sales (London) Ltd (Dealer), Silver End, Essex	09/71
				P.Sykes (Dealer), Worsborough Dale, Yorkshire for scrap	09/71
RTL1556	540845	3586	OLD665		
				Camplins European Catering Company, London SW9, as a catering unit	03/69
				Organisation moved to SE22	02/73
				Organisation moved to Sutton, Surrey	10/76
				Withdrawn	09/77
				Sold	03/78
				E.Brakell (Dealer), Cheam, Surrey	10/82
RTL1557	540844	9216	OLD666		
				Kingsbury Motors Hire Limited, London NW9, for film and advertising work	06/68
				Used in film "The Husbands"	06/69
				With fictitious fleet number RTL557 was burnt out for episode of ITV 'On the Buses'	09/71
				Chassis dumped on Kingsbury Motors premises	01/72
RTL1558	540898	5955	OLD777		
				Wombwell Diesel Company (Dealer), Wombwell, Yorkshire	12/69
RTL1559	540890	3613	OLD778		
				Wombwell Diesel Company (Dealer), Wombwell, Yorkshire	12/69
RTL1560	540918	3604	OLD779		
				Bird's Commercial Motors (Dealer), Stratford-upon-Avon, Warwickshire	01/70
RTL1561	540849	3701	OLD780		
				Wombwell Diesel Company (Dealer), Wombwell, Yorkshire	11/69
RTL1562	540950	3786	OLD781		
				Bird's Commercial Motors (Dealer), Stratford-upon-Avon, Warwickshire	01/70
RTL1563	540820	9148	OLD782		
			23 sri 3423	Ceylon Transport Board, Colombo, Ceylon	12/68
				Still in existence but withdrawn	02/77
RTL1564	540908	3916	OLD783		
			23 sri 3186	Ceylon Transport Board, Colombo, Ceylon	04/68
RTL1565	540919	5347	OLD784		
				Passenger Vehicle Sales (London) Ltd (Dealer), Upminster, Essex	08/66
				Barton Transport Limited, Chilwell, Nottinghamshire 1083	08/66
				Withdrawn	03/71
				Amos (Dealer), Onibury, Ludlow	04/71
				L & N.D.Rennies t/a Lion and Comfort Coaches, Dunfermline	06/71
				Withdrawn and returned to Amos	09/71
				Harry's Coaches Limited, Cheltenham, Gloucestershire	12/71
				Withdrawn after low bridge accident at Bishops Cleeve	01/73
				G.Lister (Dealer), Bolton	02/73
RTL1566	540940	3612	OLD785		
				Wombwell Diesel Company (Dealer), Wombwell, Yorkshire	11/69
RTL1567	540941	3583	OLD786		
				Wombwell Diesel Company (Dealer), Wombwell, Yorkshire	05/69
RTL1568	540931	9153	OLD787		
			23 sri 3124	Ceylon Transport Board, Colombo, Ceylon	11/67
				Still in existence now fitted with a Leyland 0680 Power Plus engine	02/77
				Rebuilt as a CTB half cab lorry	by 04/81
				Noted at CTB Ratmalana depot	04/81
RTL1569	540959	3534	OLD788		
				Passenger Vehicle Sales (London) Ltd (Dealer), Upminster, Essex	08/67
				Used on a shuttle service to and from the British Fair at the Canadian National Exhibition grounds	
				during a British week in Toronto, Ontario, Canada	10/67
				British Promotions, Boston, Massachusetts, USA	10/67
				Hired by McGinn Bus Company, Lynn, Near Boston	by 12/67
				Hired by Back Bay Merchants Association for free shoppers' service	12/68
				In use as a boutique bus	04/69
				B.A. Stockton, Stockton Motors (Dealer), Huntsville, Alabama	04/69
				Bill's Inc, 2006 S.Parkway, Huntsville for continued use as a boutique bus	04/69

With a background of various types of other road transport RTL1174 rests at its owners Spittalfield garage on the 26th July 1969. The chassis has obviously recently received a respray with silver coloured paint but it is a pity that the radiator shell has been degraded with a paint finish in line with the operators darker colour. The date of fitting the platform doors is unknown but their inclusion is a welcome addition for its operation so far north. (A.R. Packer)

From left to right RTL754, RTW371 and RTL1000 are seen in the yard of W. north, Sherburn-in-Elmet in the final months before all were broken up in February 1966. The RTW has last been used as a learner bus with London Transport, being garaged at Garston which accounts for the Green Line 'London' blind fitted in the destination box. (John Gascoine)

RTL1570	541000	3904	OLD789		
			23 sri 3187	Ceylon Transport Board, Colombo, Ceylon	04/68
RTL1571	540861	6067	OLD790		
				Passenger Vehicle Sales (London) Ltd (Dealer), Upminster, Essex	03/67
				Barton Transport Limited, Chilwell, Nottinghamshire 1089	04/69
				Withdrawn	08/69
				East Midlands Transport Society, cut down to panalless single decker	08/70
				Broken up as means of raising funds from sale of scrap	09/70
RTL1572	541008	9154	OLD791		
				Passenger Vehicle Sales (London) Ltd (Dealer), Upminster, Essex	08/67
				"1800 Restaurant",. Boston, Massachusetts, USA	12/67
				Heavily vandalised and sold	08/70
				Noted derelict in a contractor's yard in East Boston	01/71
RTL1573	540949	5964	OLD792		
				Pickersgill & Laverick (Dealer), Cudworth, Yorkshire	02/70
RTL1574	541057	5984	OLD793		
				Wombwell Diesel Company (Dealer), Wombwell, Yorkshire	06/69
RTL1575	540828	9147	OLD794		
				Wombwell Diesel Company (Dealer), Wombwell, Yorkshire after mechanical units	
				had been removed at Stonebridge Garage for Ceylon Transport Board	04/69
RTL1576	540808	9150	OLD795		
			23 sri 3375	Ceylon Transport Board, Colombo, Ceylon	12/68
RTL1577	540990	9160	OLD796		
				Passenger Vehicle Sales (London) Ltd (Dealer), Canvey Island, Essex	12/67
				Barton Transport Limited, Chilwell, Nottinghamshire 1111	12/67
				Withdrawn	03/72
				Unidentified dealer, Long Eaton, as a store shed	—/72
				Scrapped	by —/84
RTL1578	540978	5990	OLD797		
				Wombwell Diesel Company (Dealer), Wombwell, Yorkshire after mechanical units	
				had been removed at Stonebridge Garage for Ceylon Transport Board	12/69
RTL1579	541122	3593	OLD798		
				Pickersgill & Laverick (Dealer), Cudworth, Yorkshire	02/70
RTL1580	540979	4958	OLD799		
				Bird's Commercial Motors (Dealer), Stratford-upon-Avon, Warwickshire	01/70

The first RT family chassis manufactured by Leyland was used as the basis for RTL501 entering service in June 1948. Still fitted with its original Park Royal body when disposed of, even after two overhauls while in the ownership of London Transport, it is now seen at Saltcoats on the 28th July 1964 minus its roof route box. An interesting comparison can be made of the style and application of the fleet name when this print is compared to that of RTL883 which appears elsewhere in the book. (A.R. Packer)

RTL1581	540999	9151	OLD800			
					Burnt out 16/6/58 at Clay Hall Garage	
					Chassis scrapped	11/58
					Body dismantled at Aldenham	11/58
RTL1582	541058	3585	OLD801			
					Bird's Commercial Motors (Dealer), Stratford-upon-Avon, Warwickshire	01/70
RTL1583	541094	3592	OLD802			
					Wombwell Diesel Company (Dealer), Wombwell, Yorkshire	11/69
RTL1584	541149	3686	OLD803			
					Wombwell Diesel Company (Dealer), Wombwell, Yorkshire	12/69
RTL1585	541084	4919	OLD804			
					Pickersgill & Laverick (Dealer), Cudworth, Yorkshire	02/70
RTL1586	540989	3658	OLD805			
					Wombwell Diesel Company (Dealer), Wombwell, Yorkshire	11/69
RTL1587	541047	9161	OLD806			
				23 sri 3388	Ceylon Transport Board, Colombo, Ceylon	12/68
					Still in existence but withdrawn	02/77
RTL1588	541123	3449	OLS807			
					Pickersgill & Laverick (Dealer), Cudworth, Yorkshire	02/70
RTL1589	541148	6042	OLD808			
					Pickersgill & Laverick (Dealer), Cudworth, Yorkshire, after mechanical units had been removed at Stonebridge Garage for Ceylon Transport Board	06/69
RTL1590	541074	3630	OLD809			
					Pickersgill & Laverick (Dealer), Cudworth, Yorkshire	02/70
RTL1591	541095	5953	OLD810			
					Wombwell Diesel Company (Dealer), Wombwell, Yorkshire after mechanical units had been removed at Stonebridge Garage for Ceylon Transport Board	12/69
RTL1592	541457	5977	OLD811			
					Wombwell Diesel Company (Dealer), Wombwell, Yorkshire	11/69
RTL1593	541139	5312	OLD812			
				23 sri 1967	Ceylon Transport Board, Colombo, Ceylon	10/65
RTL1594	541454	5346	OLD814			
					Wombwell Diesel Company (Dealer), Wombwell, Yorkshire	04/69
RTL1595	541163	3434	OLD815			
				23 sri 2097	Ceylon Transport Board, Colombo, Ceylon	01/66

RTL16 in company with a Yeates bodied coach now looks slightly forlorn as it resides on the grass, standing next to a building clad in corrugated material. Stephenson Bros. of High Etherley had acquired the vehicle in August 1958 and withdrew it from service in December 1966 and it was then used as a means for providing spare parts.

RTL1596	541073	3578	OLD816		
				Wombwell Diesel Company (Dealer), Wombwell, Yorkshire after mechanical units had been removed at Stonebridge Garage for Ceylon Transport Board	11/69
RTL1597	541138	3580	OLD817		
				Wombwell Diesel Company (Dealer), Wombwell, Yorkshire	12/69
RTL1598	541481	5232	OLD818		
			23 sri 1891	Ceylon Transport Board, Colombo, Ceylon	09/65
RTL1599	541515	3713	OLD819		
				Wombwell Diesel Company (Dealer), Wombwell, Yorkshire after mechanical units had been removed at Stonebridge Garage for Ceylon Transport Board	12/69
RTL1600	541514	4713	OLD820		
				Harper Bros,. Heath Hayes, Cannock, Staffordshire 7	06/65
				Involved in an accident and received the MCW body from another RTL of Harpers	—/66
				Harper Bros., taken over by Midland Red and now operating on Hire to Midland Red	09/74
				Withdrawn	10/74
				Longbridge Engineering (Dealer), Longbridge	—/75
RTL1601	540467	3704	OLD536		
				Wombwell Diesel Company (Dealer), Wombwell, Yorkshire	11/69
RTL1602	540495	5368	OLD831		
				Wombwell Diesel Company (Dealer), Wombwell, Yorkshire	10/69
RTL1603	540715	3642	OLD832		
				Pickersgill & Laverick (Dealer), Cudworth, Yorkshire	02/70
RTL1604	540473	5960	OLD833		
				Pickersgill & Laverick (Dealer), Cudworth, Yorkshire	02/70
RTL1605	540709	9140	OLD834		
			23 sri 3386	Ceylon Transport Board, Colombo, Ceylon	12/68
RTL1606	540496	5247	OLD835		
			23 sri 1955	Ceylon Transport Board, Colombo, Ceylon	10/65
RTL1607	540472	3776	OLD836		
				Wombwell Diesel Company (Dealer), Wombwell, Yorkshire	05/69
RTL1608	540640	5268	OLD837		
			23 sri 1969	Ceylon Transport Board, Colombo, Ceylon	10/65
RTL1609	540518	3428	OLD838		
			23 sri 2052	Ceylon Transport Board, Colombo, Ceylon	12/65
RTL1610	540960	3735	OLD839		
				Wombwell Diesel Company (Dealer), Wombwell, Yorkshire	12/69
RTL1611	541085	3635	OLD840		
				Pickersgill & Laverick (Dealer), Cudworth, Yorkshire	02/70
RTL1612	541009	3715	OLD841		
			23 sri 2024	Ceylon Transport Board, Colombo, Ceylon	12/65
				Still in existence but withdrawn	02/77
RTL1613	541256	5982	OLD842		
				Pickersgill & Laverick (Dealer), Cudworth, Yorkshire	02/70
RTL1614	540930	3573	OLD843		
				Wombwell Diesel Company (Dealer), Wombwell, Yorkshire after mechanical units had been removed at Stonebridge Garage for Ceylon Transport Board	12/69
RTL1615	540631	5322	OLD844		
			23 sri 1906	Ceylon Transport Board, Colombo, Ceylon	09/65
RTL1616	541017	3685	OLD845		
				Empress Cleaning Services (Ilford) Limited, Barkingside, Essex	12/68
				Withdrawn after accident	12/68
				Dumped out of use at rear of Marconi Factory, Basildon, Essex	03/71
RTL1617	541018	3466	OLD846		
			23 sri 1887	Ceylon Transport Board, Colombo, Ceylon	09/65
RTL1618	541164	5962	OLD847		
				Passenger Vehicle Sales (London) Ltd (Dealer), Upminster, Essex	06/66
				Barton Transport Limited, Chilwell, Nottinghamshire 1046	06/66
				Withdrawn	08/71
				Fisher & Ford (Dealer), Carlton	09/71
RTL1619	541241	5333	OLD848		
				Pickersgill & Laverick (Dealer), Cudworth, Yorkshire	02/70
RTL1620	541242	3859	OLD849		
			23 sri 3387	Ceylon Transport Board, Colombo, Ceylon	12/68
				Still in use now fitted with a Leyland 0680 Power Plus engine, numbered RL92	04/81
RTL1621	541474	3745	OLD850		
				Passenger Vehicle Sales (London) Ltd (Dealer), Upminster, Essex	03/67
				Hadley, Quarry Bank, Staffordshire,	04/67
				Withdrawn and sold for scrap	08/67
				Gordon (Breakers), Amblecote	08/67
RTL1622	541456	3792	OLD851		
			23 sri 3185	Ceylon Transport Board, Colombo, Ceylon	04/68

RTL1623	541455	9223	OLD852		
				Wombwell Diesel Company (Dealer), Wombwell, Yorkshire after mechanical units had been removed at Stonebridge Garage for Ceylon Transport Board	04/69
RTL1624	541264	3781	OLD853		
			23 sri 3160	Ceylon Transport Board, Colombo, Ceylon	12/67
RTL1625	541048	3661	OLD854		
				Wombwell Diesel Company (Dealer), Wombwell, Yorkshire	11/69
RTL1626	541483	9226	OLD855		
				Passenger Vehicle Sales (London) Ltd (Dealer), Upminster, Essex	08/67
				Leyland Motors Ltd (Dealers), London W1	08/67
				Exported to USA	—/—
				Royal Coach Motor Hotels, Dallas, Texas as a courtesy bus	by 01/71
				Later open top, in unknown scrapyard	—/—
				Friendze Stores Inc., Abeline, Texas	by 05/95
				Still in use	05/98
RTL1627	541257	3561	OLD856		
				Bird's Commercial Motors (Dealer), Stratford-upon-Avon, Warwickshire	01/70
RTL1628	541265	9170	OLD857		
				Passenger Vehicle Sales (London) Ltd (Dealer), Upminster, Essex	10/67
				Leyland Motors Ltd (Dealer), London W1	10/67
				Exported to USA, new owner not known	10/67
				Seashore Trolley Museum, Kennebunkport, Maine, in poor condition	by 06/92
				Still there	05/93
RTL1629	541482	3628	OLD858		
				Passenger Vehicle Sales (London) Ltd (Dealer), Canvey Island, Essex	12/68
RTL1630	541513	5351	OLD859		
				Pickersgill & Laverick (Dealer), Cudworth, Yorkshire	02/70
RTL1631	541475	5364	OLD860		
				Pickersgill & Laverick (Dealer), Cudworth, Yorkshire	02/70

The Grand Bahamas Port Authority used a small number of RTLs and appeared to be proud that the buses once operated in London. Local advertising was added to the buses at a later date. RTL715 still carries its last London operational garage code WL – and a full set of route blinds from that garage. A local registration plate is provided for its new use on sightseeing tours of Grand Bahama Island and the bus is seen parked beside 'The Pub on the Mall'. (M.M.Bateman collection)

RTW

DIRECTORY

Stevenson's of Uttoxeter have always operated a very mixed fleet of different chassis and bodybuilder's combinations of buses and coaches. They first purchased ex-London Transport buses of April 1957 when two Craven bodied RTs were acquired through the dealer Bird's of Stratford-upon-Avon. In 1965 KLB908 originally RTW178 but now identified as fleet number 11 was added to the fleet and fitted with platform doors before entering service. It was in January 1978 that it moved into the preservation movement and is now a regular entry to many rallies. (R. F. Mack)

RTW1	472472	3360	KGK501		
				Pickersgill & Laverick (Dealer), Cudworth, Yorkshire	11/68
RTW2	490635	3394	KGK502		
			23 sri 2584	Ceylon Transport Board, Colombo, Ceylon	12/66
				Withdrawn	02/78
RTW3	490636	3370	KGK503		
			23 sri 2768	Ceylon Transport Board, Colombo, Ceylon	01/67
				Withdrawn	03/77
RTW4	490640	3291	KGK504		
				Pickersgill & Laverick (Dealer), Cudworth, Yorkshire	12/70
RTW5	491533	3369	KGK505		
			23 sri 2579	Ceylon Transport Board, Colombo, Ceylon	11/66
				Withdrawn	12/72
RTW6	490638	3396	KGK506		
			23 sri 2710	Ceylon Transport Board, Colombo, Ceylon	12/66
				Withdrawn	12/72
RTW7	485020	3355	KGK507		
			23 sri 2590	Ceylon Transport Board, Colombo, Ceylon	12/66
				Withdrawn	06/73
RTW8	491537	3373	KGK508		
			23 sri 2691	Ceylon Transport Board, Colombo, Ceylon	12/66
				Withdrawn	01/73
RTW9	491536	3380	KGK509		
				Pickersgill & Laverick (Dealer), Cudworth, Yorkshire	09/70
RTW10	491535	2967	KGK510		
				Wombwell Diesel Company (Dealer), Wombwell, Yorkshire	11/69
RTW11	490637	3386	KGK511		
				Pickersgill & Laverick (Dealer), Cudworth, Yorkshire	11/68
RTW12	492080	3320	KGK512		
			23 sri 2692	Ceylon Transport Board, Colombo, Ceylon	12/66
				Withdrawn	06/73
RTW13	490641	3393	KGK513		
				Pickersgill & Laverick (Dealer), Cudworth, Yorkshire	11/68
RTW14	491538	3382	KGK514		
			23 sri 2996	Ceylon Transport Board, Colombo, Ceylon	08/67
				Withdrawn	11/78
RTW15	492172	3381	KGK515		
			23 sri 2694	Ceylon Transport Board, Colombo, Ceylon	12/66
				Withdrawn	12/72
RTW16	492339	3397	KGK516		
			23 sri 2589	Ceylon Transport Board, Colombo, Ceylon	12/66
				Withdrawn	10/78
RTW17	492336	2913	KGK517		
				Pickersgill & Laverick (Dealer), Cudworth, Yorkshire	04/71
RTW18	492173	3392	KGK518		
				W.North (Dealer), Sherburn-in-Elmet, Yorkshire	08/68
				Still there	06/69
RTW19	492337	3356	KGK519		
			23 sri 2585	Ceylon Transport Board, Colombo, Ceylon	12/66
				Withdrawn	01/80
			27 sri 4622	Sold rebuilt as a private lorry	01/80
RTW20	492171	3368	KGK520		
			23 sri 2588	Ceylon Transport Board, Colombo, Ceylon	12/66
				Withdrawn	10/74
RTW21	492496	3372	KGK521		
			23 sri 2620	Ceylon Transport Board, Colombo, Ceylon	12/66
				Withdrawn	03/77
RTW22	492312	3329	KGK522		
				Bird's Commercial Motors (Dealer), Stratford-upon-Avon, Warwickshire	01/66
				Stephenson Brothers, High Etherley, Bishop Auckland, Co. Durham	02/66
				Kirkby & Sons (Dealer), Anston	09/70
				Superb Coaches, (Birmingham), Limited, Warwickshire	09/70
				Withdrawn and converted to a goods vehicle	10/72
RTW23	492495	3391	KGK523		
			23 sri 2581	Ceylon Transport Board, Colombo, Ceylon	11/66
				Withdrawn	01/73
RTW24	492977	2905	KGK524		
				Wombwell Diesel Company (Dealer), Wombwell, Yorkshire	12/69
RTW25	492588	3308	KGK525		
				Wombwell Diesel Company (Dealer), Wombwell, Yorkshire	04/69
RTW26	492978	3383	KGK526		
				Viola Coaches, London SE22	06/66

RTW27	492587	3390	KGK527

Pickersgill & Laverick (Dealer), Cudworth, Yorkshire — 12/68

RTW28	490639	2990	KGK528

Pickersgill & Laverick (Dealer), Cudworth, Yorkshire — 03/71

RTW29	493112	3377	KGK529

Wombwell Diesel Company (Dealer), Wombwell, Yorkshire — 12/69
M.Bowers, Beddington, Surrey, for preservation — by 01/70
B.Monk, Hatfield, Herts, for continued preservation — 08/72
A.Hallpike, Bristol, for continued preservation — 01/73
R.Adams, Wick, near Bristol for continued preservation — —/84
Still owned — 08/97

RTW30	493247	2971	KGK530

Pickersgill & Laverick (Dealer), Cudworth, Yorkshire — 04/71

RTW31	493111	2919	KGK531

Wombwell Diesel Company (Dealer), Wombwell, Yorkshire — 06/70

RTW32	492976	3376	KGK532
			23 sri 2592

Ceylon Transport Board, Colombo, Ceylon — 12/66
Withdrawn — 03/77

RTW33	493246	3389	KGK533
			23 sri 2716

Ceylon Transport Board, Colombo, Ceylon — 12/66
Withdrawn — 01/79

RTW34	493249	3015	KGK534
			23 sri 1894

Ceylon Transport Board, Colombo, Ceylon — 09/65
Withdrawn — 01/73

RTW35	493245	3375	KGK535
			23 sri 2618

Ceylon Transport Board, Colombo, Ceylon — 12/66
Withdrawn — 12/78

RTW36	491534	3387	KGK536

Pickersgill & Laverick (Dealer), Cudworth, Yorkshire — 11/68

RTW37	493336	2978	KGK537

Bird's Commercial Motors (Dealer), Stratford-upon-Avon, Warwickshire — 02/65
Porthcawl Omnibus Co, Porthcawl, Glamorgan — 02/65
Licenced — 03/65
Withdrawn after collision with tree which took placed 10/67 — 03/68
W.H.Way (Dealer), Cardiff Docks — 03/68
Still there — 11/76
Trevor Wigley (Breaker), Carlton and scrapped — 05/79

RTW456 on Buckmaster Coaches livery was owned for a short period of two years before moving into the fairground fraternity. It is seen parked with other road users in Leighton Buzzard clearly showing the lighting arrangement of the route boxes. (John Gascoine)

RTW38	492975	3371	KGK538		12/66
			23 sri 2677	Ceylon Transport Board, Colombo, Ceylon	
				Fitted with CTB 33 seat single deck bodywork	between 1973-75
				Withdrawn	01/79
RTW39	493334	2920	KGK539		
				Wombwell Diesel Company (Dealer), Wombwell, Yorkshire	12/69
RTW40	493289	2911	KGK540		
				Pickersgill & Laverick (Dealer), Cudworth, Yorkshire	12/70
RTW41	493469	2949	KGK541		
				Pickersgill & Laverick (Dealer), Cudworth, Yorkshire	03/71
RTW42	493288	2917	KGK542		
				Pickersgill & Laverick (Dealer), Cudworth, Yorkshire	03/71
RTW43	493332	2926	KGK543		
				Wombwell Diesel Company (Dealer), Wombwell, Yorkshire	01/70
RTW44	493470	2941	KGK544		
				Pickersgill & Laverick (Dealer), Cudworth, Yorkshire	07/70
RTW45	493468	2968	KGK545		
				Pickersgill & Laverick (Dealer), Cudworth, Yorkshire	12/70
RTW46	494045	2974	KGK546		
				Pickersgill & Laverick (Dealer), Cudworth, Yorkshire	07/70
RTW47	494049	2960	KGK547		
				23 sri 1897	Ceylon Transport Board, Colombo, Ceylon	09/65
				Withdrawn	06/73
RTW48	494047	2910	KGK548		
				Pickersgill & Laverick (Dealer), Cudworth, Yorkshire	08/70
				R.Hill, Wakefield for preservation	11/70
				Gone	12/77
RTW49	493248	2915	KGK549		
				Wombwell Diesel Company (Dealer), Wombwell, Yorkshire	12/69
RTW50	492338	2931	KGK550		
				Pickersgill & Laverick (Dealer), Cudworth, Yorkshire	03/71
RTW51	492586	2945	KGK551		
				Wombwell Diesel Company (Dealer), Wombwell, Yorkshire	12/69
RTW52	493287	3378	KGK552		
				23 sri 2718	Ceylon Transport Board, Colombo, Ceylon	12/66
				Withdrawn	12/75
RTW53	493471	2922	KGK553		
				Pickersgill & Laverick (Dealer), Cudworth, Yorkshire	03/71
RTW54	493333	2935	KGK554		
				Pickersgill & Laverick (Dealer), Cudworth, Yorkshire	08/70
RTW55	494046	2901	KGK555		
				Wombwell Diesel Company (Dealer), Wombwell, Yorkshire	12/69
RTW56	493335	2923	KGK556		
				F.Ridler (Dealer), Whitton, Middlesex	03/65
				N.Beldoz (Breaker), Hertford	03/65
				Scrapped	07/65
RTW57	494048	2909	KGK557		
				Wombwell Diesel Company (Dealer), Wombwell, Yorkshire	12/69
RTW58	493467	2902	KGK558		
				Pickersgill & Laverick (Dealer), Cudworth, Yorkshire	03/71
RTW59	494050	3384	KGK559		
				23 sri 2617	Ceylon Transport Board, Colombo, Ceylon	12/66
				Withdrawn	01/78
RTW60	494079	2969	KGK560		
				Pickersgill & Laverick (Dealer), Cudworth, Yorkshire	04/71
RTW61	494080	2929	KGK561		
				Wombwell Diesel Company (Dealer), Wombwell, Yorkshire	12/69
RTW62	494081	2953	KGK562		
				Pickersgill & Laverick (Dealer), Cudworth, Yorkshire	08/70
RTW63	494082	3398	KGK563		
				23 sri 2586	Ceylon Transport Board, Colombo, Ceylon	12/66
				Withdrawn	05/78
RTW64	494083	2984	KGK564		
				Pickersgill & Laverick (Dealer), Cudworth, Yorkshire	03/71
RTW65	494084	3364	KGK565		
				23 sri 2580	Ceylon Transport Board, Colombo, Ceylon	11/66
				Withdrawn	12/72
RTW66	494185	2991	KGK566		
				F.Ridler (Dealer), Whitton, Middlesex	07/65
				N. Beldoz (Breaker), Hertford	07/65
				Scrapped	07/65

RTW67	494186	3317	KGK567		
				Pickersgill & Laverick (Dealer), Cudworth, Yorkshire	03/71
RTW68	494187	3331	KGK568		
			23 sri 2591	Ceylon Transport Board, Colombo, Ceylon	12/66
				Withdrawn	05/78
RTW69	494188	3030	KGK569		
				Pickersgill & Laverick (Dealer), Cudworth, Yorkshire	08/70
RTW70	494261	3009	KGK570		
				Pickersgill & Laverick (Dealer), Cudworth, Yorkshire	03/71
RTW71	494262	2906	KGK571		
				Pickersgill & Laverick (Dealer), Cudworth, Yorkshire	09/70
RTW72	494263	2932	KGK572		
				Wombwell Diesel Company (Dealer), Wombwell, Yorkshire	12/69
RTW73	494264	2954	KGK573		
				Pickersgill & Laverick (Dealer), Cudworth, Yorkshire	08/70
RTW74	494265	3103	KGK574		
			23 sri 1896	Ceylon Transport Board, Colombo, Ceylon	09/65
				Withdrawn	10/78
RTW75	494266	2912	KGK575		
				E.Brakell , T.Robertson, T.Hornby, Cheam, Surrey for preservation	01/70
				Star Construction Group, Chadwell St Mary, for preservation and promotional work	07/88
				Wright & Biddell, Rainham, Essex for continued preservation	08/93
				Still owned	04/98
RTW76	494267	2966	KGK576		
				Wombwell Diesel Company (Dealer), Wombwell, Yorkshire	12/69
RTW77	494268	2964	KGK577		
				Pickersgill & Laverick (Dealer), Cudworth, Yorkshire	12/70
RTW78	494269	2908	KGK578		
				Pickersgill & Laverick (Dealer), Cudworth, Yorkshire	12/70
RTW79	494270	2963	KGK579		
				Wombwell Diesel Company (Dealer), Wombwell, Yorkshire	06/70
RTW80	494271	2952	KGK580		
				Pickersgill & Laverick (Dealer), Cudworth, Yorkshire	03/71
RTW81	494272	3121	KGK581		
			23 sri 2770	Ceylon Transport Board, Colombo, Ceylon	01/67
				Withdrawn	03/77
RTW82	494501	2947	KGK582		
				W.North (Dealer), Sherburn-in-Elmet, Yorkshire	08/66
				Johnson, (Breakers), South Elmsall, Yorkshire	02/67
RTW83	494629	2943	KGK583		
				Pickersgill & Laverick (Dealer), Cudworth, Yorkshire	08/70

A. H. Kearsey and later Marchants, both of Cheltenham operated RTW137 before it was finally withdrawn from use in April 1973. It carries fleet number 68 within a circle beneath its offside sidelight together with a very small 'A' and is seen manoeuvring in a typical environment associated with an operator of smaller fleets.

RTW84	494630	2927	KGK584		
				T. Collins (Dealer), Stepney, London E1	12/70
				Still there	01/71
RTW85	494631	2980	KGK585		
			23 sri 2152	Ceylon Transport Board, Colombo, Ceylon	03/66
				Withdrawn	03/77
RTW86	494632	2996	KGK586		
			23 sri 1981	Ceylon Transport Board, Colombo, Ceylon	11/65
				Withdrawn	01/79
RTW87	494633	3016	KGK587		
				Trollope & Colls Limited (Contractor), London EC3 as staff bus	09/65
				Moved to their Scottish associated company, Kintyre Concrete Products Limited, Irvine, Ayrshire	
				as staff bus	10/65
				Kintyre renamed Trollope Industries (Scotland) Limited, Irvine, Ayrshire	—/6-
				Still owned	01/68
				Withdrawn	11/69
RTW88	494716	2946	KGK588		
				Wombwell Diesel Company (Dealer), Wombwell, Yorkshire	11/69
RTW89	494717	2928	KGK589		
				Pickersgill & Laverick (Dealer), Cudworth, Yorkshire	04/71
RTW90	494718	3395	KGK590		
			23 sri 2619	Ceylon Transport Board, Colombo, Ceylon	12/66
				Still owned	04/81
RTW91	494719	2939	KGK591		
				Wombwell Diesel Company (Dealer), Wombwell, Yorkshire	01/70
RTW92	494720	2938	KGK592		
				Pickersgill & Laverick (Dealer), Cudworth, Yorkshire	03/71
RTW93	494803	2930	KGK593		
			23 sri 2686	Ceylon Transport Board, Colombo, Ceylon	12/66
				Still owned	04/81
RTW94	494804	3071	KGK594		
			23 sri 2681	Ceylon Transport Board, Colombo, Ceylon	12/66
				Still owned	04/81
RTW95	494805	2965	KGK595		
			23 sri 2334	Ceylon Transport Board, Colombo, Ceylon	06/66
RTW96	494806	3014	KGK596		
			CA 6669	City Tramways, Cape Town, South Africa 732	06/65
				Still in service	04/74
RTW97	494807	3053	KGK597		
			23 sri 2163	Ceylon Transport Board, Colombo, Ceylon	03/66
				Still owned	04/81
RTW98	494808	2916	KGK598		
			23 sri 2587	Ceylon Transport Board, Colombo, Ceylon	12/66
				Withdrawn	10/74
RTW99	494809	2934	KGK599		
				Pickersgill & Laverick (Dealer), Cudworth, Yorkshire	07/70
RTW100	494810	3008	KGK600		
				Wombwell Diesel Company (Dealer), Wombwell, Yorkshire after mechanical units	
				had been removed at Stonebridge Garage for Ceylon Transport Board	01/70
RTW101	494921	3082	KGK601		
				Bird's Commercial Motors (Dealer), Stratford-upon-Avon, Warwickshire	07/65
				A1 Service, (Stewart, Saltcoats), Ardrossan, Ayrshire	11/65
				To service	03/66
				Withdrawn	12/70
RTW102	494922	2904	KGK602		
				Pickersgill & Laverick (Dealer), Cudworth, Yorkshire	03/71
RTW103	494923	2903	KGK603		
				Wombwell Diesel Company (Dealer), Wombwell, Yorkshire	07/70
RTW104	494924	2925	KGK604		
				Pickersgill & Laverick (Dealer), Cudworth, Yorkshire	07/70
RTW105	494925	2924	KGK605		
				Pickersgill & Laverick (Dealer), Cudworth, Yorkshire	04/71
RTW106	494926	2933	KGK606		
				Pickersgill & Laverick (Dealer), Cudworth, Yorkshire	03/71
RTW107	494927	2958	KGK607		
			23 sri 2025	Ceylon Transport Board, Colombo, Ceylon	12/65
				Withdrawn	01/78
RTW108	494928	2994	KGK608		
				Pickersgill & Laverick (Dealer), Cudworth, Yorkshire	12/70
RTW109	494977	2921	KGK609		
				Pickersgill & Laverick (Dealer), Cudworth, Yorkshire	12/70

RTW110	494978	2957	KGK610		
				Bird's Commercial Motors (Dealer), Stratford-upon-Avon, Warwickshire	02/65
				Andy's Clappers Beat Group, Birmingham, Warwickshire	by 03/65
				Harper Bros., Heath Hayes, Staffordshire for spares	c09/66
RTW111	494979	2962	KGK611		
			23 sri 1982	Ceylon Transport Board, Colombo, Ceylon	11/65
				Withdrawn	01/78
RTW112	494980	3018	KGK612		
			23 sri 1983	Ceylon Transport Board, Colombo, Ceylon	11/65
				Rebuilt with CTB single deck bodywork	—/—
				Withdrawn	01/79
RTW113	494981	3026	KGK613		
			23 sri 2684	Ceylon Transport Board, Colombo, Ceylon	12/66
				Withdrawn	01/75
RTW114	494982	2979	KGK614		
			23 sri 1984	Ceylon Transport Board, Colombo, Ceylon	11/65
				Withdrawn	01/73
RTW115	494983	2914	KGK615		
				Wombwell Diesel Company (Dealer), Wombwell, Yorkshire	12/69
RTW116	494984	3006	KGK616		
				Pickersgill & Laverick (Dealer), Cudworth, Yorkshire	08/70
RTW117	495660	2940	KGK617		
				Bird's Commercial Motors (Dealer), Stratford-upon-Avon, Warwickshire	02/65
				Kenfig Motors Limited, Kenfig Hill, Bridgend, Glamorgan	02/65
				Licenced	03/65
				Withdrawn	06/70
				Passenger Vehicle Sales (London) Ltd (Dealer), Canvey Island, Essex	06/70
				Barraclough, (Breaker), Barnsley, Yorkshire	06/70
RTW118	495661	2961	KGK618		
				Pickersgill & Laverick (Dealer), Cudworth, Yorkshire	09/70
RTW119	495662	3100	KGK619		
			23 sri 1985	Ceylon Transport Board, Colombo, Ceylon	11/65
				Withdrawn	12/78
RTW120	495663	2918	KGK620		
				Pickersgill & Laverick (Dealer), Cudworth, Yorkshire	04/71
RTW121	495683	3056	KGK621		
			23 sri 2051	Ceylon Transport Board, Colombo, Ceylon	12/65
				Fitted with CTB single deck bodywork	by 02/77
				Still extant	04/81
RTW122	495684	2956	KGK622		
				Pickersgill & Laverick (Dealer), Cudworth, Yorkshire	09/70

With the addition of a substantial door arrangement to the rear platform, RTW489 is seen with front roof damage while parked at Nazeing. Its use is clearly advertised together with much road grime and overspill of diesel.

RTW123	495685	3044	KGK623		
				Pickersgill & Laverick (Dealer), Cudworth, Yorkshire	09/70
RTW124	495686	2951	KGK624		
				Bird's Commercial Motors (Dealer), Stratford-upon-Avon, Warwickshire	03/65
				Red Rover, Aylesbury, Buckinghamshire 5	03/65
				Later numbered RR5	by 10/66
				Withdrawn	11/70
				Unknown operator	—/71
				D.Nash (Dealer), Holmer Green, Buckinghamshire and partially scrapped	c11/71
				E.Brakell (Dealer), Cheam, Surrey for mechanical spares	11/72
				Remain to T.Nicholson (Dealer)	05/73
RTW125	495728	3005	KGK625		
				W.North (Dealer), Sherburn-in-Elmet, Yorkshire	08/66
				Johnson, (Breakers), South Elmsall, Yorkshire	02/67
RTW126	495729	3003	KGK626		
			23 sri 1986	Ceylon Transport Board, Colombo, Ceylon	11/65
				Still owned	04/81
RTW127	495730	3007	KGK627		
				N.Watson, Chippewa, Ontario, Canada who formed Doubledeck Tours Limited for tours of the Niagara Falls area	05/65
				Broiler factory (Restaurant), Maple Leaf Village, Niagara Falls, Canada parked inside the restaurant with serving hatch cut into nearside lower saloon	by —/78
				Restaurant became "Komedy Karaet"	—/—
				Still there	—/91
				Restaurant became Paradise Restaurant, Hai Phon Chinese Food Takeout, no engine or front wheels	by 06/96
				Land area now fenced off for redevelopment, bus probably moved off	06/96
RTW128	495731	3019	KGK628		
			BA 4805	N.Watson, Chippewa, Ontario, Canada who formed Doubledeck Tours Limited for tours of the Niagara Falls area in LT livery with Preston Coat of Arms on sides	05/65
			BA 583	David Hay Limited, Richmond Hill, Ontario, Canada	between 01/84 and 11/85
			BW1 196	David Hay Limited, Richmond Hill, Ontario, Canada	—/—
			HOGEE 7	Hogee's Double Decker Services, Mississauga, Ontario, Canada	—/87
			026 RXV	R.Mitchinson, Kincardine, Ontario as a fish and chip shop and	c—/93
				Double Deck Tours Ltd., Niagara Falls, Ontario (in dealer capacity)	by 09/92
				Parked at Queen Street/Kincardine Avenue, Kincardine still in use	09/95
RTW129	495732	2986	KGK629		
			23 sri 2616	Ceylon Transport Board, Colombo, Ceylon	12/66
				Withdrawn	12/72
RTW130	495776	3084	KGK630		
				Ford & Walton Limited, London E15	02/66
RTW131	495767	2973	KGK631		
				Pickersgill & Laverick (Dealer), Cudworth, Yorkshire	08/70
RTW132	495768	3000	KGK632		
			23 sri 2689	Ceylon Transport Board, Colombo, Ceylon	12/66
				Withdrawn	06/73
RTW133	495769	3088	KGK633		
			23 sri 1961	Ceylon Transport Board, Colombo, Ceylon	10/65
				Withdrawn	01/73
RTW134	495770	2992	KGK634		
			23 sri 1987	Ceylon Transport Board, Colombo, Ceylon	11/65
				Withdrawn	01/73
RTW135	495771	3142	KGK635		
				Bird's Commercial Motors (Dealer), Stratford-upon-Avon, Warwickshire	03/65
				A1 Service, (T.Hunter, Kilmarnock), Ardrossan, Ayrshire	04/65
				Into service	10/65
				Withdrawn	04/68
				Frews (Breakers), Kilmarnock	04/68
RTW136	495772	2981	KGK636		
			23 sri 2077	Ceylon Transport Board, Colombo, Ceylon	01/66
				Lions Club, Nugegoda, Colombo, as static display	04/81
RTW137	495773	2948	KGK637		
				Bird's Commercial Motors (Dealer), Stratford-upon-Avon, Warwickshire	03/65
				A.H.Kearsey, Cheltenham , Gloucestershire, 68A	09/65
				Marchants, Cheltenham, Gloucestershire upon take over of Kearsey's business	06/68
				Withdrawn	04/73
				Jamieson (Dealer), Dunscroft	—/74
RTW138	495774	3025	KGK638		
			23 sri 1956	Ceylon Transport Board, Colombo, Ceylon	10/65
				Withdrawn	06/73
RTW139	495775	3072	KGK639		
				W.North (Dealer), Sherburn-in-Elmet, Yorkshire	08/66
				Johnson, (Breakers), South Elmsall, Yorkshire	02/67

RTW140	495873	2982	KGK640		
			23 sri 1988	Ceylon Transport Board, Colombo, Ceylon	11/65
				Withdrawn	01/73
RTW141	495874	2999	KGK641		
			23 sri 2026	Ceylon Transport Board, Colombo, Ceylon	12/65
				Withdrawn	01/73
RTW142	495875	3059	KGK642		
			23 sri 2091	Ceylon Transport Board, Colombo, Ceylon	01/66
RTW143	495876	3040	KGK643		
				Pickersgill & Laverick (Dealer), Cudworth, Yorkshire	04/71
RTW144	495877	2977	KGK644		
			23 sri 1989	Ceylon Transport Board, Colombo, Ceylon	11/65
				Withdrawn	12/72
RTW145	495878	2998	KGK645		
			23 sri 2683	Ceylon Transport Board, Colombo, Ceylon	12/66
				Withdrawn	06/78
RTW146	495879	3011	KGK646		
			23 sri 2081	Ceylon Transport Board, Colombo, Ceylon	01/66
				Still in existence but withdrawn	02/77
				Scrapped	—/8-
RTW147	495880	3145	KGK647		
			23 sri 2093	Ceylon Transport Board, Colombo, Ceylon	01/66
				Still in existence but withdrawn	02/77
RTW148	495881	3017	KGK648		
			Y2I 847	N.Watson, Chippewa, Canada, who formed Doubledeck Tours Limited for tours of the Niagara Falls area, in full LT livery with Preston Coat of Arms on sides	05/65
				Village by the Grange, McCall Street, Toronto, Canada	09/79
				Vandalised	09/79
				David Hay Limited, Richmond Hill, Ontario, Canada and used in connection with St. Anne's Flea Market, Yonge Street	05/83
			BA6 583	Alltour Marketing Support Services Ltd., Mississauga, Ontario, Canada	by 05/86
				Nestle Enterprises, Toronto and converted to open top, used as a promotional vehicle	—/89
				Loran Hagen, Toronto	—/89
			XOI 548	V.Lansdown Scarborough, Ontario, Canada as a fish and chip shop	10/92
				Still owned and in use	09/95
RTW149	495882	2959	KGK649		
				Pickersgill & Laverick (Dealer), Cudworth, Yorkshire	07/70
RTW150	495950	2989	KGK650		
				Pickersgill & Laverick (Dealer), Cudworth, Yorkshire	12/70

RTW87 resided in Scotland and was used in a non-psv capacity throughout its years of exile. It was photographed on the 10th September 1966 having only received an external repaint. (V. C. Jones)

RTW					
RTW151	495951	3024	KLB881		
				Arlington Motors (Dealer), Potters Bar, Middlesex	12/65
				Anglo-Continental Tours, Torquay (Le Roy Organisation), Tunbridge Wells, Kent	12/65
				J.Crump t/a Denham Coaches, Iver Heath, Middlesex	04/67
				Holgars Coaches, Hillingdon, Middlesex	07/70
				Withdrawn	—/71
				Winlow's Autos (Dealer), Kew Station yard, Middlesex	05/71
				Gone	06/71
				Denyer (Dealer), Stondon Massey, Essex	02/73
				R.Wright and R.Humphrey as The Thamesmead Preservation Group, Woolwich, London	12/79
				R.Wright, Rainham for continued preservation	by 12/85
				Still owned	08/97
RTW152	495952	2937	KLB882		
			23 sri 2645	Ceylon Transport Board, Colombo, Ceylon	12/66
				Withdrawn	02/77
RTW153	495954	3013	KLB883		
			23 sri 2332	Ceylon Transport Board, Colombo, Ceylon	06/66
RTW154	495953	3055	KLB884		
				Pickersgill & Laverick (Dealer), Cudworth, Yorkshire	09/70
RTW155	495955	3037	KLB885		
			23 sri 2610	Ceylon Transport Board, Colombo, Ceylon	12/66
				Withdrawn	10/74
RTW156	495958	2907	KLB886		
				Wombwell Diesel Company (Dealer), Wombwell, Yorkshire	06/70
RTW157	495959	2942	KLB887		
				H.A.Turner, Hanover, West Germany, converted to a travelling showroom to promote Burberry and other British fashion houses in Germany	03/66
RTW158	495956	3152	KLB888		
				Pickersgill & Laverick (Dealer), Cudworth, Yorkshire	04/71
RTW159	495957	3069	KLB889		
				Bird's Commercial Motors (Dealer), Stratford-upon-Avon, Warwickshire	07/65
				Superb Coaches Limited, Birmingham, Warwickshire	09/65
				Withdrawn	12/67
RTW160	496082	2970	KLB890		
				Pickersgill & Laverick (Dealer), Cudworth, Yorkshire	03/71
RTW161	496083	3070	KLB891		
			CA 59108	City Tramways Co., Cape Town, South Africa 733	06/65
				Still in service	04/74
RTW162	496085	3131	KLB892		
			23 sri 2056	Ceylon Transport Board, Colombo, Ceylon	12/65
				Withdrawn	03/72
RTW163	496080	3094	KLB893		
			23 sri 2062	Ceylon Transport Board, Colombo, Ceylon	01/66
				Withdrawn	08/72
RTW164	496084	3076	KLB894		
			23 sri 1953	Ceylon Transport Board, Colombo, Ceylon	10/65
				Still owned	04/81
RTW165	496086	3078	KLB895		
			23 sri 2078	Ceylon Transport Board, Colombo, Ceylon	01/66
				Withdrawn	06/78
RTW166	496239	3113	KLB896		
				Wombwell Diesel Company (Dealer), Wombwell, Yorkshire	12/69
RTW167	496081	2997	KLB897		
			23 sri 2076	Ceylon Transport Board, Colombo, Ceylon	01/66
				Withdrawn	05/72
RTW168	496088	3043	KLB898		
				Pickersgill & Laverick (Dealer), Cudworth, Yorkshire	09/70
RTW169	496237	3010	KLB899		
			23 sri 1990	Ceylon Transport Board, Colombo, Ceylon	11/65
				Withdrawn	12/75
RTW170	496235	2950	KLB900		
			23 sri 2764	Ceylon Transport Board, Colombo, Ceylon	01/67
				Withdrawn	03/77
RTW171	496089	2972	KLB901		
			23 sri 2333	Ceylon Transport Board, Colombo, Ceylon	06/66
RTW172	496087	3042	KLB902		
			23 sri 2027	Ceylon Transport Board, Colombo, Ceylon	12/65
				Withdrawn	03/77
RTW173	496238	3093	KLB903		
				Pickersgill & Laverick (Dealer), Cudworth, Yorkshire	08/70
RTW174	496242	3110	KLB904		
				Pickersgill & Laverick (Dealer), Cudworth, Yorkshire	12/70

RTW175	496240	3087	KLB905		
			CA 59114	City Tramways Co., Cape Town, South Africa 734	06/65
				Still in service	04/74
RTW176	496241	3057	KLB906		
				Isadore Margo, t/a Margo's Coaches of Penge, London SE20	10/65
				Racing car transporter, London SE17	02/68
				Saunders (Dealer) London SE5	10/68
				Broken up	by 12/68
RTW177	496236	3051	KLB907		
			23 sri 2574	Ceylon Transport Board, Colombo, Ceylon	11/66
				Withdrawn	03/77
RTW178	496243	3041	KLB908		
				Bird's Commercial Motors (Dealer), Stratford-upon-Avon, Warwickshire	07/65
				J.Stevenson, Spath, Uttoxeter, Staffordshire 11	07/65
				Fitted with platform doors	—/66
				Renumbered 11A and withdrawn	10/77
				K.E.Garnall, M.J. Gamble and A.J.Sewell as the 908 Group for preservation	01/78
				A.Sewell, Markfield, Leicestershire for continued preservation and use with promotional work	—/91
				T.Stubbs, Winshills, Burton-on-Trent for continued reservation	—/96
				Still owned	04/98
RTW179	496244	3134	KLB909		
				Pickersgill & Laverick (Dealer), Cudworth, Yorkshire	03/71
RTW180	496294	2976	KLB910		
			23 sri 1991	Ceylon Transport Board, Colombo, Ceylon	11/65
				Still owned	04/81
RTW181	496295	3148	KLB911		
			23 sri 2578	Ceylon Transport Board, Colombo, Ceylon	11/66
				Still owned	04/81
RTW182	496296	3048	KLB912		
			23 sri 2720	Ceylon Transport Board, Colombo, Ceylon	12/66
				Withdrawn	05/78
RTW183	496297	2995	KLB913		
				Bird's Commercial Motors (Dealer), Stratford-upon-Avon, Warwickshire	03/65
				S.Field, Blackheath, Staffordshire	03/65
				Withdrawn	12/69
RTW184	496298	3090	KLB914		
				Bird's Commercial Motors (Dealer), Stratford-upon-Avon, Warwickshire	04/65
				A1 Service, (T.Hunter, Kilmarnock), Ardrossan, Ayrshire	04/65
				Into service	07/65
				Withdrawn	01/71

Standing within the operator's yard at Aylesbury, RTW124 now carries alien fleet number RR5. As with many of the vehicles disposed around this era a life expectancy of around five to six years with their initial new owner was regarded as the average. RR5 saw use with Red Rover for the period March 1965 through to early 1971 before being disposed of. (John Gascoine Collection)

Scottish Ideal Homesteads Limited of Barrhead used RTW304 after its transfer from the parent company in June 1966. Nothing further is documented about this vehicle although it is seen here on the 9th September 1966 parked within a residential estate almost looking as if a publicity photograph is being taken. (V. C. Jones)

RTW185	496299	3083	KLB915		
				F.Clayton, Worcester Park, Surrey, for preservation	05/71
				Clayton moved to Baynards, Sussex	—/—
				Still owned	10/97
RTW186	496300	3052	KLB916		
			CA 59117	City Tramways Co., Cape Town, South Africa 735	06/65
				Still in service	04/74
RTW187	496301	3112	KLB917		
				Bird's Commercial Motors (Dealer), Stratford-upon-Avon, Warwickshire	03/66
				Mason's Coaches, Darlaston, Staffordshire CT21	07/66
				Withdrawn	12/70
RTW188	496302	3004	KLB918		
			23 sri 1992	Ceylon Transport Board, Colombo, Ceylon	11/65
				Withdrawn	06/78
RTW189	496303	2955	KLB919		
				Wombwell Diesel Company (Dealer), Wombwell, Yorkshire	12/69
RTW190	496304	3002	KLB920		
			23 sri 2347	Ceylon Transport Board, Colombo, Ceylon	06/66
RTW191	496305	3102	KLB921		
				Pickersgill & Laverick (Dealer), Cudworth, Yorkshire	07/70
RTW192	496306	3156	KLB922		
			23 sri 1964	Ceylon Transport Board, Colombo, Ceylon	10/65
				Still owned	04/81
RTW193	496307	3108	KLB923		
				Pickersgill & Laverick (Dealer), Cudworth, Yorkshire	12/70
RTW194	496308	3022	KLB924		
			23 sri 2064	Ceylon Transport Board, Colombo, Ceylon	01/66
				Withdrawn	06/75
RTW195	496309	3101	KLB925		
				Isadore Margo, t/a Margo's Coaches of Penge, Penge, London SE20	09/65
				Bilsby Brothers (Breakers), St. Leonards, Sussex	03/68
RTW196	496310	3097	KLB926		
			23 sri 1993	Ceylon Transport Board, Colombo, Ceylon	11/65
				Withdrawn	02/77
RTW197	496311	3104	KLB927		
			23 sri 2066	Ceylon Transport Board, Colombo, Ceylon	01/66
				Withdrawn	—/74
RTW198	496312	2985	KLB928		
			23 sri 2028	Ceylon Transport Board, Colombo, Ceylon	12/65
				Withdrawn	05/72

RTW199	496313	3105	KLB929		
			23 sri 1962	Ceylon Transport Board, Colombo, Ceylon	10/65
				Withdrawn	01/73
RTW200	496314	2936	KLB930		
				Pickersgill & Laverick (Dealer), Cudworth, Yorkshire	04/71
RTW201	496315	2975	KLB931		
				Pickersgill & Laverick (Dealer), Cudworth, Yorkshire	07/70
RTW202	496316	2983	KLB932		
			23 sri 1994	Ceylon Transport Board, Colombo, Ceylon	11/65
				Withdrawn	01/78
RTW203	496317	3074	KLB933		
			23 sri 2575	Ceylon Transport Board, Colombo, Ceylon	11/66
				Withdrawn	02/73
RTW204	496318	2993	KLB934		
			23 sri 2721	Ceylon Transport Board, Colombo, Ceylon	12/66
				Still in existence but withdrawn	02/77
RTW205	496319	3089	KLB935		
			23 sri 2070	Ceylon Transport Board, Colombo, Ceylon	01/66
				Withdrawn	03/76
RTW206	496320	2988	KLB936		
			23 sri 2090	Ceylon Transport Board, Colombo, Ceylon	01/66
				Withdrawn	10/74
RTW207	496321	3012	KLB937		
			23 sri 2158	Ceylon Transport Board, Colombo, Ceylon	03/66
				Withdrawn	01/78
RTW208	496322	2944	KLB938		
				Decca Radio & T.V., London SW8, was to have been mobile showroom, but not preceded with	06/65
				Home Parade (Breaker), London SE11	05/67
RTW209	496323	3036	KLB939		
			23 sri 2102	Ceylon Transport Board, Colombo, Ceylon	01/66
				Withdrawn	06/73
RTW210	496324	3332	KLB940		
				W.North (Dealer), Sherburn-in-Elmet, Yorkshire	08/68
				Still there in poor condition	12/70
RTW211	496325	3085	KLB941		
			23 sri 2067	Ceylon Transport Board, Colombo, Ceylon	01/66
				Withdrawn	03/77
RTW212	496326	2987	KLB942		
			23 sri 2151	Ceylon Transport Board, Colombo, Ceylon	03/66
				Withdrawn	03/77
RTW213	496327	3111	KLB943		
			23 sri 2150	Ceylon Transport Board, Colombo, Ceylon	03/66
				Withdrawn	03/77
			27 sri 1422	Rebuilt as a private lorry	03/77
RTW214	496328	3155	KLB944		
				Pickersgill & Laverick (Dealer), Cudworth, Yorkshire	12/68
RTW215	496329	3021	KLB945		
				Pickersgill & Laverick (Dealer), Cudworth, Yorkshire	04/71
RTW216	496330	3095	KLB946		
			23 sri 2069	Ceylon Transport Board, Colombo, Ceylon	01/66
				Withdrawn	12/75
RTW217	496331	3050	KLB947		
			23 sri 2065	Ceylon Transport Board, Colombo, Ceylon	01/66
				Withdrawn	02/73
RTW218	496332	3106	KLB948		
				Bird's Commercial Motors (Dealer), Stratford-upon-Avon, Warwickshire	04/65
				Stephenson Brothers, High Etherley, Bishop Auckland, Co. Durham	04/65
				Kirkby & Sons (Dealer), Anston	09/70
				Superb Coaches, (Birmingham) Limited, Warwickshire	09/70
				Withdrawn	09/71
				Noted in scrap yard at Appleby-Magna, Leicestershire	04/73
RTW219	496333	3117	KLB949		
			23 sri 2029	Ceylon Transport Board, Colombo, Ceylon	12/65
				Withdrawn	01/73
RTW220	496381	3029	KLB950		
				Pickersgill & Laverick (Dealer), Cudworth, Yorkshire	12/70
RTW221	496382	3098	KLB951		
			23 sri 2030	Ceylon Transport Board, Colombo, Ceylon	12/65
				Withdrawn	06/73
RTW222	496444	3086	KLB952		
			23 sri 2080	Ceylon Transport Board, Colombo, Ceylon	01/66
				Withdrawn	11/72

RTW223	496445	3054	KLB953		
				Pickersgill & Laverick (Dealer), Cudworth, Yorkshire	03/71
RTW224	496456	3157	KLB954		
			23 sri 2088	Ceylon Transport Board, Colombo, Ceylon	01/66
				Withdrawn	09/73
RTW225	496457	3001	KLB955		
			23 sri 2083	Ceylon Transport Board, Colombo, Ceylon	01/66
				Withdrawn	03/77
RTW226	496458	3166	KLB956		
			23 sri 2032	Ceylon Transport Board, Colombo, Ceylon	12/65
				Withdrawn	06/73
RTW227	496459	3118	KLB957		
			23 sri 1965	Ceylon Transport Board, Colombo, Ceylon	10/65
				Withdrawn	01/78
RTW228	496460	3023	KLB958		
			23 sri 2094	Ceylon Transport Board, Colombo, Ceylon	01/66
				Withdrawn	02/77
RTW229	496461	3114	KLB959		
				Pickersgill & Laverick (Dealer), Cudworth, Yorkshire	12/70
RTW230	496462	3124	KLB960		
			23 sri 2679	Ceylon Transport Board, Colombo, Ceylon	12/66
				Withdrawn	01/76
RTW231	496463	3049	KLB961		
			23 sri 1995	Ceylon Transport Board, Colombo, Ceylon	11/65
				Still extant	04/81
RTW232	496464	3061	KLB962		
				Pickersgill & Laverick (Dealer), Cudworth, Yorkshire	04/71
RTW233	496465	3073	KLB963		
			23 sri 2173	Ceylon Transport Board, Colombo, Ceylon	03/66
				Withdrawn	01/73
RTW234	496466	3045	KLB964		
			23 sri 1903	Ceylon Transport Board, Colombo, Ceylon	09/65
				Withdrawn	01/78
RTW235	496467	3139	KLB965		
			23 sri 2063	Ceylon Transport Board, Colombo, Ceylon	01/66
				Withdrawn	01/78
RTW236	496468	3273	KLB966		
			23 sri 1963	Ceylon Transport Board, Colombo, Ceylon	10/65
				Fitted with CTB single deck bodywork	02/77
				Withdrawn	01/79
				Still extant	04/81
RTW237	496469	3064	KLB967		
				Pickersgill & Laverick (Dealer), Cudworth, Yorkshire	12/70
RTW238	496470	3063	KLB968		
			23 sri 2576	Ceylon Transport Board, Colombo, Ceylon	11/66
				Still extant	04/81
RTW239	496471	3077	KLB969		
			23 sri 2095	Ceylon Transport Board, Colombo, Ceylon	01/66
				Withdrawn	01/73
RTW240	496472	3115	KLB970		
			23 sri 2092	Ceylon Transport Board, Colombo, Ceylon	01/66
				Withdrawn	01/76
			27 sri 6960	Rebuilt as a private lorry	—/82
RTW241	496473	3066	KLB971		
			23 sri 2031	Ceylon Transport Board, Colombo, Ceylon	12/65
				Withdrawn	10/78
RTW242	496474	3133	KLB972		
			23 sri 2328	Ceylon Transport Board, Colombo, Ceylon	06/66
				Fitted with CTB single deck bodywork	by 04/81
				Still extant	04/81
RTW243	496475	3031	KLB973		
			23 sri 2084	Ceylon Transport Board, Colombo, Ceylon	01/66
				Withdrawn	06/73
RTW244	496476	3137	KLB974		
			23 sri 2573	Ceylon Transport Board, Colombo, Ceylon	11/66
				Withdrawn	11/72
RTW245	496477	3060	KLB975		
			23 sri 1881	Ceylon Transport Board, Colombo, Ceylon	09/65
				Withdrawn	01/76
RTW246	500157	3027	KLB976		
				Pickersgill & Laverick (Dealer), Cudworth, Yorkshire	09/70
RTW247	500158	3159	KLB977		
				Pickersgill & Laverick (Dealer), Cudworth, Yorkshire	04/71

RTW248	500159	3122	KLB978		
			23 sri 2577	Ceylon Transport Board, Colombo, Ceylon	11/66
				Withdrawn	06/78
RTW249	500160	3141	KLB979		
				Bird's Commercial Motors (Dealer), Stratford-upon-Avon, Warwickshire	04/65
				A.Hornsby t/a Primrose Coaches, Scunthorpe, Lincolnshire	c07/65
				Withdrawn	05/71
				Omnibus Promotions (Dealer)	—/71
RTW250	500161	3068	KLB980		
				Pickersgill & Laverick (Dealer), Cudworth, Yorkshire	08/70
RTW251	500162	3107	KXW351		
			23 sri 2041	Ceylon Transport Board, Colombo, Ceylon	12/65
				Withdrawn	07/80
RTW252	500163	3020	KXW352		
			23 sri 2033	Ceylon Transport Board, Colombo, Ceylon	12/65
				Withdrawn	01/73
RTW253	500164	3039	KXW353		
			23 sri 2040	Ceylon Transport Board, Colombo, Ceylon	12/65
				Withdrawn	01/73
RTW254	501001	3119	KXW354		
				Wombwell Diesel Company (Dealer), Wombwell, Yorkshire after mechanical units had been removed at Stonebridge Garage for Ceylon Transport Board	05/69
RTW255	501003	3399	KXW355		
			23 sri 2569	Ceylon Transport Board, Colombo, Ceylon	11/66
				Withdrawn	02/77
RTW256	501002	3143	KXW356		
				Passenger Vehicle Sales (London) Ltd (Dealer), Upminster, Essex	02/66
				G.W.Osborne & Sons, Tollesbury, Essex	03/66
				Numbered 29	12/66
				Withdrawn	03/73
				Blackbrooker as a mobile caravan Elephant & Castle, London	06/73
				Wombwell Diesel Company (Dealer), Wombwell, Yorkshire	06/75
RTW257	501004	3028	KXW357		
			23 sri 1895	Ceylon Transport Board, Colombo, Ceylon	09/65
				Ftted with CTB single deck bodywork	by 02/77
				Still extant	04/81
RTW258	501005	3092	KXW358		
			23 sri 2719	Ceylon Transport Board, Colombo, Ceylon	12/66
				Withdrawn	12/78
RTW259	501006	3129	KXW359		
				Pickersgill & Laverick (Dealer), Cudworth, Yorkshire	08/70

A1 Service of Ardrossan Ayrshire with T.Hunter of Kilmarnock as the owning member used RTW184 for a little over five years. It is kept company with a variety of other double deck buses including a Craven bodied RT in this view taken on a cold and wet day at the Ardrossan terminus. Only the duty running number plate holders have been removed and an exterior repaint applied which alter its appearance from its earlier years of operation within the capital.

RTW260	501007	3163	KXW360			
			23 sri 2177	Ceylon Transport Board, Colombo, Ceylon		03/66
				Withdrawn		12/77
RTW261	501008	3136	KXW361			
			23 sri 2606	Ceylon Transport Board, Colombo, Ceylon		12/66
				Withdrawn		01/80
RTW262	501009	3091	KXW362			
			23 sri 2693	Ceylon Transport Board, Colombo, Ceylon		12/66
RTW263	501010	3033	KXW363			
			23 sri 2998	Ceylon Transport Board, Colombo, Ceylon		08/67
				Withdrawn		11/78
RTW264	501011	3120	KXW364			
			23 sri 2352	Ceylon Transport Board, Colombo, Ceylon		06/66
				Still extant		04/81
RTW265	501012	3146	KXW365			
			23 sri 1996	Ceylon Transport Board, Colombo, Ceylon		11/65
				Withdrawn		01/80
RTW266	501013	3038	KXW366			
			23 sri 2351	Ceylon Transport Board, Colombo, Ceylon		06/66
				Withdrawn		06/75
RTW267	501014	3205	KXW367			
				F.Ridler (Dealer), Whitton, Middlesex		07/65
				N.Beldoz (Dealer), Hertford and scrapped		07/65
RTW268	501015	3126	KXW368			
			23 sri 1970	Ceylon Transport Board, Colombo, Ceylon		10/65
				Withdrawn		10/74
RTW269	501016	3116	KXW369			
			23 sri 2690	Ceylon Transport Board, Colombo, Ceylon		12/66
				Still in service		02/77
RTW270	501017	3168	KXW370			
			23 sri 2175	Ceylon Transport Board, Colombo, Ceylon		03/66
				Withdrawn		06/73
RTW271	501018	3032	KXW371			
				Pickersgill & Laverick (Dealer), Cudworth, Yorkshire		04/71
RTW272	501019	3209	KXW372			
			23 sri 2072	Ceylon Transport Board, Colombo, Ceylon		01/66
				Withdrawn		01/76
RTW273	501020	3034	KXW373			
			23 sri 2034	Ceylon Transport Board, Colombo, Ceylon		12/65
				Fitted with CTB single deck bodywork		by 02/77
				Still extant		04/81
RTW274	501105	3138	KXW374			
			23 sri 2058	Ceylon Transport Board, Colombo, Ceylon		01/66
				Withdrawn		12/75
RTW275	501106	3096	KXW375			
				Pickersgill & Laverick (Dealer), Cudworth, Yorkshire		12/70
RTW276	501107	3158	KXW376			
			23 sri 2566	Ceylon Transport Board, Colombo, Ceylon		11/66
				Withdrawn		06/73
RTW277	501108	3099	KXW377			
				Wombwell Diesel Company (Dealer), Wombwell, Yorkshire		07/70
RTW278	501111	3046	KXW378			
				Pickersgill & Laverick (Dealer), Cudworth, Yorkshire		03/71
RTW279	501110	3284	KXW379			
			23 sri 2604	Ceylon Transport Board, Colombo, Ceylon		12/66
				Withdrawn		01/78
RTW280	501109	3144	KXW380			
			23 sri 2089	Ceylon Transport Board, Colombo, Ceylon		01/66
				Withdrawn		01/73
RTW281	501112	3282	KXW381			
				Pickersgill & Laverick (Dealer), Cudworth, Yorkshire		12/70
RTW282	501113	3227	KXW382			
			23 sri 2068	Ceylon Transport Board, Colombo, Ceylon		01/66
				Withdrawn		11/76
RTW283	501114	3127	KXW383			
				W.North (Dealer), Sherburn-in-Elmet, Yorkshire		08/68
				Laverty, Neilston		10/68
				W.North (Dealer), Sherburn-in-Elmet, Yorkshire		03/70
				Tweedie, Glasgow		04/70
				Withdrawn after fire damage		10/70
				P.Sheffield, Cleethorpes, Lincolnshire		10/70
				Enser & Foster (Furniture Manufacturers), Wigan, Lancashire		—/72

RTW284	501115	3210	KXW384		
				Cresta Coaches Limited, London SW19	09/65
				Fisher & Ford (Dealer), Barnsley, Yorkshire	03/69
RTW285	501116	3281	KXW385		
			23 sri 2353	Ceylon Transport Board, Colombo, Ceylon	06/66
				Still in service	02/77
				Withdrawn and used by CTB for spares	by 04/81
RTW286	501117	3080	KXW386		
				W.North (Dealer), Sherburn-in-Elmet, Yorkshire	08/66
				Johnson, (Breakers), South Elmsall, Yorkshire	02/67
RTW287	501118	3195	KXW387		
				Pickersgill & Laverick (Dealer), Cudworth, Yorkshire	04/71
RTW288	501119	3197	KXW388		
				Pickersgill & Laverick (Dealer), Cudworth, Yorkshire	09/70
RTW289	501120	3215	KXW389		
			23 sri 2165	Ceylon Transport Board, Colombo, Ceylon	03/66
				Withdrawn	11/72
RTW290	501368	3250	KXW390		
			23 sri 2572	Ceylon Transport Board, Colombo, Ceylon	11/66
				Withdrawn	01/74
RTW291	501369	3294	KXW391		
			23 sri 2570	Ceylon Transport Board, Colombo, Ceylon	11/66
				Withdrawn	06/73
RTW292	501370	3286	KXW392		
			23 sri 2642	Ceylon Transport Board, Colombo, Ceylon	12/66
				Withdrawn	12/72
RTW293	501371	3237	KXW393		
			23 sri 2609	Ceylon Transport Board, Colombo, Ceylon	12/66
				Withdrawn	01/78
RTW294	501372	3047	KXW394		
			23 sri 2075	Ceylon Transport Board, Colombo, Ceylon	01/66
				Withdrawn	12/78
RTW295	501373	3079	KXW395		
			23 sri 1997	Ceylon Transport Board, Colombo, Ceylon	11/65
				Withdrawn	01/73
RTW296	501413	3188	KXW396		
			23 sri 2348	Ceylon Transport Board, Colombo, Ceylon	06/66
				Fitted with CTB single deck bodywork	by 02/77
				Withdrawn and sold	01/79
			26 sri 9122	Rebuilt as a private lorry	01/79
RTW297	501414	3246	KXW397		
			23 sri 2772	Ceylon Transport Board, Colombo, Ceylon	01/67
				Withdrawn	12/78
RTW298	501415	3247	KXW398		
				W.North (Dealer), Sherburn-in-Elmet, Yorkshire	08/68
				Still there, in poor condition	12/70
RTW299	501416	3169	KXW399		
			23 sri 2607	Ceylon Transport Board, Colombo, Ceylon	12/66
				Withdrawn	12/78
RTW300	501417	3222	KXW400		
			23 sri 2643	Ceylon Transport Board, Colombo, Ceylon	12/66
				Withdrawn	11/73
RTW301	501418	3198	KXW401		
				Passenger Vehicle Sales (London) Ltd (Dealer), Upminster, Essex	02/66
				Hall t/a Broadway Coaches, Wickford, Essex	03/66
				Withdrawn	—/70
				Passenger Vehicle Sales (London) Ltd (Dealer), Silver End, Essex	—/70
				Barraclough (Dealer), Royston, Yorkshire and scrapped	—/70
RTW302	501419	3227	KXW402		
			23 sri 2644	Ceylon Transport Board, Colombo, Ceylon	12/66
				Withdrawn	12/72
RTW303	501420	3167	KXW403		
				Pickersgill & Laverick (Dealer), Cudworth, Yorkshire	11/68
RTW304	501421	3239	KXW404		
				Agent Engineering Company Limited, Crayford, Kent	01/66
				Scottish Ideal Homesteads Limited, Barrhead, Renfrewshire transferred from parent company and used as a staff bus	06/66
RTW305	501422	3218	KXW405		
			23 sri 2567	Ceylon Transport Board, Colombo, Ceylon	11/66
				Withdrawn	01/78
RTW306	501423	3241	KXW406		
			23 sri 2571	Ceylon Transport Board, Colombo, Ceylon	11/66
				Withdrawn	06/73

RTW307	501424	3035	KXW407		
			23 sri 2605	Ceylon Transport Board, Colombo, Ceylon	12/66
				Withdrawn	03/77
			27 sri 899	Rebuilt as a private lorry	—/7-
RTW308	501592	3176	KXW408		
			23 sri 2326	Ceylon Transport Board, Colombo, Ceylon	06/66
				Withdrawn	01/76
RTW309	501593	3154	KXW409		
			23 sri 2053	Ceylon Transport Board, Colombo, Ceylon	12/65
				Withdrawn	06/73
RTW310	501594	3065	KXW410		
				F.Ridler (Dealer), Whitton, Middlesex	07/65
				N.Beldoz (Breakers), Hertford and broken up	07/65
RTW311	501595	3161	KXW411		
			23 sri 2682	Ceylon Transport Board, Colombo, Ceylon	12/66
				Withdrawn	10/79
RTW312	501596	3216	KXW412		
			23 sri 2641	Ceylon Transport Board, Colombo, Ceylon	12/66
				Withdrawn	02/78
RTW313	501597	3164	KXW413		
				Wombwell Diesel Company (Dealer), Wombwell, Yorkshire after mechanical units had been removed at Stonebridge Garage for Ceylon Transport Board	05/69
RTW314	501598	3243	KXW414		
			23 sri 2346	Ceylon Transport Board, Colombo, Ceylon	06/66
				Withdrawn	06/73
RTW315	501599	3171	KXW415		
			23 sri 2688	Ceylon Transport Board, Colombo, Ceylon	12/66
				Withdrawn	05/78
RTW316	501600	3132	KXW416		
			23 sri 2156	Ceylon Transport Board, Colombo, Ceylon	03/66
				Withdrawn	10/79
RTW317	501601	3256	KXW417		
			23 sri 2711	Ceylon Transport Board, Colombo, Ceylon	12/66
				Withdrawn	01/76

With superficial damage RTW402 has an upper saloon passenger who has found the best seat in the bus next to the gaping hole where window glazing has been removed. RT3339 minus its roof box and fleet number but identified by its registration 23 SRI 1297 is parked further along the roadway which appears to be some sort of bus terminus somewhere in Ceylon. Both buses are still adorned by their London transport radiator badge while the paintwork of the RTW shows signs of wear and is fading.

RTW318	501602	3135	KXW418		
			23 sri 2337	Ceylon Transport Board, Colombo, Ceylon	06/66
				Withdrawn	06/78
RTW319	501603	3203	KXW419		
				Pickersgill & Laverick (Dealer), Cudworth, Yorkshire	03/71
RTW320	501703	3147	KXW420		
				Pickersgill & Laverick (Dealer), Cudworth, Yorkshire	03/71
RTW321	501704	3128	KXW421		
			23 sri 2706	Ceylon Transport Board, Colombo, Ceylon	12/66
				Withdrawn	06/73
RTW322	501705	3217	KXW422		
				Pickersgill & Laverick (Dealer), Cudworth, Yorkshire	09/70
RTW323	501706	3184	KXW423		
			23 sri 2345	Ceylon Transport Board, Colombo, Ceylon	06/66
				Withdrawn	12/73
RTW324	501707	3150	KXW424		
			23 sri 2155	Ceylon Transport Board, Colombo, Ceylon	03/66
				Withdrawn	05/78
				Elk Arc, Colombo, chassis only acquired for spares	by 04/81
RTW325	501708	3255	KXW425		
			23 sri 2568	Ceylon Transport Board, Colombo, Ceylon	11/66
				Withdrawn	06/78
RTW326	501709	3260	KXW426		
			23 sri 2763	Ceylon Transport Board, Colombo, Ceylon	01/67
				Withdrawn	12/73
RTW327	501710	3194	KXW427		
			23 sri 2608	Ceylon Transport Board, Colombo, Ceylon	12/66
				Withdrawn	06/73
RTW328	501711	3207	KXW428		
			23 sri 2343	Ceylon Transport Board, Colombo, Ceylon	06/66
				Withdrawn	06/73
RTW329	501712	3232	KXW429		
				Arlington Motors (Dealer), Potters Bar, Middlesex	01/66
				Gor-Ray Skirts Limited, Enfield, Middlesex as staff transport	01/66
				Hawespares (Dealer), Green Street, Green, Kent	12/74
				R.Gale, Totnes, Devon for preservation	by 11/75
				Unknown preservationist	06/77
				M.Biddell, Woodford Bridge for continued preservation	01/86
RTW330	501713	3252	KXW430		
			23 sri 2708	Ceylon Transport Board, Colombo, Ceylon	12/66
				Withdrawn	01/78
RTW331	501803	3186	KXW431		
				W.North (Dealer), Sherburn-in-Elmet, Yorkshire	08/68
				Holder t/a Charlton-on-Otmoor Services, Charlton-on-Otmoor, Oxfordshire	09/69
				Delicenced	by 11/72
				Lister (Dealer), Bolton	—/73
				Unknown contractor, Wakefield, Yorkshire	01/74
				Disposed	06/77
RTW332	501804	3211	KXW432		
				Pickersgill & Laverick (Dealer), Cudworth, Yorkshire	12/70
RTW333	501805	3058	KXW433		
				Pickersgill & Laverick (Dealer), Cudworth, Yorkshire	12/70
RTW334	501806	3125	KXW434		
			23 sri 2162	Ceylon Transport Board, Colombo, Ceylon	03/66
				Withdrawn	12/78
RTW335	501807	3220	KXW435		
				J.Schwalen, Hywema Lifts, Solingen, West Germany and used as a hospitality bus	02/66
				C.Ireland (Dealer), Kirgston-upon-Hull	c 09/97
				D.Chabaud t/a London Street, as agent, Romagne, Vienne, France	09/97
				Sold to film company in Paris	09/97
RTW336	501808	3238	KXW436		
			23 sri 3000	Ceylon Transport Board, Colombo, Ceylon	08/67
				Withdrawn	01/73
RTW337	501809	3324	KXW437		
			23 sri 2325	Ceylon Transport Board, Colombo, Ceylon	06/66
				Withdrawn	01/78
RTW338	501810	3081	KXW438		
			23 sri 2085	Ceylon Transport Board, Colombo, Ceylon	01/66
				Fitted with CTB single deck bodywork	by 02/77
				Withdrawn	01/80
			17 sri 5485	Sold and rebuilt as a private lorry	—/8-

RTW339	501811	3153	KXW439		
			23 sri 2171	Ceylon Transport Board, Colombo, Ceylon	03/66
				Withdrawn	06/78
RTW340	501812	3075	KXW440		
			23 sri 3005	Ceylon Transport Board, Colombo, Ceylon	08/67
				Withdrawn	11/73
RTW341	501813	3160	KXW441		
				Barton Transport Limited, Chilwell, Nottinghamshire 1035	12/65
				Withdrawn	09/71
				Unidentified owner	09/71
RTW342	501814	3175	KXW442		
				W.North (Dealer), Sherburn-in-Elmet, Yorkshire	08/68
				Clyde Coast Services, (W.Shield, Saltcoats), Saltcoats, Ayrshire	05/69
				Transferred to CCS member McGregor, Saltcoats	—/—
				Withdrawn	by 06/72
				Tiger Coaches (Dealer), Salsburgh	08/72
RTW343	501815	3140	KXW443		
			23 sri 2059	Ceylon Transport Board, Colombo, Ceylon	01/66
				Withdrawn	06/80
RTW344	501816	3162	KXW444		
				W.North (Dealer), Sherburn-in-Elmet, Yorkshire	08/68
				Still there in poor condition	12/70
				In a scrapyard at Carlton, Yorkshire	01/71
RTW345	501817	3181	KXW445		
			23 sri 2159	Ceylon Transport Board, Colombo, Ceylon	03/66
				Withdrawn	01/73
RTW346	501818	3062	KXW446		
				Pickersgill & Laverick (Dealer), Cudworth, Yorkshire	08/70
RTW347	501819	3123	KXW447		
				Bird's Commercial Motors (Dealer), Stratford-upon-Avon, Warwickshire	01/66
				St. Michael's School, Ingoldisthorpe, Norfolk	01/66
				Sold	—/70
RTW348	501820	3224	KXW448		
			23 sri 2765	Ceylon Transport Board, Colombo, Ceylon	01/67
				Withdrawn	10/74
RTW349	501821	3271	KXW449		
				W.North (Dealer), Sherburn-in-Elmet, Yorkshire	08/68
				Anderson Coaches, Westerhope operated in Curtis Coaches of Dudley livery	10/68
				Withdrawn	10/70
				Moor-Dale Motor Services, Newcastle	04/71
				G.Lister (Dealer), Bolton, Lancashire	12/72
				Curtis Coaches, Dudley, Northumberland	12/72
				Withdrawn	04/73
				Used as towing vehicle with rear platform cut away	06/73
				Rollinson (Breaker), Barnsley, Yorkshire	11/73
RTW350	501822	3149	KXW450		
			23 sri 2071	Ceylon Transport Board, Colombo, Ceylon	01/66
				Still extant	04/81
RTW351	501823	3229	LLU501		
			23 sri 2633	Ceylon Transport Board, Colombo, Ceylon	12/66
				Withdrawn	01/78
RTW352	501824	3151	LLU502		
				W.North (Dealer), Sherburn-in-Elmet, Yorkshire	08/68
				Still there	06/69
RTW353	501825	3180	LLU503		
				F.Ridler (Dealer), Whitton, Middlesex	07/65
				N.Beldoz (Breakers), Hertford and broken up	07/65
RTW354	501826	3349	LLU504		
			23 sri 2597	Ceylon Transport Board, Colombo, Ceylon	12/66
				Withdrawn	10/74
RTW355	501827	3183	LLU505		
			23 sri 2630	Ceylon Transport Board, Colombo, Ceylon	12/66
				Fitted with CTB single deck bodywork	by 02/77
				Stll extant	04/81
RTW356	502125	3177	LLU506		
			23 sri 2596	Ceylon Transport Board, Colombo, Ceylon	12/66
				Withdrawn	12/78
RTW357	502126	3258	LLU507		
			23 sri 2157	Ceylon Transport Board, Colombo, Ceylon	03/66
				Withdrawn	03/77
RTW358	502127	3221	LLU508		
				Pickersgill & Laverick (Dealer), Cudworth, Yorkshire	11/68

RTW359	502128	3173	LLU509		
				Pickersgill & Laverick (Dealer), Cudworth, Yorkshire	12/70
RTW360	502129	3262	LLU510		
			23 sri 2680	Ceylon Transport Board, Colombo, Ceylon	12/66
				Withdrawn	12/78
RTW361	502130	3174	LLU511		
			23 sri 2035	Ceylon Transport Board, Colombo, Ceylon	12/65
				Fitted with CTB single deck bodywork	by 02/77
				Withdrawn	01/80
RTW362	502131	3165	LLU512		
				Pickersgill & Laverick (Dealer), Cudworth, Yorkshire	07/70
RTW363	502132	3172	LLU513		
			23 sri 2556	Ceylon Transport Board, Colombo, Ceylon	11/66
				Withdrawn	12/72
RTW364	502133	3272	LLU514		
			23 sri 1959	Ceylon Transport Board, Colombo, Ceylon	10/65
				Withdrawn	12/75
RTW365	502134	3245	LLU515		
			23 sri 2696	Ceylon Transport Board, Colombo, Ceylon	12/66
				Still in existence now fitted with a Leyland 0680 Power Plus engine	04/81
RTW366	502135	3208	LLU516		
			23 sri 2631	Ceylon Transport Board, Colombo, Ceylon	12/66
				Still extant	04/81
RTW367	502136	3279	LLUl517		
				Roydonian Coaches, Roydon, Yorkshire	03/66
				Scrapped by Rodonion	03/72
RTW368	502304	3302	LLU518		
			23 sri 2161	Ceylon Transport Board, Colombo, Ceylon	03/66
				Withdrawn	11/76
RTW369	502305	3179	LLU519		
			23 sri 2167	Ceylon Transport Board, Colombo, Ceylon	03/66
				Withdrawn	03/77
RTW370	502306	3109	LLU520		
				Bird's Commercial Motors (Dealer), Stratford-upon-Avon, Warwickshire	07/65
				A1 Service, (Stewart, Stevenston), Ardrossan, Ayrshire 36A	08/65
				To service	10/65
				Withdrawn	10/71
				Lawson (Breakers), Stevenston, Ayrshire	12/70
RTW371	502307	3214	LLU521		
				W.North (Dealer), Sherburn-in-Elmet, Yorkshire	10/65
				Broken up	03/66
RTW372	502308	3259	LLU522		
			23 sri 2628	Ceylon Transport Board, Colombo, Ceylon	12/66
				Withdrawn	06/73
RTW373	502309	3242	LLU523		
				C.Hoyle (Breaker), Wombwell, Yorkshire	10/65
				Noted less engine and front axle, dumped on waste ground, alongside A1, North of Baldock	10/65
RTW374	502310	3300	LLU524		
			23 sri 2599	Ceylon Transport Board, Colombo, Ceylon	12/66
				Withdrawn	06/78
RTW375	502311	3219	LLU525		
			23 sri 3026	Ceylon Transport Board, Colombo, Ceylon	08/67
				Withdrawn	06/78
RTW376	502312	3295	LLU526		
			23 sri 2086	Ceylon Transport Board, Colombo, Ceylon	01/66
				Withdrawn	01/76
RTW377	502313	3228	LLU527		
			23 sri 2149	Ceylon Transport Board, Colombo, Ceylon	03/66
				Withdrawn	03/77
RTW378	502314	3189	LLU528		
			23 sri 2560	Ceylon Transport Board, Colombo, Ceylon	11/66
				Withdrawn	07/75
RTW379	502315	3261	LLU529		
			23 sri 2638	Ceylon Transport Board, Colombo, Ceylon	12/66
				Withdrawn	12/73
RTW380	502449	3264	LLU530		
			23 sri 2563	Ceylon Transport Board, Colombo, Ceylon	11/66
				Withdrawn	08/72
RTW381	502450	3130	LLU531		
			23 sri 2166	Ceylon Transport Board, Colombo, Ceylon	03/66
				Withdrawn	06/73

RTW382	502451	3213	LLU532		
			23 sri 2557	Ceylon Transport Board, Colombo, Ceylon	11/66
				Withdrawn	01/79
RTW383	502452	3263	LLU533		
			23 sri 2767	Ceylon Transport Board, Colombo, Ceylon	01/67
				Withdrawn	03/77
RTW384	502453	3204	LLU534		
			23 sri 2715	Ceylon Transport Board, Colombo, Ceylon	12/66
				Withdrawn	06/78
RTW385	502454	3269	LLU535		
			23 sri 3021	Ceylon Transport Board, Colombo, Ceylon	08/67
				Withdrawn	12/75
RTW386	502455	3187	LLU536		
			23 sri 2601	Ceylon Transport Board, Colombo, Ceylon	12/66
				Still extant	04/81
RTW387	502456	3274	LLU537		
				Cresta Coaches, London SW19	02/66
				Fisher & Ford (Dealer), Barnsley, Yorkshire	03/69
RTW388	502457	3201	LLU538		
			23 sri 2349	Ceylon Transport Board, Colombo, Ceylon	06/66
				Withdrawn	05/72
RTW389	502458	3234	LLU539		
				Pickersgill & Laverick (Dealer), Cudworth, Yorkshire	08/70
RTW390	502459	3212	LLU540		
			23 sri 2627	Ceylon Transport Board, Colombo, Ceylon	12/66
				Withdrawn	10/79
RTW391	502530	32890	LLU541		
			23 sri 2079	Ceylon Transport Board, Colombo, Ceylon	01/66
				Still extant	04/81
RTW392	502531	3185	LLU542		
			23 sri 2678	Ceylon Transport Board, Colombo, Ceylon	12/66
				Withdrawn	06/73
RTW393	502532	3190	LLU543		
			23 sri 2331	Ceylon Transport Board, Colombo, Ceylon	06/66
				Withdrawn	03/77
RTW394	502533	3330	LLU544		
			23 sri 2626	Ceylon Transport Board, Colombo, Ceylon	12/66
				Withdrawn	03/77

RTW249 was operated by A. Hornsby who traded as Primrose Coaches and were based at Scunthorpe, Lincolnshire. Quite clearly they were one of the few operators who made use of the front via and destination boxes as originally intended.

RTW395	502534	3206	LLU545		
				Pickersgill & Laverick (Dealer), Cudworth, Yorkshire	11/68
RTW396	502535	3233	LLU546		
			23 sri 2624	Ceylon Transport Board, Colombo, Ceylon	12/66
				Withdrawn	06/73
RTW397	502536	3230	LLU547		
			23 sri 2169	Ceylon Transport Board, Colombo, Ceylon	03/66
				Withdrawn	01/80
RTW398	502537	3192	LLU548		
				Wombwell Diesel Company (Dealer), Wombwell, Yorkshire	12/69
RTW399	502538	3193	LLU549		
				Wombwell Diesel Company (Dealer), Wombwell, Yorkshire	12/69
RTW400	502539	3170	LLU550		
				W.North (Dealer), Sherburn-in-Elmet, Yorkshire	08/68
				Laverty, Neilston	10/68
				Returned to W.North (Dealer), Sherburn-in-Elmet, Yorkshire	04/69
				Sheffield, Cleethorpes, Lincolnshire	05/69
				Withdrawn	05/70
				Arskin (Breaker), Barnsley, Yorkshire	by 05/70
RTW401	502540	3253	LLU551		
			23 sri 2753	Ceylon Transport Board, Colombo, Ceylon	01/67
				Withdrawn	01/80
RTW402	502541	3270	LLU552		
			23 sri 2338	Ceylon Transport Board, Colombo, Ceylon	06/66
				Withdrawn	by —/77
				Still in existence as a lorry with Ceylon Transport Board	by 04/81
RTW403	502542	3231	LLU553		
				Wombwell Diesel Company (Dealer), Wombwell, Yorkshire	12/69
RTW404	502543	3244	LLU554		
			23 sri 2330	Ceylon Transport Board, Colombo, Ceylon	06/66
				Withdrawn	03/76
RTW405	502544	3266	LLU555		
				Bird's Commercial Motors (Dealer), Stratford-upon-Avon, Warwickshire	03/66
				A.G.Anderton (Andy's Coaches), Nechells Park Road, Birmingham	05/66
				Withdrawn	02/68
				Gordon (Breakers), Amblecote	02/68
RTW406	502545	3249	LLU556		
			23 sri 2634	Ceylon Transport Board, Colombo, Ceylon	12/66
				Withdrawn	01/78
RTW407	502546	3257	LLU557		
				Wombwell Diesel Company (Dealer), Wombwell, Yorkshire	11/69
RTW408	502547	3276	LLU558		
			23 sri 2047	Ceylon Transport Board, Colombo, Ceylon	12/65
				Withdrawn	01/73
RTW409	502548	3233	LLU559		
			23 sri 2724	Ceylon Transport Board, Colombo, Ceylon	12/66
				Withdrawn	01/73
RTW410	502549	3226	LLU560		
				Pickersgill & Laverick (Dealer), Cudworth, Yorkshire	12/70
RTW411	502778	3287	LLU561		
			23 sri 2178	Ceylon Transport Board, Colombo, Ceylon	03/66
				Withdrawn	03/77
RTW412	502779	3275	LLU562		
			23 sri 2709	Ceylon Transport Board, Colombo, Ceylon	12/66
				Withdrawn	03/77
RTW413	502780	3289	LLU563		
				Passenger Vehicle Sales (London) Ltd (Dealer), Upminster, Essex	04/66
				Super Coaches, Upminster, Essex	04/66
				Transferred to R.Wordsworth t/a Upminster & District	11/68
				Passenger Vehicle Sales (London) Ltd Contract Fleet 61 on contract to Lesney Products as staff bus	01/69
				Barraclough (Dealer), Royston, Yorkshire	11/70
RTW414	502781	3351	LLU564		
			23 sri 2695	Ceylon Transport Board, Colombo, Ceylon	12/66
				Withdrawn	01/76
RTW415	502782	3292	LLU565		
			23 sri 2565	Ceylon Transport Board, Colombo, Ceylon	11/66
				Withdrawn	06/75
RTW416	502783	3304	LLU566		
				Pickersgill & Laverick (Dealer), Cudworth, Yorkshire	04/71
RTW417	502784	3240	LLU567		
				A.J..MacLagan (Mobile Showroom), London N3	05/68
				Firma-Inmode as mobile Boutique for Carnaby Street clothes, Haarlem, Holland	06/68
				Scrap yard at Vyfhuizen, Haarlem, Holland with roof damage	04/69

RTW418	502785	3328	LLU568			
			23 sri 2559	Ceylon Transport Board, Colombo, Ceylon		11/66
				Withdrawn		06/73
RTW419	502786	3298	LLU569			
			23 sri 2636	Ceylon Transport Board, Colombo, Ceylon		12/66
				Withdrawn		10/79
RTW420	502787	3337	LLUI570			
			23 sri 2603	Ceylon Transport Board, Colombo, Ceylon		12/66
				Withdrawn		06/80
RTW421	502788	3321	LLU571			
			23 sri 2713	Ceylon Transport Board, Colombo, Ceylon		12/66
				Still extant		04/81
RTW422	502789	3322	LLU572			
			23 sri 2558	Ceylon Transport Board, Colombo, Ceylon		11/66
				Withdrawn		12/72
RTW423	502790	3283	LLU573			
			23 sri 2554	Ceylon Transport Board, Colombo, Ceylon		11/66
				Withdrawn		06/74
RTW424	502791	3067	LLU574			
			23 sri 1950	Ceylon Transport Board, Colombo, Ceylon		10/65
				Withdrawn		10/75
RTW425	502792	3199	LLU575			
			23 sri 2598	Ceylon Transport Board, Colombo, Ceylon		12/66
				Withdrawn		03/77
RTW426	502793	3314	LLU576			
				Wombwell Diesel Company (Dealer), Wombwell, Yorkshire		07/70
RTW427	502794	3365	LLU577			
			23 sri 2640	Ceylon Transport Board, Colombo, Ceylon		12/66
				Withdrawn		12/72
RTW428	502795	3310	LLU578			
				Pickersgill & Laverick (Dealer), Cudworth, Yorkshire		11/68
RTW429	502796	3366	LLU579			
				Passenger Vehicle Sales (London) Ltd (Dealer), Upminster, Essex		04/66
				W.North (Dealer), Sherburn-in-Elmet, Yorkshire		04/66
				O.K. Motor Services (W.Emmerson), Bishop Auckland, Co. Durham		04/66
				Withdrawn		11/72
				G.Lister (Dealer), Bolton		11/72
				C.Platt and D.Bailey Chorley for preservation and kept in OK livery		02/73
				G.Lister (Dealer), Bolton		06/74
				Redford (Fruit Farmer), Longforgan, Near Dundee for use by fruit pickers		06/74
				Scrapped at a Muirhouses farm		—/80
RTW430	502797	3196	LLU580			
				Wombwell Diesel Company (Dealer), Wombwell, Yorkshire after mechanical units had been removed at Stonebridge Garage for Ceylon Transport Board		05/69
RTW431	504191	3388	LLU581			
			23 sri 2625	Ceylon Transport Board, Colombo, Ceylon		12/66
				Still in existence but withdrawn		02/77
RTW432	504192	3363	LLU582			
			23 sri 3001	Ceylon Transport Board, Colombo, Ceylon		08/67
				Still extant		04/81
RTW433	504193	3178	LLU583			
				Pickersgill & Laverick (Dealer), Cudworth, Yorkshire		12/70
RTW434	504194	3299	LLU584			
				Wombwell Diesel Company (Dealer), Wombwell, Yorkshire		12/69
RTW435	504195	3316	LLU585			
			23 sri 2623	Ceylon Transport Board, Colombo, Ceylon		12/66
				Withdrawn		01/76
RTW436	504196	3278	LLU586			
			23 sri 2687	Ceylon Transport Board, Colombo, Ceylon		12/66
				Still extant		04/81
RTW437	504197	3236	LLU587			
				Pickersgill & Laverick (Dealer), Cudworth, Yorkshire		03/71
RTW438	504198	3285	LLU588			
			23 sri 2340	Ceylon Transport Board, Colombo, Ceylon		06/66
				Withdrawn		06/73
RTW439	504199	3359	LLU589			
				F.Rider (Dealer), Whitton, Middlesex		07/65
				N.Beldoz (Breaker), Hertford and broken up		07/65
RTW440	504200	3268	LLU590			
			23 sri 2045	Ceylon Transport Board, Colombo, Ceylon		12/65
				Withdrawn		01/73

RTW441	504201	3191	LLU591		
				Pickersgill & Laverick (Dealer), Cudworth, Yorkshire	08/70
RTW442	504202	3354	LLU592		
				Pickersgill & Laverick (Dealer), Cudworth, Yorkshire	03/71
RTW443	504203	3248	LLU593		
			23 sri 2622	Ceylon Transport Board, Colombo, Ceylon	12/66
				Withdrawn	02/78
RTW444	504204	3374	LLU594		
			23 sri 2329	Ceylon Transport Board, Colombo, Ceylon	06/66
				Withdrawn	05/78
RTW445	504500	3315	LLU595		
				Pickersgill & Laverick (Dealer), Cudworth, Yorkshire	07/70
RTW446	504314	3323	LLU596		
			23 sri 2723	Ceylon Transport Board, Colombo, Ceylon	12/66
				Still extant	04/81
RTW447	504315	3267	LLU597		
			23 sri 2564	Ceylon Transport Board, Colombo, Ceylon	11/66
				Withdrawn	12/72
RTW448	504316	3296	LLU598		
			23 sri 2327	Ceylon Transport Board, Colombo, Ceylon	06/66
				Fitted with single deck bodywork	02/77
				Withdrawn	01/78
RTW449	504317	3340	LLU599		
			23 sri 2685	Ceylon Transport Board, Colombo, Ceylon	12/66
				Withdrawn	05/78
RTW450	504318	3353	LLU600		
				Pickersgill & Laverick (Dealer), Cudworth, Yorkshire	09/70
RTW451	504319	3306	LLU941		
			23 sri 2153	Ceylon Transport Board, Colombo, Ceylon	03/66
				Withdrawn	03/77
RTW452	504320	3303	LLU942		
			23 sri 2555	Ceylon Transport Board, Colombo, Ceylon	11/66
				Withdrawn	11/72
RTW453	504321	3200	LLU943		
				Pickersgill & Laverick (Dealer), Cudworth, Yorkshire	12/68
RTW454	504322	3182	LLU944		
			23 sri 2562	Ceylon Transport Board, Colombo, Ceylon	11/66
				Withdrawn	01/78
RTW455	504323	3348	LLU945		
			23 sri 2714	Ceylon Transport Board, Colombo, Ceylon	12/66
RTW456	504324	3202	LLU946		
				Passenger Vehicle Sales (London) Ltd (Dealer), Upminster, Essex	05/66
				Buckmaster Coaches, Leighton Buzzard	06/66
				Withdrawn	04/68
				T.Smith & Sons, (Showman), Dunstable, Bedfordshire, noted at Pinner Fair	06/68
				St. Albans Fair	06/68
				Ivinghoe Fair	10/68
				Ivinghoe Fair	07/69
				Ivinghoe Fair	09/69
RTW457	504325	3385	LLU947		
				Pickersgill & Laverick (Dealer), Cudworth, Yorkshire	03/71
RTW458	504326	3336	LLU948		
			23 sri 2341	Ceylon Transport Board, Colombo, Ceylon	06/66
				Withdrawn	10/74
RTW459	504327	3343	LLU949		
			23 sri 2174	Ceylon Transport Board, Colombo, Ceylon	03/66
				Withdrawn	06/73
RTW460	504328	3361	LLU950		
			23 sri 2635	Ceylon Transport Board, Colombo, Ceylon	12/66
				Withdrawn	12/73
RTW461	504329	3254	LLU951		
			23 sri 2632	Ceylon Transport Board, Colombo, Ceylon	12/66
				Fitted with CTB single deck bodywork	by 02/77
				Withdrawn	01/79
RTW462	504330	3293	LLU952		
			23 sri 2621	Ceylon Transport Board, Colombo, Ceylon	12/66
				Withdrawn	06/75
RTW463	504331	3307	LLU953		
			23 sri 2600	Ceylon Transport Board, Colombo, Ceylon	12/66
				Withdrawn	06/78
RTW464	504332	3342	LLU954		
			23 sri 2697	Ceylon Transport Board, Colombo, Ceylon	12/66
				Withdrawn	03/77

RTW465	504333	3265	LLU955		
			23 sri 2595	Ceylon Transport Board, Colombo, Ceylon	12/66
				Withdrawn	11/78
RTW466	504334	3301	LLU956		
			23 sri 2722	Ceylon Transport Board, Colombo, Ceylon	12/66
				Withdrawn	05/78
RTW467	504335	3235	LLU957		
				RTW 467 Group, Greenford, Middlesex, later to Thornton Heath	03/67
RTW468	504336	3309	LLU958		
				Pickersgill & Laverick (Dealer), Cudworth, Yorkshire	11/68
RTW469	504337	3326	LLU959		
				Pickersgill & Laverick (Dealer), Cudworth, Yorkshire	01/69
RTW470	504338	3338	LLU960		
			23 sri 2712	Ceylon Transport Board, Colombo, Ceylon	12/66
				Withdrawn	03/77
RTW471	504595	3327	LLU961		
			23 sri 2717	Ceylon Transport Board, Colombo, Ceylon	12/66
				Withdrawn	05/78
RTW472	504596	3288	LLU962		
			23 sri 2324	Ceylon Transport Board, Colombo, Ceylon	06/66
				Withdrawn	12/78
RTW473	504597	3362	LLU963		
				Pickersgill & Laverick (Dealer), Cudworth, Yorkshire	12/68
RTW474	504598	3319	LLU964		
			23 sri 2639	Ceylon Transport Board, Colombo, Ceylon	12/66
				Withdrawn	01/76
RTW475	504599	3325	LLU965		
				Pickersgill & Laverick (Dealer), Cudworth, Yorkshire	03/71
RTW476	504600	3344	LLU966		
			23 sri 2629	Ceylon Transport Board, Colombo, Ceylon	12/66
				Withdrawn	05/75
RTW477	504601	3345	LLU967		
				W.North (Dealer), Sherburn-in-Elmet, Yorkshire	08/68
				Still there in poor condition	12/70
				In a scrapyard at Carlton, Yorkshire	01/71
RTW478	504602	3312	LLU968		
				Pickersgill & Laverick (Dealer), Cudworth, Yorkshire	09/70
RTW479	504603	3305	LLU969		
			23 sri 2676	Ceylon Transport Board, Colombo, Ceylon	12/66
				Withdrawn	10/74
RTW480	504604	3358	LLU970		
			23 sri 2336	Ceylon Transport Board, Colombo, Ceylon	06/66
				Withdrawn	10/74
RTW481	504605	3297	LLU971		
			23 sri 2344	Ceylon Transport Board, Colombo, Ceylon	06/66
				Withdrawn	11/78
RTW482	504606	3225	LLU972		
				Wombwell Diesel Company (Dealer), Wombwell, Yorkshire after mechanical units	
				had been removed at Stonebridge Garage for Ceylon Transport Board	04/69
RTW483	504607	3350	LLU973		
			23 sri 2769	Ceylon Transport Board, Colombo, Ceylon	01/67
				Still extant	04/81
RTW484	504608	3334	LLU974		
			23 sri 2771	Ceylon Transport Board, Colombo, Ceylon	01/67
				Still extant	04/81
RTW485	504609	3335	LLU975		
			23 sri 2593	Ceylon Transport Board, Colombo, Ceylon	12/66
				Withdrawn	03/77
RTW486	504610	3379	LLU976		
				F.Ridler (Dealer), Witton, Middlesex	07/65
				N. Beldoz (Breaker), Hertford and broken up	07/65
RTW487	504611	3315	LLU977		
				Pickersgill & Laverick (Dealer), Cudworth, Yorkshire	03/71
RTW488	504612	3318	LLU978		
				Pickersgill & Laverick (Dealer), Cudworth, Yorkshire	03/71
RTW489	504613	3311	LLU979		
				Wrighton & Sklan Limited, (Furniture Manufacturers), Nazeing, Essex and converted to a	
				mobile showroom	03/66
				Salisbury Hall Garages (Dealer), Walthamstow, London	05/67
				Slade Green Autos (Dealer)	—/71
				Enser & Foster (Furniture Manufacturers), Wigan, Lancashire	by —/71
				Believed sold	—/72

G. W. Osborne & Sons of Tollesbury, Essex owned RTW256 from March 1966 until sold in June 1973 for further use as a mobile caravan. The bodywork finished in a rather attractive livery scheme is only marred by the nearside roof damage sustained with its use in rural Essex. It is seen on the operator's premises on the 5th October 1969. (V. C. Jones)

RTW490	504614	3367	LLU980		
			23 sri 2561	Ceylon Transport Board, Colombo, Ceylon	11/66
				Withdrawn	12/75
RTW491	504615	3333	LLU981		
				Pickersgill & Laverick (Dealer), Cudworth, Yorkshire	04/71
RTW492	504616	3352	LLU982		
			23 sri 2339	Ceylon Transport Board, Colombo, Ceylon	06/66
				Withdrawn	01/73
RTW493	504617	3290	LLU983		
			23 sri 2637	Ceylon Transport Board, Colombo, Ceylon	12/66
				Withdrawn	06/73
RTW494	504618	3341	LLU984		
			23 sri 2594	Ceylon Transport Board, Colombo, Ceylon	12/66
RTW495	504619	3346	LLU985		
				Wombwell Diesel Company (Dealer), Wombwell, Yorkshire	11/69
RTW496	504620	3347	LLU986		
			23 sri 2707	Ceylon Transport Board, Colombo, Ceylon	12/66
				Withdrawn	06/78
RTW497	504621	3251	LLU987		
				Passenger Vehicle Sales (London) Ltd (Dealer), Upminster, Essex	06/66
				Buckmaster Coaches, Leighton Buzzard, Bedfordshire	06/66
				Withdrawn	06/69
				Smith (Dealer), Leighton Buzzard, Bedfordshire	07/71
				F.A.Hewer, Leighton Buzzard, Bedfordshire for preservation	01/73
				B.G. Mapperson, Coventry for continued preservation	by 06/75
				A.Potter, Edgware for continued preservation	10/79
				Still owned	03/98
RTW498	504622	3400	LLU998		
			23 sri 1998	Ceylon Transport Board, Colombo, Ceylon	11/65
				Withdrawn	12/75
RTW499	504623	3357	LLU989		
			23 sri 2766	Ceylon Transport Board, Colombo, Ceylon	01/67
				Withdrawn	03/77
RTW500	504624	3339	LLU990		
			23 sri 2602	Ceylon Transport Board, Colombo, Ceylon	12/66
				Withdrawn	03/77

NOTE

All the buses exported to Ceylon were sold through the U.K. Crown Agents.

Cape Electric Tramways of Cape Town were the owners of the South African buses covered by this book and they were operated by the City Tramways Department and two associated operating companies.

RTW329 is now preserved and looks much different from when photographed in the yard beside Richmond station two decades earlier in company with another ex-London bus. Its previous use as a staff bus with Gor-Ray Skirts Ltd. no doubt contributed to its selection as a preservation project but even so much work needs to be carried out to bring it back to something approaching its original condition.
(John A.S. Hambley)

APPENDIX I

Yearly summary of RTL and RTW vehicle disposals

RTL CLASS

1952

RTL1222

1958

RTL1/2/4-18, 20/1/3-31/3-49, 51/2/4/5/9, 63, 71/8, 81/4, 94, 100/5, 116-8, 125/6, 131, 155, 162/8, 171, 185-9, 191/3/5-7, 203/4/6/7, 210/1/3/6-8, 220/1/6, 230/2/4/6/9, 242/5, 252/4/7/9, 263/4, 273/5, 280/2/7/8, 413, 463, 477, 481, 490/1, 501, 511/3/5/6/9, 520, 530/7, 1008, 1349, 1490/7, 1510, 1527, 1538, 1581

1959

RTL57/8, 61/2, 76/9, 80/2/3/7, 91/3/5/7/9, 102-4/6/8/9, 111/3/5, 133/5/6/8, 149, 153/9, 160/7, 192/4, 202/9, 212/4/5/9, 224/5/7/8, 231/3/5, 240/3/9-51/3/5/8, 261/2/5/7-72/4/6/8/9, 281/3/4/6, 290-2/7/8, 302/3/5/6/7/9, 311/8, 323/8, 332/6, 357/8, 362, 401, 411, 460/4, 485, 523/5, 550, 1348, 1359, 1369, 1377, 1403, 1413, 1431/4/9, 1444, 1464/6, 1470/2, 1487, 1492/4, 1505, 1515

1960

RTL174

1961

RTL300, 320, 349, 355/6, 361/4, 393/7, 404, 423, 433, 446/9, 541/5, 1017, 1029, 1042, 1068

1962

RTL129, 1209, 1256

1963

RTL1052, 1064/5/9, 1071, 1082/4, 1095/7/9, 1108, 1111/4/6/9, 1120/9, 1133/6, 1141/8, 1163/7, 1174/6/7, 1182, 1191, 1208, 1210/4/7, 1265, 1276, 1311

1964

RTL3, 32, 60/4/7/9, 89, 92, 107, 114, 127, 147, 151/2/4/6, 169, 170/3/8, 182, 200/5/8, 222, 237, 344, 366, 398, 445, 454, 479, 552, 1020, 1038/9, 1044/9, 1050/5/6/8, 1060/7, 1074/6-9, 1086/9-91/6/8, 1100-3, 1110/2/5/7/8, 1122/8, 1130/5/8, 1142/3, 1150/3/9, 1160/9, 1173/5, 1184/8, 1196/7, 1207, 1212/3, 1245, 1250/8, 1262/4/6/8, 1273/5/7-9, 1285, 1290/7, 1300/7, 1310, 1322-5/7/9, 1334/9, 1346/7, 1350-4/6-8, 1361/4/5/7, 1370/2/3/5/8, 1380-2/4/5/9, 1393-7, 1417/9, 1448, 1455, 1463/8

1965

RTL72/4, 90, 119, 177, 260, 296, 324, 331/4, 373/4/7, 385/9, 396, 402/5, 444/7/8, 450/5, 462/5/7/8, 471/2/4/5/8, 483/4/6-9, 492, 500/8, 512/4/8, 528, 532/5, 558, 576, 585, 592, 600/7/8, 610/2/5/8, 621/3, 633/5/9, 641/6/9, 654/5/9, 669, 672/9, 680, 690/4/7, 706/8, 714-7, 728, 737, 740/6, 768, 784, 876, 970, 1000, 1012, 1025, 1053/7, 1062/3/6, 1070/2/5, 1080/7, 1093, 1104/6/9, 1113, 1123/5, 1132/4/7, 1144/7, 1151/4/5, 1162/5/6, 1179, 1181/7, 1199, 1203/5, 1211, 1246/9, 1252/5, 1260, 1314/6, 1374, 1386, 1404/5/9, 1411, 1421, 1449-52/4, 1461/9, 1473/4/6-8, 1480-2/4, 1491/5/6/8, 1500/1/3/4, 1516, 1520-2/4, 1530/3/5/7/9-41/3/6, 1550/3, 1593/8, 1600/6/8/9, 1612/5/7

1966

RTL295, 304, 325, 408, 419, 421/6, 443, 461/6/9, 470, 482, 496/7, 503, 510, 522, 551/7, 561, 572/9, 588, 591/4/7/8, 603/6, 611/7, 630/2, 640/3/7, 650, 660/2/6/8, 673-5, 698, 700, 711, 721/2/5/9, 730/3/5, 742/5/8, 750/4/5/8, 765, 780/6, 792, 800/7, 812, 822/4/7/9, 838, 841/2/5/7/8, 852, 863/5-8, 877/9, 833/4/6/8/9, 893/6, 900/1, 916/7, 923/6, 949, 951/8, 975/9, 980/3, 1479, 1483/5/6/8/9, 1493, 1508, 1517, 1523, 1532, 1542, 1565, 1595, 1618

1967

RTL19, 22, 70, 123, 139, 199, 317, 322/6, 335, 359, 380, 391, 406, 410, 452/7, 517, 521, 539, 548, 553-5, 565-8, 573-5/8, 580/4/6/7/9, 590/5/6/9, 601/4/5, 613/4/9, 622/4/5/8/9, 631/4/6-8, 642/5/8, 651-3/6/8, 661/3/5/7, 670/1/6/8, 682/3/5/6/8/9, 691-3/5/6/9, 701-5/7/9, 712/3/8/9, 723/4/6/7, 731/2/6/8/9, 741/3/7/9, 751-3/6/9-64-6/7/9-77/9, 781-3/5/8, 793/4/6/7/9, 801-3/5/6/8, 810/1/3-5/7/9, 820/3/5/8, 831-7, 840/4/6/9, 851/4/5/7-62/9-71/3-5/8, 880/2/5/7, 891/2/7/8, 903/4/8/9, 911-5/8-22/4/9, 930/6/8, 940/2/5/6, 953/4/6/7, 960/1/3/6/7, 971/3/4/6/8, 981/2/8/9, 991/2/4/5/8/9, 1004/5, 1014-6, 1021/2/7/8, 1030/1/3/6, 1040/7, 1051/4, 1073, 1081/5, 1094, 1105, 1121, 1131, 1140, 1152/7/8, 1164, 1170-2/8, 1183/6/9, 1192/4/5, 1204, 1221/4-6/8-30/8, 1240, 1261/3, 1274, 1281/3, 1291/2, 1306, 1315, 1335, 1345, 1355, 1511, 1568/9, 1571/2/7, 1621/4/6/8

1968

RTL53, 65/6/8, 77, 86/88, 101, 110/2, 122/4/8, 134/7, 141/2/8, 150/8, 166, 179, 180/3, 201, 241/7, 294, 313/5/6/9, 329, 372, 395, 403, 441, 480, 498, 534/6, 540, 556/9, 560/4/9-71, 581/3, 609, 616, 620/7, 657, 681/7, 744, 757, 778, 789, 791/5, 816/8, 821/6, 830/9, 843, 850/3/6, 864, 872, 881, 890/4/5, 902/5/6, 932/4/7/9, 941/3/4/7/8, 950/2/5/9, 962/5, 977, 984/5/7, 990/3/6/7, 1002/3/7/9-11/9, 1023/6, 1034/5/7, 1045/6/8, 1059, 1061, 1083/8, 1092, 1107, 1126/7, 1139, 1146/9, 1156, 1168, 1180, 1190/3/8, 1200-2/6, 1216/9, 1220/3/7, 1231/3/4/6/9, 1241/3/4, 1251/7, 1267, 1270-2, 1280/2/4/6-8, 1293/4/6/8, 1302-5, 1319, 1320/6, 1333/6, 1341/4, 1360/6/8, 1388, 1390/1, 1407, 1414-6/8, 1435/6, 1441, 1462/7, 1506, 1557, 1563/4, 1570/6, 1587, 1605, 1616, 1620/2/9

1969

RTL50/6, 73/5, 85, 96/8, 1201/1, 130/2, 140/3-6, 157, 161/4/5, 172/5/6, 181/4, 190, 223/9, 238, 244/6/8, 256, 266, 285/9, 293/9, 301/8, 310/2/4, 321/7, 337/9-42/5-8, 350-3, 360/3, 367-70/5/6/8/9, 381-4/6-8, 390/2/4, 407/9, 412/4-8, 40/2/4/7-31/5/7-9, 442, 451/6/9, 473, 493/5/9, 502/4/5/9, 526/7, 538, 542/3/7/9, 562/3, 577, 582, 593, 602, 626, 644, 664, 677, 684, 710, 720, 734, 787, 790/8, 804/9, 899, 907, 910, 925/7/8, 931/3/5, 964/8/9, 972, 986, 1001/6, 1013, 1024, 1032, 1041/3, 1124, 1145,

1161, 1185, 1215/8, 1235/7, 1247/8, 1253, 1295/9, 1301/9, 1312/3/7/8, 1321/8, 1330/2/7/8, 1340/3, 1362/3, 1371/6/9, 1383/7, 1392/8-1402/6/8, 1410/2, 1420/2/4-30/3/7/8, 1440/2/3/5-7, 1453/6-60/5, 1471/5, 1502/7/9, 1513/8, 1525/8/9, 1531/6, 1544/5/7-9, 1551/2/4-6/8/9, 1561/6/7, 1574/5/8, 1583/4/6/9, 1591/2/4/6/7/9, 1601/2/7, 1610/4, 1623/5

1970

RTL163, 198, 277, 330/3/8, 343, 354, 365, 371, 399, 400, 425, 432/4/6, 440, 453/8, 476, 494, 506/7, 524/9, 531/3, 544/6, 1018, 1242, 1254/9, 1269, 1289, 1308, 1331, 1342, 1423, 1432, 1499, 1512/4/8, 1526, 1534, 1560/2, 1573/9, 1580/2/5/9, 1590, 1603/4, 1611/3/9, 1627, 1630/1

1971

RTL1232

Total number of RTL's disposed in year sequence.

1952	1
1958	133
1959	120
1960	1
1961	20
1962	3
1963	35
1964	147
1965	191
1966	122
1967	311
1968	210
1969	273
1970	63
1971	1
	——
	1631
	——

RTW CLASS

1965

RTW34/7, 47, 56, 66, 74, 86/7, 96, 101/7, 110-2/4/7/9, 121/4/6-8, 133-5/7/8, 140/1/4/8, 151/9, 161/2/4/9, 172/5/6/8, 180/3/4/6/8, 192/5/6/8/9, 202, 218/9, 221/6/7, 231/4/6, 241/5/9, 251-3/7, 265/7, 273, 284, 295, 309, 310, 341, 353, 361/4, 370/1/3, 408, 424, 439, 440, 486, 498

1966

RTW2/5-8, 12/5/6/9-23/6, 32/3/5/8, 52/9, 63/5/8, 82/5, 90/3-5/7/8, 113, 125/9, 130/2/6/9, 142/5-7, 152/3/5/7, 163/5, 171/7, 181/2/7, 190/4/7, 203-7/9, 211-3/6/7, 222/4/5/8, 230/3/5/8-40/2-4/8, 255/6/8, 260-2/4/6/9, 270/2/4/6/9, 280/2/5/6/9-94/6/9-302/4-8, 311/2/4-8, 321/3-5/7-30/4/5/7-9, 343/5/7, 350/1/4-7, 360/3/5-9, 372/4/6-82/4/6-8, 390-4/6/7, 402/4-6/9, 411-5/8-23/5/7/9, 431/5/6/8, 443/4/6-9, 451/2/4-6/8-66, 470-2/4/6/9-81/5/9, 490/2-4/6/7, 500

1967

RTW3, 14, 81, 170, 263, 297, 326, 336, 340/8, 375, 383/5 401, 432, 467, 483/4, 499

1968

RTW1, 11/3/8, 27, 36, 168, 208, 210/4, 283, 298, 303, 331, 342/4/9, 352/8, 395, 400, 417, 428, 453, 468, 473/7

1969

RTW10, 24/5/9, 39, 49, 51/5/7, 61, 72/6, 88, 115, 166/7, 189, 254, 313, 398/9, 403/7, 430/4, 469, 482, 495

1970

RTW4/9, 31, 40/3-6/8, 54, 62/9, 71/3/5/7-9, 83/4, 91/9, 100/3/4/8/9, 116/8, 122/3, 131, 149, 150/4/6, 173/4, 191/3, 201, 220/9, 237, 246, 250/9, 268, 275/7, 281/8, 322, 332/3, 346, 359, 362, 389, 410, 426, 433, 441/5, 450, 478

1971

RTW17, 28, 30, 41/2, 50/3/8, 60/4/7, 70, 80/9, 92, 102/5/6, 120, 143, 158, 160, 179, 185, 200, 215, 223, 232, 247, 271/8, 287, 319, 320, 416, 437, 442, 457, 475, 487/8, 491

Total number of RTW's disposed in year sequence.

1965	87
1966	231
1967	19
1968	27
1969	28
1970	66
1971	42
	——
	500
	——

APPENDIX II

Known sold RTL class vehicles to have been initially exported:

<u>To Ceylon</u>
RTL22, 53/7-63/5/6/9, 71/4/6-84/6/7, 90-5/7/9-106/8-13/5-9, 123-7, 131/4/6/7, 141/2/7/8, 150/3-5/8-60/2/6/7, 171/7-80/2/3/5-9, 191-7, 201-7/9-21/4-8, 230-7/9-43/5/9-55/7-9, 261-5/7/8, 271-5/9-84/6-8, 290-2/4-8, 300/2/3/6/7/9, 311/8-20/3-5/8, 331/2/4/5, 349, 355/6, 361/4, 372/7, 385/9, 391/3/5/7, 402-5/8, 410/3/9, 421/3/6, 433, 441/6-50/2/5/7, 461-9, 471/2/4/5/7-84/6-92/7/8, 503, 510-3/5-20/2/8, 530/2/4-7/9-41/5/8, 556-61/5/6/8-73/6, 581/3/5/6/8/9, 594/9, 603/9, 611/2/4/6-8, 620/1/7/8, 630-2/4, 643/5/8-50/7/8, 663/6/7, 673/8, 681-3/6/7/9, 692/3/6-8, 700/1/4/5/9, 711/3/9, 723/6/8, 732/5, 743/4/9, 751-3/7/9, 763/4/9, 770/4/8-82/5/8/9, 791/3/5/7, 801/5, 813/5-9, 821/5/6/8, 830/3/9, 843/4/9, 850/3/5/6/8/9, 864, 871-5, 881, 890/1/4/5/8, 902-6, 911/2/5/9, 920/2/4/9, 932/4/6-9, 941/3/4/6-8, 950-2/5/7/9, 962/3/5-7, 973/4/7/8, 982/4/5/7, 990/1/3/4/6/7/9, 1002/3/5/7-12/5/7/9, 1021/2/5/7/9-31/4/5/8, 1040/2/5-8, 1053/7-9, 1061-3/6/8, 1070/2/3/5/9-81/3/5/7-94/8, 1100/4/6/7/9, 1113/8, 1123/5-7, 1132/4/5/7-40/4/6/7/9, 1151/4-60/2/4/6, 1170/2/3/5/8-81/6-90/3/5/6/8-206, 1211-3/6/9-21/3/5-30/3/4/6/9, 1240/3/4/6/9, 1251/2/7, 1261/7, 1270-2, 1280/2/4/6-8, 1291/3/4/6, 1300/2-5/7, 1314/6/9, 1320/4, 1333/6/9, 1341/4/5, 1350/2/4/7-60/5-9, 1372-5/7/8, 1380/5, 1390, 1404/7/9, 1413-7, 1421, 1434/9, 1441/9, 1452/5, 1461/2/6/7/9, 1472-4/6, 1480/1, 1490/1/5-8, 1500/4/6/8, 1510/7, 1520-4/7, 1530/2/3/5/8, 1541-3/6, 1550, 1563/4/8, 1570/6, 1587 1593/5/8, 1605/6/8/9, 1612/5/7, 1620/2/4

<u>To South Africa</u>
RTL32, 64/7, 89, 107, 151, 165/9, 170/3, 208, 344, 366, 373/4, 396, 444, 458, 496, 508, 514, 597, 600/6, 615, 640/7, 668, 675/9, 680, 694, 706, 716/7, 722, 730, 742/5, 750, 786, 792, 822, 838, 841/5, 868, 879, 884/6, 896, 979, 1069, 1071, 1082/4, 1097/9, 1120/8, 1153, 1167, 1182, 1191, 1208, 1210/4, 1250, 1260/4/6, 1273, 1297, 1310, 1322/5, 1334, 1346, 1351/3/6, 1361, 1370, 1381/2/6/9, 1394-7, 1419, 1451/4, 1468, 1477/8, 1484, 1501/3, 1516, 1553

<u>To Yugoslavia</u>
RTL114, 152/6, 200, 222, 454, 1020, 1039, 1044, 1055/6, 1060, 1077, 1086, 1101-3, 1110/2, 1122, 1130, 1142/3, 1150, 1184, 1197, 1207, 1258, 1262/8, 1275/7/8, 1285, 1290, 1327, 1347, 1384, 1393, 1448

<u>To USA</u>
RTL129, 328, 538, 551, 564, 601, 721, 755, 893, 921, 1014, 1037, 1168, 1194, 1231, 1306, 1388, 1572, 1626/8

<u>To Canada</u>
RTL470, 506, 531, 579, 598, 695, 1051, 1076, 1105, 1152, 1176, 1315, 1569

The RTL's exported to Yugoslavia were used on several feeder services from different points round Sarajevo to link up to the outer termini of the capital's tram services. At the Ilidza terminus RTL1110 is seen operation on route (Linija in the local language), 28. This country area terminus has very primitive facilities provided for the travelling public. Note the fleet number 42 carried on the London Transport plate attached to the engine bonnet. (John G.S. Smith)

To Jersey
RTL260, 411, 460, 485, 523/5, 909, 960, 988, 1348, 1405, 1411, 1505, 1515

To Bahamas
RTL608, 639, 674, 715, 807, 866, 877

To France
RTL313, 1026, 1549

To Netherlands
RTL139, 1435

To Australia
RTL547

To Belgium
RTL626

To Eire
RTL835

To Switzerland
RTL3

Known sold RTW class vehicles to have been initially exported:

To Ceylon
RTW2/3/5-8, 12/4-6/9-21/3, 32-5/8, 47, 52/9, 63/5/8, 74, 81/5/6, 90/3-5/7/8, 107, 111-4/9, 121/6/9, 132-4/6/8, 140-2/4-7, 152/3/5, 162-5/7/9-72/7, 180-2/8, 190/2/4/6-9, 202-7/9, 211-3/6/7/9, 221/2/4-8, 230/1/3-6/8-45/8, 251-3/5/7/8, 260-6/8-70/2-4/6/9, 280/2/5/9-97, 300/2/5-9, 311/2/4-8, 321/3-8, 330/4/6-40/3/5/8, 350/1/4-7, 360/1/3-6/8/9, 372/4-86/8, 390-4/6/7, 401/2/4/6/8/9, 411/2/4/5/8-25/7, 431/2/5/6/8, 440/3/4/6-9, 451/2/4/5/8-66, 470-2/4/6/9-81/3-5, 490/2-4/6/8-500

To South Africa
RTW96, 161, 175, 186

To Canada
RTW127/8, 148

To West Germany
RTW157, 335

To Netherlands
RTW417

After extensive enquiries the identity of this RTL still remains a mystery. Photographed in February 1974 it is seen standing behind the Royal Starlight Hotel, Bray, County Wicklow. Painted in an all-over matt red livery it carries Irish Caterers very conspicuously between docks together with a Republic of Ireland Co. Wicklow registration. (M.Dryhurst)

APPENDIX III

Original registration number, body builder and body number details

RTL		Reg		Body builder	Body no	
RTL1	to RTL12	JXN313	to JXN324	Park Royal	2214	to 2225
RTL13	RTL22	JXN333	JXN342	Park Royal	2234	2240
					4401	4403
RTL23		JXN344		Park Royal	4408	
RTL24	RTL116	JXN347	JXN439	Park Royal	4412	4415
					4418	4486
					4488	4509
RTL117	RTL252	KGK781	KGK916	Park Royal	4510	4534
					4552	4599
					4613	4638
					4662	4696
RTL253	RTL254	KGK929	KGK930	Park Royal	4727	4728
RTL255	RTL285	KGU201	KGU231	Park Royal	4729	4759
RTL286	RTL331	KGU244	KGU289	Park Royal	4772	4817
RTL332	RTL340	KGU401	KGU409	Park Royal	4829	4837
RTL341	RTL363	KGU417	KGU439	Park Royal	4845	4867
RTL364	RTL413	KGU451	KGU500	Park Royal	4879	4903
					4934	4958
RTL414	RTL443	KLB601	KLB630	Park Royal	4959	4988
RTL444	RTL459	KLB639	KLB654	Park Royal	3420	3435
RTL460	RTL492	KLB679	KLB711	Park Royal	3495	3527
RTL493	RTL500	KXW277	KXW284	Park Royal	3593	3600
RTL501		JXC20		Park Royal	1936	
RTL502	RTL517	KXW285	KXW300	Park Royal	3601	3616
RTL518	RTL524	KXW344	KXW350	Park Royal	3360	3666
RTL525	RTL528	KYY521	KYY524	Park Royal	3667	3670
RTL529	RTL539	KYY558	KYY568	Park Royal	3704	3714
RTL540	RTL550	KYY633	KYY643	Park Royal	3779	3789
RTL551	RTL650	KGU1	KGU100	Metro-Cammell	3951	4050
RTL651	RTL750	KXW1	KXW100	Metro-Cammell	4051	4150
RTL751	RTL850	KYY721	KYY820	Metro-Cammell	4151	4250
RTL851	RTL950	LLU841	LLU940	Metro-Cammell	4251	4350
RTL951	RTL1000	LUC326	LUC375	Metro-Cammell	4351	4400
RTL1001	RTL1006	KYY644	KYY649	Park Royal	3790	3795
RTL1007	RTL1017	KYY705	KYY715	Park Royal	3851	3861
RTL1018	RTL1039	LLU772	LLU793	Park Royal	3898	3919
RTL1040	RTL1051	LLU819	LLU830	Park Royal	3945	3950
					5403	5408
RTL1052	RTL1057	LUC23	LUC28	Park Royal	5441	5446
RTL1058	RTL1060	LUC41	LUC43	Park Royal	5459	5461
RTL1061	RTL1072	LUC68	LUC79	Park Royal	5486	5497
RTL1073	RTL1088	LUC250	LUC265	Park Royal	5443	5558
RTL1089	RTL1094	LUC282	LUC287	Park Royal	5575	5580
RTL1095	RTL1109	LUC305	LUC319	Park Royal	5598	5612
RTL1110	RTL1147	LYF34	LYF71	Park Royal	5652	5689
RTL1148	RTL1226	LYF89	LYF167	Park Royal	5707	5785
RTL1227	RTL1293	LYR759	LYR825	Park Royal	6282	6345
RTL1294	RTL1301	LYR828	LYR835	Park Royal	6351	6358
RTL1302	RTL1306	LYR936	LYR940	Park Royal	6359	6363
RTL1307		LYR935		Weyman	7706	
RTL1308	RTL1313	LYR956	LYR961	Park Royal	6379	6384
RTL1314	RTL1325	MLL676	MLL687	Park Royal	6522	6533
RTL1326	RTL1332	MLL697	MLL703	Park Royal	6543	6549
RTL1333	RTL1336	MXX32	MXX35	Park Royal	6560	6563
RTL1337*		MXX40		Park Royal	6568	
RTL1338	RTL1407	MXX61	MXX130	Park Royal	6589	6658
RTL1408	RTL1413	MXX215	MXX220	Park Royal	6659	6664
RTL1414	RTL1426	NLE501	NLE513	Park Royal	6665	6677
RTL1427	RTL1465	NLE701	NLE739	Park Royal	6678	
					8295	
					6711	6716
RTL1466	RTL1468	NLE751	NLE753	Park Royal	8255	8257

RTL1469	RTL1474		NXP955	NXP960		Park Royal	9026	9031
RTL1475	RTL1480		OLD571	OLD576		Park Royal	9032	9037
RTL1481	RTL1557		OLD590	OLD666		Park Royal	9051	9127
RTL1558	RTL1593		OLD777	OLD812		Park Royal	9128	9163
RTL1594	RTL1600		OLD814	OLD820		Park Royal	9165	9171
RTL1601			OLD536			Weyman	8991	
RTL1602	RTL1631		OLD831	OLD860		Weyman	9197	9226

* Body and registration transferred to RT4668, new Park Royal body, number 9164 fitted and new registration number OLD813.

RTW1	to	RTW150	KGK501	to	KGK650	Leyland	2901 to	3050
RTW151		RTW250	KLB881		KLB980	Leyland	3051	3150
RTW251		RTW350	KXW351		KXW450	Leyland	3151	3250
RTW351		RTW450	LLU501		LLU600	Leyland	3251	3350
RTW451		RTW500	LLU941		LLU990	Leyland	3351	3400

RTL1361 now carries registration number CA9002 and fleet number 202 for its use with the Golden Arrow Bus Service of Cape Town. Protection for the radiator has been provided with the addition of a metal bar placed horizontally just above the registration plate. Although with added side lights, rebuilt indicator boxes and a new colour scheme of orange and pale cream, its London ancestry cannot be disguised. (G. Bruce Shields)

RTL315 is seen in the ownership of William Warne & Company Limited and parked at their premises in Gascoigne Road, Barking on the 6th June 1970. Its precise use is unknown at present but an attractive livery scheme was afforded the bus all the same. (John G.S. Smith)